Learn English for Adult Beginners

7 Steps to Master Grammar, Achieve Fluency, and Expand Your Vocabulary with 1,000 New Words & Phrases

7 ESL Books in 1

Explore To Win

THIS COLLECTION INCLUDES THE FOLLOWING BOOKS:

Foundations of English Grammar:
Master Basic English Grammar Concepts for Effective Communication

Building Vocabulary:
Expand Your Vocabulary with Essential Words and Phrases for Everyday Use

Mastering Sentence Structure:
Learn to Build Simple, Compound, and Complex Sentences with Confidence

Increasing Comprehension:
Improve Reading Comprehension with Strategies for Understanding and Interpretation

Effective Communication:
Develop Conversational Skills and Overcome Language Barriers in Daily Interactions

Practical Writing Skills:
Master Paragraphs, Essays, Emails, and More for Effective Written Communication

Achieving Fluency:
Reach English Fluency with Immersive Learning Techniques and Confidence-Building Practices

Table of Contents

BOOK 5
EFFECTIVE COMMUNICATION

BOOK 6
PRACTICAL WRITING SKILLS

BOOK 7
ACHIEVING FLUENCY _____ 275

$1000+ FREE BONUSES

~~$297~~ FREE

**Learn English
Video Course**

~~$197~~ FREE

**English Pronunciation
Video Course**

~~$147~~ FREE

**Learn English in 30
Minutes Video Guide**

~~$97~~ FREE

**English Flash
Pack**

~~$97~~ FREE

**USA Travel Guide + Living
in the USA Cultural Guide**

~~$47~~ FREE

**English Stories
Audiobooks**

~~$27~~ FREE

**20 Native English
Conversations Narrated**

~~$150~~ FREE

**Premium English
Learning Software**

Scan QR code to claim
your bonuses

— OR —

visit bit.ly/3Yh6EGy

Introduction

Welcome to the ultimate guide for mastering English as an adult beginner! We are excited to introduce **"Learn English for Adult Beginners: 7 Steps to Master Grammar, Achieve Fluency, and Expand Your Vocabulary with 1,000 New Words & Phrases"**—a comprehensive resource designed to elevate your English language skills with a structured and engaging approach.

Our mission is to empower you with the essential tools you need to succeed in your English language journey, providing you with in-depth content, practical exercises, and strategies that boost your confidence and proficiency.

Why This Book Matters

Have you ever felt challenged by the intricacies of learning English? Do you find it difficult to communicate effectively in a language that's not your first? You're not alone. Many adult learners face these hurdles, but the good news is that mastering English doesn't have to be overwhelming.

Imagine confidently using English in daily conversations, understanding complex texts, and expressing your thoughts with clarity. With this book, you will achieve all that and more. We've crafted this all-encompassing guide to help you navigate the nuances of the English language, ensuring you build a solid foundation and advance your skills within just four weeks.

What You Will Gain

This book is specifically tailored for adult learners who are beginning their English language journey. Whether you're learning English for work, travel, or personal development, this guide is designed to meet your needs. Here's what you can expect to gain:

Comprehensive Content

Our book covers everything from foundational grammar to advanced communication techniques. Each section is presented clearly and accessible, making complex concepts easier to grasp. You'll find detailed explanations, examples, and practice exercises that reinforce your learning and ensure you retain the information effectively.

Sentence Structure Mastery

Understanding and constructing proper sentences is at the core of effective communication. This book offers step-by-step guidance on mastering sentence structure, helping you to form sentences with confidence. You'll learn to create simple, compound, and complex sentences, as well as how to avoid common errors that can hinder your fluency.

Enhanced Comprehension Skills

We go beyond just vocabulary and grammar by focusing on comprehension skills, ensuring you can understand and engage with English texts. Through various techniques and exercises, you'll learn to infer meaning, identify main ideas, and draw conclusions from written material, enhancing your overall reading ability.

Practical Communication Techniques

Communication is key, and this book provides you with practical tools to improve your conversational English. From asking questions to expressing opinions, you'll learn how to interact confidently in different settings, whether it's at work, in social situations, or online.

User-Friendly Design

This book is structured to make your learning experience as smooth as possible. Clear headings, subheadings, and well-organized content allow you to navigate through the material easily. Each chapter builds upon the last, ensuring a logical progression that makes learning both intuitive and effective.

Supplementary Learning Resources

To further support your learning, we've included supplementary materials such as flashcards, quizzes, and a study planner. These resources are designed to cater to different learning styles, helping you reinforce your knowledge and track your progress.

Meet Your Guide

The authors of this book are experienced educators and language experts who have dedicated their careers to teaching English to adult learners. With their guidance, you'll receive practical tips and strategies that make learning English both accessible and enjoyable.

How to Use This Book

This book is your companion over the next four weeks, but you can pace yourself according to your schedule. Each chapter is designed to gradually increase in difficulty, ensuring you gain a thorough understanding of English language concepts as you progress.

1. Follow the 4-Week Plan

Our 4-week plan is carefully structured to maximize your learning potential. Each day, you'll spend time reading, practicing exercises, and reviewing key points, ensuring a balanced and comprehensive approach to mastering English.

2. Engage with the Exercises

Practical exercises are crucial for reinforcing what you've learned. Take the time to complete these exercises and check your answers. They will help solidify your knowledge and prepare you for real-world applications.

3. Use the Supplementary Resources

We provide additional resources to enhance your study sessions, including flashcards for vocabulary building and quizzes to test your comprehension. These tools are designed to help you retain information and measure your progress effectively.

4. Review and Reflect

After each chapter, review the summary and reflect on what you've learned. This reflection helps to reinforce your understanding and identify areas where you may need to revisit certain concepts.

5. Set Realistic Goals

Set achievable goals at the start of each week. Break down your study sessions into manageable intervals, ensuring you cover all necessary material without feeling overwhelmed.

6. Stay Consistent

Consistency is key in language learning. Dedicate a specific time each day to your studies, creating a routine that fits your lifestyle. Regular practice will lead to better retention and a more rewarding learning experience.

7. Seek Support When Needed

Don't hesitate to seek help if you encounter difficulties. Engaging with other learners, joining study groups, or seeking online resources can provide additional insights and encouragement.

BOOK 1

Foundations of English Grammar

Master Basic English Grammar Concepts
for Effective Communication

Explore to Win

Chapter 1: Introduction to English Grammar

"Grammar is the logic of speech, even as logic is the grammar of reason."

— Richard Chenevix Trench

Have you ever thought about why English sentences are put together the way they are or why some words change in different situations? In this chapter, we will learn the basics of English grammar, which will help you communicate better.

We'll start with the alphabet, vowels, and consonants and then move on to simple grammar rules. By the end of this chapter, you'll understand why grammar is essential for learning English and how it helps with everything else you will study in this book.

Introduction to the Alphabet

The alphabet is the starting point for learning any language, including English. It is where you begin when learning English. The English alphabet has 26 letters. Each letter makes its sound and has a special job in the language. If you are new to English, it's very important to know and understand the alphabet. It helps you read, write, and learn how to say and spell words correctly.

In this section, we will look closely at the English alphabet. You will get to know each letter, its sound, and how it is used in words. We'll also talk about the difference between big letters (uppercase) and small letters (lowercase).

The Basics: The 26 Letters of the English Alphabet

The English alphabet consists of 26 letters arranged in a specific order. Each letter has two forms: uppercase (capital) and lowercase (small). Here is the complete alphabet:

Uppercase	Lowercase
A	a
B	b
C	c
D	d
E	e

F	f
G	g
H	h
I	i
J	j
K	k
L	l
M	m
N	n
O	o
P	p
Q	q
R	r
S	s
T	t
U	u
V	v
W	w
X	x
Y	y
Z	z

Visual Representation of the Alphabet

To help you learn the alphabet, here's a picture that shows how each letter looks in both big (uppercase) and small (lowercase) forms. This is helpful for beginners who are learning to tell the difference between the two.

THE ALPHABET

Apple **Aa**	**Bb**	Cat **Cc**	**Dd**
Ee	**Ff**	**Gg**	**Hh**
Ii	**Jj**	**Kk**	**Ll**
Mm	**Nn**	**Oo**	**Pp**
Qq	**Rr**	**Ss**	**Tt**
Uu	**Vv**	**Ww**	**Xx**
Yy	**Zz**		

Uppercase vs. Lowercase Letters: When and Why They Are Used

Understanding the difference between uppercase and lowercase letters is fundamental to reading and writing in English. Here's a breakdown of when and why each form is used:

Uppercase Letters:

- **At the Beginning of Sentences:** Every sentence in English begins with an uppercase letter.

- Example: "The cat is on the roof."
- **Proper Nouns:** Names of people, places, brands, days of the week, and months start with an uppercase letter.
  - Example: "John lives in New York."
- **Titles:** Titles of books, movies, songs, and articles typically capitalize the first letter of each important word.
  - Example: "The Great Gatsby"
- **Acronyms:** Acronyms are abbreviations formed from the initial letters of words and are written in uppercase.
  - Example: "NASA" (National Aeronautics and Space Administration)

Lowercase Letters:

- **Within Sentences:** Lowercase letters are used for the majority of the text within a sentence.
  - Example: **"She enjoys reading."**
- **Common Nouns:** Words that are not names of specific people, places, or things are written in lowercase.
  - Example: **"apple," "city," "book"**
- **After the First Letter in Proper Nouns:** Only the first letter of a proper noun is capitalized. The rest are lowercase.
  - Example: **"America," "Jessica"**

Vowels and Consonants

Understanding vowels and consonants is very important for learning English. These are the basic sounds that make up the words you use every day. Without them, we couldn't have language because they are the key parts that help us create meaning when we speak and write. In this section, we'll learn what vowels and consonants are, how they work together, and why they are so important in English.

What Are Vowels?

Vowels are the main part of every word in English. The vowels are A, E, I, O, U, and sometimes Y (like in the words "gym" or "fly"). Unlike consonants, which need your tongue, lips, or teeth to make the sound, vowels are made with an open mouth. This means that the air flows freely without being blocked by any part of the mouth.

Characteristics of Vowels:

- **Every English word has at least one vowel:** It is impossible to form an English word without a vowel.

- **Vowels can stand alone:** In English, vowels can form complete words on their own, like "I" or "a."
- **Vowel sounds vary:** Vowels can have both short and long sounds, depending on how they are used in a word.

The Importance of Vowels in Word Formation

Vowels are important for making syllables, which are the parts that build words. A syllable is a piece of a word that usually has a vowel sound. English words can have one or more syllables, and each syllable must have at least one vowel.

Single Syllable Words:

Words with just one syllable have one vowel sound.

- Examples: **"cat," "dog," "fish."**

Multi-Syllable Words:

Words with more than one syllable have more than one vowel sound.

- Examples: **"table" (two syllables: ta-ble), "elephant" (three syllables: el-e-phant), "computer" (three syllables: com-pu-ter).**

Understanding Vowel Placement in Words:

The placement of vowels in a word can change the word's meaning, pronunciation, and even its grammatical function.

- **Examples:**
    - **"bat" (a tool for hitting in sports) vs. "bait" (something used to lure animals or fish).**
    - **"hat" (a piece of clothing) vs. "hate" (a strong dislike).**

What Are Consonants?

Vowels are essential for making syllables, which are the parts that make up words. A syllable is a small part of a word that usually has a vowel sound. English words can have one or more syllables, and each syllable needs to have at least one vowel.

Characteristics of Consonants:

- **Consonants usually need vowels:** Consonants alone cannot form words; they typically need vowels to create meaningful sounds.
- **Consonants can be hard or soft:** Some consonants can produce different sounds depending on their placement in a word.

- **Consonant blends:** In English, consonants can be combined to create unique sounds, such as "bl" in "blue" or "tr" in "tree."

Consonant-Vowel Blends: The Building Blocks of Words

In English, consonants and vowels often come together to make syllables and words. These combinations are important for creating the sounds we use when we speak. Understanding how consonants and vowels work together will help you pronounce words correctly and spell them better.

Common Consonant-Vowel Blends:

Blend	Example Word	
Bl	"Blue"	/bluː/
Tr	"Tree"	/triː/
Gr	"Green"	/griːn/
Cl	"Clap"	/klæp/
Sp	"Spin"	/spɪn/

Basic Phonetic Sounds

Phonetics is the study of the sounds we make when we speak. When you learn English, knowing phonetics is important because it helps you say words the right way. In this section, we will learn about the basic sounds in English, focusing on how vowels and consonants make different sounds. We'll also see how these sounds come together to make syllables and words.

This section is made easy for beginners, using simple language and clear examples to help you understand. We'll use pictures and tables to make the information easier and more fun to learn.

What Is Phonetics?

Phonetics is the study of the sounds we make when we speak. When you learn English, knowing phonetics is important because it helps you say words the right way. In this section, we will learn about the basic sounds in English, focusing on how vowels and consonants make different sounds. We'll also see how these sounds come together to make syllables and words.

This section is made easy for beginners, using simple language and clear examples to help you understand. We'll use pictures and tables to make the information easier and more fun to learn.

Why Is Phonetics Important?

- **Improves pronunciation:** Knowing the correct sounds helps you pronounce words accurately.

- **Enhances listening skills:** Understanding phonetics helps you recognize and differentiate between similar sounds.
- **Aids in spelling:** Phonetics can also assist in predicting the spelling of unfamiliar words.

Vowel Sounds in Phonetics

Vowels are the letters A, E, I, O, U, and sometimes Y. They are essential in creating the sounds in words, and they can produce different sounds depending on their placement in a word. Let's explore the basic vowel sounds:

Short Vowel Sounds:

Short vowels are quick and pronounced with a short sound. They often appear in simple, one-syllable words.

Vowel	Short Sound	Example Word	
A	/æ/	"cat"	/kæt/
E	/ɛ/	"bed"	/bɛd/
I	/ɪ/	"sit"	/sɪt/
O	/ɒ/	"hot"	/hɒt/
U	/ʌ/	"cup"	/kʌp/

Long Vowel Sounds:

Long vowels "say their name," meaning they sound like the name of the letter itself. These sounds are often found in words with silent "e" at the end or when two vowels are together.

Vowel	Long Sound	Example Word	
A	/eɪ/	"cake"	/keɪk/
E	/iː/	"see"	/siː/
I	/aɪ/	"bike"	/baɪk/
O	/oʊ/	"home"	/hoʊm/
U	/juː/	"cute"	/kjuːt/

Phonetic Rules: Understanding English Pronunciation

English pronunciation follows some basic rules that can help you guess how a word will sound. Even though there are some exceptions, knowing these rules will help you pronounce words better.

Phonetic Rules for Vowels:

- **Silent "e":** When a word ends in a silent "e," the vowel before it is usually long (e.g., "cake" /keɪk/).

- **Two vowels together:** When two vowels appear together, the first vowel is usually long, and the second is silent (e.g., "boat" /boʊt/).

- **R-controlled vowels:** When a vowel is followed by an "r," it often changes the vowel sound (e.g., "car" /kɑr/).

Phonetic Rules for Consonants:

- **Hard and soft "C":** "C" sounds like "k" before "a," "o," or "u" (e.g., "cat" /kæt/), and like "s" before "e," "i," or "y" (e.g., "city" /ˈsɪti/).

- **Hard and soft "G":** "G" sounds like "g" before "a," "o," or "u" (e.g., "go" /goʊ/), and like "j" before "e," "i," or "y" (e.g., "giant" /ˈdʒaɪənt/).

The Role of Phonetics in Learning English

Phonetics is very important for learning English. By understanding the sounds of the language, you can make your pronunciation, listening, and speaking skills better. Phonetics also helps you feel more confident when reading aloud and talking with others.

Key Benefits of Learning Phonetics:

- **Improved Pronunciation:** Knowing the correct sounds helps you speak more clearly and accurately.

- **Better Listening Skills:** Recognizing different sounds helps you understand spoken English more easily.

- **Enhanced Reading Abilities:** Phonetic knowledge makes it easier to sound out unfamiliar words when reading.

Practical Tips for Practicing Phonetics:

- **Listen to Native Speakers:** Pay attention to how native speakers pronounce words. Try to mimic their pronunciation.

- **Use Phonetic Transcriptions:** When learning new words, write down their phonetic transcription and practice saying them out loud.

- **Record Yourself:** Record your voice while reading a passage and compare it to a native speaker's pronunciation. Identify areas for improvement.

Importance of Grammar in Communication

Grammar is the set of rules that tells us how to use and arrange words in sentences. It's like the structure of a building, keeping everything in place and making sure each part works well. In communication, grammar is essential because it helps make sure your message is clear and understood. Without good grammar, sentences can be confusing or difficult to understand.

For people learning English, knowing grammar is very important for speaking and writing well. In this section, we'll discuss why grammar matters, how it helps communication, and how it improves both writing and speaking. We'll use simple language, clear examples, and pictures to make these ideas easy to understand.

What Is Grammar?

Grammar is the set of rules that tells us how to put words together to make sentences. It includes using verbs and tenses correctly and knowing where to place commas and periods. Grammar makes sure sentences make sense, helping people share their thoughts clearly and correctly.

Why Grammar Matters:

- **Clarity:** Grammar helps to eliminate ambiguity, making sure that your message is clear and understandable.

- **Consistency:** Proper grammar provides consistency in language use, which is important for maintaining the flow and coherence of communication.

- **Professionalism:** Using correct grammar reflects well on the speaker or writer, demonstrating attention to detail and respect for the language.

The Role of Grammar in Communication

Communication is the exchange of information between individuals. It can be verbal (spoken), non-verbal (body language), or written. In all forms of communication, grammar plays a vital role in ensuring that the message is conveyed accurately.

Grammar in Verbal Communication:

When we speak, grammar helps us put our thoughts into clear sentences. It helps us choose the right tense, order words correctly, and use punctuation in speech, even though we don't see punctuation marks when talking. For example, saying "I eat breakfast" is different from "I ate breakfast" because of the tense, which is a grammar rule.

Grammar in Written Communication:

In writing, grammar is very important because the reader cannot hear your voice or see your facial expressions. Good grammar helps you share your message clearly, so there are no misunderstandings from confusing sentences.

- **Example of Ambiguity**
  - Without Grammar: "Let's eat Grandma!"
  - With Proper Grammar: "Let's eat, Grandma!"

The correct use of a comma changes the entire meaning of the sentence, showing how vital grammar is in written communication.

How Grammar Enhances Understanding

Grammar not only helps you share your thoughts clearly, but it also helps you understand others. When you read or listen to someone, their grammar helps you follow their ideas, understand what they mean, and respond correctly.

Grammar and Professional Communication

In professional settings, grammar is essential. Whether you are writing an email, making a report, or giving a presentation, good grammar shows that you are professional and know what you are doing. It shows that you care about your work and respect the language you are using.

Examples of Grammar in Professional Communication:

1. Emails:

- **Without Grammar:** "Hi I want to inform you that the meeting is rescheduled to monday thanks"
- **With Proper Grammar:** "Hi, I want to inform you that the meeting has been rescheduled to Monday. Thanks!"
- **Impact:** The second email is clear, polite, and professional, while the first one may come across as rushed or careless.

2. Reports:

- **Without Grammar:** "The sales has increased by 20 percent last quarter"
- **With Proper Grammar:** "Sales increased by 20 percent last quarter."
- **Impact:** The second sentence is concise and accurate, making the information easier to understand.

3. Presentations:

- **Without Grammar:** "We are going to talk about how to improve the companys performance"
- **With Proper Grammar:** "We are going to discuss how to improve the company's performance."
- **Impact:** The second sentence is clear and professional, setting the right tone for a presentation.

Key Differences Between English and Other Languages

When learning English as a second language, it's important to know how it is different from your native language. These differences can change how sentences are made, how words sound, and more. Sometimes, this can make learning English harder. But if you understand these differences, it will be easier to learn.

In this section, we will look at some main differences between English and other languages. We will focus on things like grammar, word order, pronunciation, and vocabulary. We will use simple explanations, examples, and pictures to help you understand, making it easier for you to learn English.

Sentence Structure: Subject-Verb-Object (SVO) Order

One of the most fundamental differences between English and many other languages is the basic sentence structure. English typically follows a Subject-Verb-Object (SVO) order, which means that the subject (who or what the sentence is about) comes first, followed by the verb (the action), and then the object (who or what receives the action).

Examples of SVO Order:

Language	Sentence	Translation	
English	"The cat (S) chased (V) the mouse (O)."	"The cat chased the mouse."	SVO
Spanish	"El gato (S) persiguió (V) al ratón (O)."	"The cat chased the mouse."	SVO
Japanese	"猫が (S) ネズミを (O) 追いかけた (V)."	"The cat chased the mouse."	SOV (Subject-Object-Verb)
Arabic	"طارد (V) القط (S) الفأر (O)."	"The cat chased the mouse."	VSO (Verb-Subject-Object)

As you can see, while English follows the SVO order, other languages like Japanese might use a Subject-Object-Verb (SOV) structure, and languages like Arabic might use a Verb-Subject-Object (VSO) structure. This difference in word order can be one of the first challenges you encounter when learning English.

Verb Tenses: Expressing Time

Another significant difference between English and many other languages is how verb tenses are used to show time. English has a more detailed system of tenses compared to some languages. This helps to clearly show when an action happens—whether it was in the past, is happening now, or will happen in the future.

Comparison of Tense Usage:

English Tense	Example Sentence	Equivalent in Other Languages	Notes
Present Simple	"She walks to school."	Spanish: "Ella camina a la escuela."	Similar structure in many languages
Present Continuous	"She is walking to school."	French: "Elle est en train de marcher."	Continuous aspects may not exist in some languages
Past Simple	"She walked to school."	Chinese: "她走路去学校了。"	Chinese often uses time markers instead of tense
Future Simple	"She will walk to school."	Japanese: "彼女は学校に行くでしょう。"	Japanese uses auxiliary words to indicate future

Some languages, like Chinese, don't change the verb to show time. Instead, they use words like "yesterday" or "tomorrow" to say when something happens. This can make learning English tenses hard for people who speak those languages because they have to learn how to change the verb to show time.

Grammar Rules: Regularity vs. Irregularity

English grammar is known for its irregularities. While some languages have more consistent and regular grammar rules, English often has exceptions that can be confusing for learners.

Comparison of Regularity in Grammar:

Grammar Aspect	English	Other Languages	Notes
Plural Formation	"Cat" to "Cats" (regular), "Child" to "Children" (irregular)	Turkish: "Kedi" to "Kediler" (regular)	English has many irregular plurals
Verb Conjugation	"Go" to "Went" (irregular), "Walk" to "Walked" (regular)	Spanish: "Ir" to "Fui" (irregular), "Caminar" to "Caminé" (regular)	English has irregular verb forms

Spelling Consistency	"Write" to "Wrote" (irregular)	Italian: "Scrivere" to "Scrissi" (regular)	English spelling can be unpredictable

In languages like Turkish, grammar rules are very regular, meaning once you learn a rule, it works the same way for the whole language. However, in English, there are many exceptions to the rules, especially with irregular verbs and plural nouns.

Chapter 2: Nouns and Pronouns

"The beginning of wisdom is to call things by their proper name."

—Confucius

Have you ever thought about how we name things around us or talk about them without repeating the same words? In this chapter, we'll learn about the basics of language—nouns and pronouns. You'll find out about different kinds of nouns, like common, proper, abstract, and collective nouns.

You'll also learn how pronouns can replace nouns to avoid repetition and make sentences smoother. By the end of this chapter, you'll know how to name and talk about people, places, things, and ideas in English, helping you communicate more clearly.

Types of Nouns: Common, Proper, Abstract, and Collective

Nouns are one of the most important parts of speech in English. They are the words we use to name everything around us—people, places, things, and ideas. Learning about the different types of nouns is critical to understanding English grammar.

In this section, we'll explore four main types of nouns: common nouns, proper nouns, abstract nouns, and collective nouns. By the end of this chapter, you'll be able to recognize and use these nouns in your writing and speaking.

1. Common Nouns

Common nouns are general names for people, places, things, or ideas. They are not specific, and they do not start with a capital letter unless they are at the beginning of a sentence. Common nouns refer to things that are not unique and can be used to describe a group or type of objects.

Examples of Common Nouns:

Category	Examples
People	"teacher," "doctor," "child"
Places	"city," "school," "park"
Things	"book," "apple," "car"
Ideas	"love," "happiness," "freedom"

How Common Nouns Are Used:

Common nouns are used when you are talking about something in a general way. For example, if you say "dog," you are talking about any dog, not a specific one. Common nouns do not start with a capital letter unless they are at the beginning of a sentence.

Examples in Sentences:

- "The dog barked loudly."
- "She went to the city."

2. Proper Nouns

Proper nouns are the specific names of people, places, things, or organizations. Unlike common nouns, proper nouns are special and always start with a capital letter, no matter where they are in a sentence. Proper nouns give more detailed information, like the name of a person, a city, a brand, or a day of the week.

Examples of Proper Nouns:

Category	Examples
People	"John," "Marie Curie," "Queen Elizabeth"
Places	"New York," "Mount Everest," "Eiffel Tower"
Things	"iPhone," "Tesla," "Mona Lisa"
Organizations	"United Nations," "Google," "Harvard University"

How Proper Nouns Are Used:

Proper nouns are used when you are referring to something specific. For example, if you say "Paris," you are talking about a specific city in France, not just any city. Proper nouns help to distinguish one particular thing from others in the same category.

Examples in Sentences:

- "John went to New York last summer."
- "She visited the Eiffel Tower in Paris."

3. Abstract Nouns

Abstract nouns refer to ideas, feelings, or qualities that you cannot touch or see. They are things that exist in our thoughts or imagination, not in the physical world. Abstract nouns are often used to talk about emotions, thoughts, or concepts that you cannot hold or see.

Examples of Abstract Nouns:

Category	Examples
Emotions	"happiness," "anger," "love"
States of Mind	"freedom," "knowledge," "peace"
Concepts	"justice," "truth," "equality"
Qualities	"bravery," "honesty," "kindness"

How Abstract Nouns Are Used:

Abstract nouns are used to express things that you can feel, think, or experience but cannot touch or see. For example, "happiness" is something you can feel, but it doesn't have a physical form that you can see or hold.

Examples in Sentences:

- **"Her kindness is appreciated by everyone."**
- **"Freedom is a fundamental right."**

4. Collective Nouns

Collective nouns are words that refer to a group of people, animals, or things seen as one unit. Even though they talk about many members, they are used as singular nouns in a sentence. Collective nouns are helpful when you want to talk about a group without mentioning each member by name.

Examples of Collective Nouns:

Category	Examples
People	"team," "family," "class"
Animals	"herd," "flock," "swarm"
Things	"collection," "fleet," "set"

How Collective Nouns Are Used:

Collective nouns are used to talk about a group as a single unit. For example, "team" refers to a group of players, but the word "team" itself is singular. Collective nouns make it easier to describe groups without listing each member.

Examples in Sentences:

- "The team won the championship."

- "A flock of birds flew across the sky."

Comparing Different Types of Nouns

Now that we've explored common, proper, abstract, and collective nouns, let's compare them to understand how they differ and how they are used in sentences.

Type of Noun	Definition	Examples	Capitalization
Common	General names for people, places, things, or ideas	"dog," "city," "happiness"	No (unless starting a sentence)
Proper	Specific names for people, places, things, or organizations	"John," "Paris," "Google"	Yes
Abstract	Names for ideas, concepts, feelings, or qualities	"love," "freedom," "justice"	No
Collective	Names for groups of people, animals, or things considered as one unit	"team," "herd," "fleet"	No

Visualizing Nouns:

Think of nouns as the foundation of a building. Just as the foundation provides stability and structure, allowing the building to stand tall, nouns give sentences their core by naming the people, places, things, or ideas that the rest of the sentence builds around.

TYPES OF NOUNS

Common Nouns

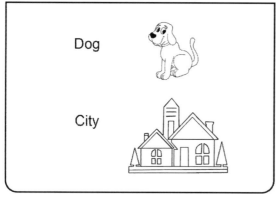

Dog

City

Proper Nouns

New york

John

Abstract Nouns

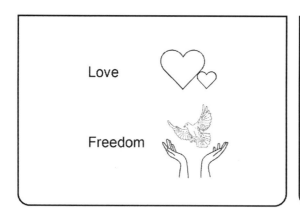

Love

Freedom

Collective Nouns

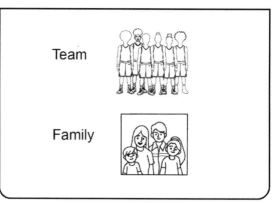

Team

Family

Usage and Rules of Pronouns

Pronouns are an important part of English grammar. They are words that replace nouns, helping us avoid saying the same nouns over and over. Without pronouns, we would have to repeat the same nouns all the time, making sentences long and hard to read. Pronouns make speaking and writing easier and clearer.

In this section, we'll learn about different types of pronouns, how to use them, and the rules they follow. By understanding pronouns, you'll be able to make your sentences smoother and more natural when you communicate in English.

What Are Pronouns?

Pronouns are words that take the place of nouns in a sentence. They refer to someone or something that has already been mentioned or is already known. Pronouns can refer to people, places, things, or ideas, and they change form depending on how they are used in the sentence.

Examples of Common Pronouns:

Type of Pronoun	Examples
Personal Pronouns	"I," "you," "he," "she," "it," "we," "they"
Possessive Pronouns	"my," "your," "his," "her," "its," "our," "their"
Reflexive Pronouns	"myself," "yourself," "himself," "herself," "itself," "ourselves," "themselves"
Relative Pronouns	"who," "whom," "which," "that"
Demonstrative Pronouns	"this," "that," "these," "those"
Interrogative Pronouns	"who," "what," "which," "whom," "whose"
Indefinite Pronouns	"anyone," "everyone," "someone," "nobody"

Why Are Pronouns Important?

Pronouns are important because they allow us to avoid redundancy and repetition. Instead of repeating the same noun over and over, we can use a pronoun to refer back to that noun. This makes sentences easier to read and understand.

Example Without Pronouns:

- "Maria went to Maria's house. Maria found that Maria's cat had knocked over a plant."

Example With Pronouns:

- "Maria went to her house. She found that her cat had knocked over a plant."

Using pronouns makes the sentence clearer and less repetitive.

Chapter 3: Verbs and Tenses

"The secret of getting ahead is getting started."

— Mark Twain

Verbs are the action words in a language—they make sentences lively by showing what is happening. In this chapter, we'll explore verbs and tenses, learning how to use verbs to describe actions in the past, present, and future.

You'll discover different types of verbs, like regular and irregular verbs, and how to change them to match the time of the action. By the end of this chapter, you'll know how to talk about time and actions clearly in English, helping you communicate better.

Introduction to Verbs and Their Functions

Verbs are very important in any language, and they are a key part of English grammar. Verbs are the words that show actions, states, or events. Without verbs, sentences would be boring and lack the movement that makes communication interesting.

In this section, we will learn what verbs are, how they work in sentences, and the different types of verbs you will see as you learn English. Whether you're talking about something happening now, in the past, or in the future, verbs help bring your sentences to life.

What Are Verbs?

A verb is a word that describes an action, state, or occurrence. It tells us what the subject of a sentence is doing or what is happening. Verbs are essential because they give meaning to sentences by indicating what is happening.

Types of Verbs:

1. Action Verbs:

Action verbs describe what the subject of a sentence does. They tell us about actions that can be seen, heard, touched, or otherwise perceived.

- **Examples:** "run," "jump," "eat," "write"
- **Example Sentences:**
  - **"She runs every morning."**
  - **"He writes a letter to his friend."**

2. State Verbs:

State verbs describe a condition or state of being. They do not describe actions but rather indicate states or conditions that exist.

- **Examples:** "be," "seem," "belong," "know"
- **Example Sentences:**
  - **"She is happy."**
  - **"They know the answer."**

3. Linking Verbs:

Linking verbs connect the subject of a sentence with additional information about the subject. They are often forms of the verb "to be."

- **Examples:** "am," "is," "are," "was," "were," "seem," "become"
- **Example Sentences:**
  - **"She is a teacher."**
  - **"The cake smells delicious."**

4. Helping (Auxiliary) Verbs:

Helping verbs are used together with a main verb to form a verb phrase. They help express tense, mood, or voice.

- **Examples:** "have," "has," "had," "do," "does," "did," "will," "shall," "can," "could," "may," "might"
- **Example Sentences:**
  - **"She has finished her homework."**
  - **"He can swim very fast."**

The Function of Verbs in Sentences

Verbs are essential because they serve as the backbone of a sentence. They tell us what is happening, when it is happening, and who is involved. Understanding how verbs function in sentences is crucial for constructing clear and meaningful sentences.

1. Verbs Indicate Action:

The most common function of a verb is to indicate an action that the subject performs. Action verbs can be physical actions, like "run" or "jump," or they can be mental actions, like "think" or "decide."

Examples of Action Verbs in Sentences:

- **"She runs in the park every morning."**

- **"They decided to go to the movies."**

In these examples, the verbs "runs" and "decided" tell us what the subjects are doing.

2. Verbs Express State of Being:

Verbs can also express a state of being, which describes the subject's condition or existence rather than an action. The most common state verb is "to be."

Examples of State Verbs in Sentences:

- **"She is tired."**
- **"They were excited about the trip."**

In these sentences, the verbs "is" and "were" describe the state of the subjects, not an action they are performing.

3. Verbs Connect Subjects to Descriptions:

Linking verbs, a subset of state verbs, connect the subject of the sentence to a word or phrase that describes the subject. They are often forms of "to be" but can also include other verbs like "seem" or "become."

Examples of Linking Verbs in Sentences:

- **"The sky is blue."**
- **"He seems happy."**

In these examples, the linking verbs "is" and "seems" connect the subjects to their descriptions.

4. Verbs Show Time and Continuity:

One of the most crucial jobs of verbs is to show when an action happens and if it is still happening. This is where tenses come in. Verbs change their form to show whether an action happened in the past, is happening now, or will happen in the future.

Examples of Verb Tenses in Sentences:

- **Present Tense: "She walks to school."** (happening now)
- **Past Tense: "She walked to school."** (happened before)
- **Future Tense: "She will walk to school."** (will happen later)

Types of Verbs: Regular and Irregular

Verbs can be classified into two main categories based on how they form their past tense: regular verbs and irregular verbs. Understanding these categories is important because it affects how verbs change when used in different tenses.

1. Regular Verbs:

Regular verbs follow a consistent pattern when forming their past tense and past participle. For most regular verbs, you simply add "-ed" to the base form of the verb.

Examples of Regular Verbs:

Base Form	Past Tense	Past Participle
"walk"	"walked"	"walked"
"talk"	"talked"	"talked"
"play"	"played"	"played"

Examples of Regular Verbs in Sentences:

- **"She walked to the store."**
- **"They played soccer yesterday."**

In these examples, the verbs "walked" and "played" are formed by adding "-ed" to the base forms "walk" and "play."

2. Irregular Verbs:

Irregular verbs do not follow a consistent pattern when forming their past tense and past participle. Instead, they change form in unpredictable ways.

Examples of Irregular Verbs:

Base Form	Past Tense	Past Participle
"go"	"went"	"gone"
"see"	"saw"	"seen"
"take"	"took"	"taken"

Examples of Irregular Verbs in Sentences:

- **"She went to the store."**
- **"They saw a movie last night."**

In these examples, the verbs "went" and "saw" do not follow the regular "-ed" pattern and instead have unique past tense forms.

Present, Past, and Future Tenses

Verb tenses are important for showing when an action happens. In English, the three main tenses are present, past, and future. These tenses help us say if something is happening now, has already happened, or will happen later. Knowing how to use these tenses correctly is vital for clear communication.

In this section, we'll learn about the present, past, and future tenses. We'll see how each tense is formed, how it's used in sentences, and some common mistakes to watch out for. We'll also include lots of examples, tables, and pictures to help you understand these ideas easily, especially if you're just starting to learn.

1. Present Tense

The present tense is used to describe actions or states that are happening now, as well as habitual actions and general truths. It's the most basic tense in English and serves as the foundation for other tenses.

Types of Present Tense:

1. Simple Present:

- **Usage:** The simple present tense is used for habitual actions, general truths, and actions happening now (in a broader sense).
- **Formation:** The base form of the verb is used, with an "s" or "es" added for the third person singular (he, she, it).

Examples:

- **"She walks to school every day."** (habitual action)
- **"The sun rises in the east."** (general truth)
- **"He plays the guitar."** (current activity)

2. Present Continuous (Progressive):

- **Usage:** The present continuous tense is used to describe actions that are happening right now or actions that are ongoing.
- **Formation:** The present continuous is formed with the present tense of the verb "to be" (am, is, are) + the "-ing" form of the main verb.

Examples:

- **"She is walking to school right now."** (action happening now)
- **"They are studying for their exams."** (ongoing action)

3. Present Perfect:

- **Usage:** The present perfect tense is used to describe actions that happened at an unspecified time before now, or actions that started in the past and continue to the present.
- **Formation:** The present perfect is formed with the present tense of the verb "to have" (have, has) + the past participle of the main verb.

Examples:

- **"She has walked to school every day this week."** (action repeated up to the present)
- **"I have finished my homework."** (completed action with relevance to now)

4. Present Perfect Continuous:

- **Usage:** The present perfect continuous tense is used to describe actions that started in the past and are still continuing or have just finished.
- **Formation:** The present perfect continuous is formed with the present perfect of the verb "to be" (have/has been) + the "-ing" form of the main verb.

Examples:

- **"She has been walking to school for an hour."** (action that started in the past and is still ongoing)
- **"They have been playing soccer all afternoon."** (action that has been happening continuously)

2. Past Tense

The past tense is used to describe actions or states that happened and were completed in the past. It's essential for telling stories, recounting events, and describing past experiences.

Types of Past Tense:

1. Simple Past:

- **Usage:** The simple past tense is used for actions that happened and were completed in the past. It's often used with time expressions like "yesterday," "last week," or "in 2010."
- **Formation:** Regular verbs form the simple past by adding "-ed" to the base form. Irregular verbs have unique past tense forms.

Examples:

- "She walked to school yesterday." (regular verb)
- "He went to the store last night." (irregular verb)

2. Past Continuous (Progressive):

- **Usage:** The past continuous tense is used to describe actions that were ongoing in the past. It's often used to set the scene in a story or describe a background action that was interrupted by another action.

- **Formation:** The past continuous is formed with the past tense of the verb "to be" (was, were) + the "-ing" form of the main verb.

Examples:

- **"She was walking to school when it started raining."** (ongoing action interrupted by another action)

- **"They were playing soccer all afternoon."** (ongoing action)

3. Past Perfect:

- **Usage:** The past perfect tense is used to describe an action that was completed before another action in the past. It's often used in complex sentences to show the sequence of events.

- **Formation:** The past perfect is formed with the past tense of the verb "to have" (had) + the past participle of the main verb.

Examples:

- **"She had walked to school before it started raining."** (action completed before another action)

- **"They had finished their homework before dinner."**

4. Past Perfect Continuous:

- **Usage:** The past perfect continuous tense is used to describe actions that were ongoing up to a certain point in the past. It's often used to emphasize the duration of an action.

- **Formation:** The past perfect continuous is formed with the past perfect of the verb "to be" (had been) + the "-ing" form of the main verb.

Examples:

- **"She had been walking for an hour before it started raining."** (ongoing action before another past action)

- **"They had been playing soccer all afternoon before it started to rain."**

3. Future Tense

The future tense is used to describe actions or states that will happen in the future. It allows us to make predictions, promises, and plans.

Types of Future Tense:

1. Simple Future:

- **Usage:** The simple future tense is used to describe actions that will happen in the future. It often uses the helping verb "will" or "shall."
- **Formation:** The simple future is formed with "will" or "shall" + the base form of the verb.

Examples:

- **"She will walk to school tomorrow."**
- **"We shall see the results next week."**

2. Future Continuous (Progressive):

- **Usage:** The future continuous tense is used to describe actions that will be ongoing at a specific point in the future.
- **Formation:** The future continuous is formed with "will be" + the "-ing" form of the main verb.

Examples:

- **"She will be walking to school at 8 AM tomorrow."** (ongoing future action)
- **"They will be playing soccer when you arrive."**

3. Future Perfect:

- Usage: The future perfect tense is used to describe actions that will be completed before a specific point in the future.
- Formation: The future perfect is formed with "will have" + the past participle of the main verb.

Examples:

- **"She will have walked to school by 9 AM tomorrow."** (completed action by a future time)
- **"They will have finished the project by next week."**

4. Future Perfect Continuous:

- **Usage:** The future perfect continuous tense is used to describe actions that will be ongoing up to a specific point in the future.
- **Formation:** The future perfect continuous is formed with "will have been" + the "-ing" form of the main verb.

Examples:

- **"She will have been walking for an hour by the time she arrives at school."**
- **"They will have been playing soccer for two hours by the time the match ends."**

Visualizing Tenses:

Think of tenses as the timeline of a journey. The past is like the road behind you, representing actions that have already happened. The present is where your vehicle is right now, capturing what's happening in the moment. The future is the road ahead, pointing to actions and events that are yet to come. Together, tenses map out when actions occur, guiding us through time.

PRESENT, PAST, AND FUTURE TENSES

Current Time 10:30 am

She walks

She walked

She will walk

Conjugation and Tense Agreement

Learning how to conjugate verbs correctly and making sure your tenses match in a sentence or paragraph are important skills in English grammar. Conjugation means changing the form of a verb to match the subject of a sentence, while tense agreement means keeping all the verbs in the right tense so your writing and speaking are clear and easy to understand.

In this section, we will look at the rules for verb conjugation and tense agreement. We will learn how to conjugate regular and irregular verbs in different tenses and talk about common mistakes that learners often make. This chapter is made easy for beginners, with simple explanations, examples, tables, and pictures to help you understand and use these ideas in your communication.

What Is Conjugation?

Conjugation means changing a verb to match the subject of a sentence. This includes making sure the verb is right for the number (singular or plural) and the person (first, second, or third person). It also means changing the verb to show the correct tense (past, present, or future).

Examples of Conjugation:

Subject	Verb: "to be" (Present Tense)	Verb: "to have" (Present Tense)
I	am	have
You	are	have
He/She/It	is	has
We	are	have
They	are	have

In the table above, you can see how the verb "to be" changes to "am," "is," and "are" depending on the subject. Similarly, the verb "to have" changes to "has" for the third person singular (he, she, it).

Conjugation of Regular Verbs

Regular verbs follow a predictable pattern when conjugated. In the present tense, they remain mostly unchanged except for adding an "-s" or "-es" in the third-person singular form. In the past tense, regular verbs typically add "-ed" to the base form.

Conjugation of Irregular Verbs

Irregular verbs do not follow a standard pattern in their conjugation. Instead, they change in unpredictable ways, especially in the past tense. Learning these verbs requires memorization, as there are no simple rules that apply to all of them.

Tense Agreement: Consistency in Time

Tense agreement means keeping the same verb tense throughout a sentence or paragraph. This means that once you choose a tense to describe an action, you should keep using it unless there's a good reason to change, like moving from talking about something that happened in the past to something that will happen in the future.

Importance of Tense Agreement:

Tense agreement is crucial because it ensures that your sentences make sense and that the timing of events is clear to the reader or listener. Inconsistent tenses can confuse the audience and make your writing or speech unclear.

Examples of Correct Tense Agreement:

Incorrect Sentence	Correct Sentence
"She is walking to school and bought lunch."	"She is walking to school and buying lunch."
"He was cooking dinner when the phone rings."	"He was cooking dinner when the phone rang."
"They will start the meeting and discussed the agenda."	"They will start the meeting and discuss the agenda."

Chapter 4: Adjectives and Adverbs

"Words are, of course, the most powerful drug used by mankind."

— Rudyard Kipling

Adjectives and adverbs make language more interesting, like adding spice to food. In this chapter, we'll learn how these descriptive words change nouns, verbs, and even other adjectives and adverbs, making your sentences more colorful and detailed.

You'll discover how to use adjectives to describe and compare things, and how adverbs can change actions, making your sentences clearer and more exact. By the end of this chapter, you'll know how to make your writing and speaking more lively, with better descriptions and stronger messages.

How To Use Adjectives and Adverbs Effectively

Adjectives and adverbs are important in English because they help us add more detail and make our sentences more interesting. While verbs and nouns build the sentence, adjectives and adverbs make it more colorful and clear. They help us describe things better and share our thoughts more precisely.

What Are Adjectives?

Adjectives are words that describe or modify nouns and pronouns. They provide additional information about the noun, such as its size, shape, color, quantity, or quality. Adjectives help answer questions like "What kind?" "Which one?" "How many?" or "How much?"

Examples of Adjectives:

Adjective	Usage in a Sentence	Explanation
"big"	"She has a big house."	Describes the size of the house.
"red"	"He wore a red shirt."	Describes the color of the shirt.
"three"	"There are three apples on the table."	Describes the quantity of apples.
"delicious"	"This is a delicious meal."	Describes the quality of the meal.

Types of Adjectives:

1. Descriptive Adjectives:

- Descriptive adjectives describe the qualities of a noun or pronoun. These are the most common types of adjectives.

- **Examples:** "tall," "blue," "happy," "soft"
- **Sentence: "She is wearing a beautiful dress."** (Describes the appearance of the dress)

2. Quantitative Adjectives:

- Quantitative adjectives indicate the quantity or amount of the noun.
- **Examples:** "few," "many," "several," "all"
- **Sentence: "He has many books."** (Indicates the number of books)

3. Demonstrative Adjectives:

- Demonstrative adjectives point out specific nouns. They include "this," "that," "these," and "those."
- **Examples:** "this," "that," "these," "those"
- **Sentence: "I like this movie."** (Points out a specific movie)

4. Possessive Adjectives:

- Possessive adjectives show ownership or possession. They include "my," "your," "his," "her," "its," "our," and "their."
- **Examples:** "my," "your," "his," "her"
- **Sentence: "This is my book."** (Shows that the book belongs to the speaker)

5. Interrogative Adjectives:

- Interrogative adjectives are used to ask questions about a noun. They include "which," "what," and "whose."
- **Examples:** "which," "what," "whose"
- **Sentence: "Which color do you prefer?"** (Asks about a specific choice of color)

What Are Adverbs?

Adverbs are words that modify verbs, adjectives, or other adverbs. They provide additional information about how, when, where, or to what extent something happens. Adverbs help answer questions like "How?" "When?" "Where?" and "To what degree?"

Examples of Adverbs:

Adverb	Usage in a Sentence	Explanation
"quickly"	"She ran quickly to catch the bus."	Describes how she ran (the verb "ran").
"yesterday"	"He arrived yesterday."	Describes when he arrived (the verb "arrived").

"here"	"Please sit here."	Describes where to sit (the verb "sit").
"very"	"The cake is very delicious."	Describes the extent of how delicious (the adjective "delicious").

Types of Adverbs:

1. Adverbs of Manner:

- Describe how an action is performed.
- **Examples:** "slowly," "happily," "carefully"
- **Sentence: "She spoke softly."** (Describes how she spoke)

2. Adverbs of Time:

- Describe when an action occurs.
- **Examples:** "now," "later," "yesterday"
- **Sentence: "He will arrive tomorrow."** (Describes when he will arrive)

3. Adverbs of Place:

- Describe where an action occurs.
- **Examples:** "here," "there," "everywhere"
- **Sentence: "The children are playing outside."** (Describes where they are playing)

4. Adverbs of Degree:

- Describe the intensity or degree of an action, adjective, or another adverb.
- **Examples:** "very," "quite," "too"
- **Sentence: "The movie was extremely interesting."** (Describes the intensity of "interesting")

5. Adverbs of Frequency:

- Describe how often an action occurs.
- **Examples:** "always," "never," "sometimes"
- **Sentence: "She always drinks coffee in the morning."** (Describes how often she drinks coffee)

Visualizing Adjectives and Adverbs:

Think of adjectives and adverbs as the paintbrushes of a picture. Adjectives add color and detail to nouns, just as a paintbrush brings life to a blank canvas by describing qualities like size, color, and shape. Adverbs, on the other hand, refine verbs, adjectives, or other adverbs, like adjusting the brightness or tone of the image, showing how, when, or to what extent something happens. Together, they enrich sentences with vivid detail and nuance.

ADJECTIVES AND ADVERBS

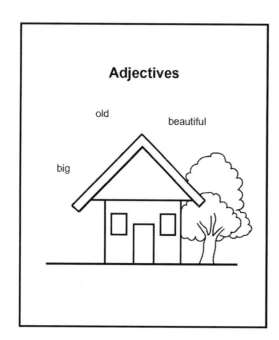

Comparative and Superlative Forms

Comparing things is an integral part of language. Whether we are looking at two items, talking about different experiences, or choosing the best option, using comparative and superlative forms of adjectives and adverbs helps us do this clearly. By learning how to make and use these comparisons, you can make your communication more precise and detailed.

What Are Comparative and Superlative Forms?

Comparative and superlative forms are special versions of adjectives and adverbs that are used to compare two or more things.

- Comparative forms are used to compare two things, showing whether one has more or less of a certain quality than the other.

- Superlative forms are used to compare three or more things, indicating which one has the most or least of a certain quality.

Examples:

Form	Adjective	Adverb	
Positive (Base)	"tall"	"quickly"	"She is tall." / "He runs quickly."
Comparative	"taller"	"more quickly"	"She is taller than her brother." / "He runs more quickly than his friend."
Superlative	"tallest"	"most quickly"	"She is the tallest in her class." / "He runs the most quickly of all the players."

Using Comparatives and Superlatives Effectively

Using comparatives and superlatives effectively means choosing the right form based on the context and ensuring that your comparisons are clear and logical. Here are some key tips:

1. Compare Similar Things:

- Make sure the items you are comparing are similar in nature.
    - **Incorrect: "This apple is bigger than that orange."**
    - **Correct: "This apple is bigger than that other apple."**

2. Use "Than" with Comparatives:

- When using the comparative form, use "than" to introduce the second item in the comparison.
    - **Example: "She is taller than her brother."**
    - **Explanation: "Than" introduces the person being compared (her brother).**

3. Use "The" with Superlatives:

- Superlatives often use "the" before the adjective or adverb because they indicate something that is the most or least of a group.
    - **Example: "She is the fastest runner on the team."**
    - **Explanation: "The" emphasizes that she is the top runner among all the team members.**

4. Avoid Double Comparisons:

- Do not use both "-er" and "more" together or "-est" and "most" together.
- **Incorrect: "She is more taller than her friend."**
- **Correct: "She is taller than her friend."**
- **Incorrect: "This is the most fastest car."**
- **Correct: "This is the fastest car."**

Chapter 5: Articles and Prepositions

"Prepositions are not words to end sentences with."

— Winston Churchill

Articles and prepositions are small but very important words that help make your sentences clear and easy to understand. In this chapter, we'll learn how articles like "a," "an," and "the" help us talk about nouns, and how prepositions like "in," "on," and "at" show how different parts of a sentence relate to each other. You'll find out how to use these words correctly, avoid common mistakes, and make your English smoother and more accurate. By the end of this chapter, you'll know how to connect ideas clearly in both writing and speaking.

Usage of 'a,' 'an,' and 'the'

Articles are small but essential words in English. They help us show whether we are talking about something specific or something general. The articles "a," "an," and "the" are important parts of English grammar, and using them correctly can make your communication clearer.

What Are Articles?

Articles are words that define a noun as specific or unspecific. In English, there are two types of articles:

1. Definite Article:

- **"The"** is the definite article and is used to refer to a specific noun that both the speaker and the listener are aware of.
- **Example: "Please pass the salt."** (The speaker and listener know which salt is being referred to.)

2. Indefinite Articles:

- **"A"** and **"an"** are indefinite articles and are used to refer to a non-specific noun, one that is not known to the listener or is being mentioned for the first time.
- **Examples:**
    - **"I saw a cat in the garden."** (The cat is not specific; it could be any cat.)
    - **"She needs an umbrella."** (Any umbrella, not a specific one.)

Common Prepositions and Their Proper Use

Prepositions are small but significant words that show how different parts of a sentence are connected. They act like links, joining nouns, pronouns, or phrases to other words. By learning how to use prepositions correctly, you can make your sentences clearer and easier to understand.

What Are Prepositions?

Prepositions are words that show how a noun (or pronoun) is connected to other parts of the sentence. They often describe relationships in time, place, direction, and manner.

Examples of Common Prepositions:

Preposition	Function	Example Sentence
"in"	Indicates location inside something	"She is in the room."
"on"	Indicates location on a surface	"The book is on the table."
"at"	Indicates a specific point	"We will meet at the park."
"to"	Indicates direction	"He is going to the store."
"for"	Indicates purpose or reason	"This gift is for you."
"with"	Indicates accompaniment	"She went to the party with her friends."

Visualizing Prepositions:

Think of prepositions as the bridges that connect different parts of a sentence. They help you understand where something is, when something happens, and how different ideas or objects relate to each other.

COMMON PREPOSITIONS

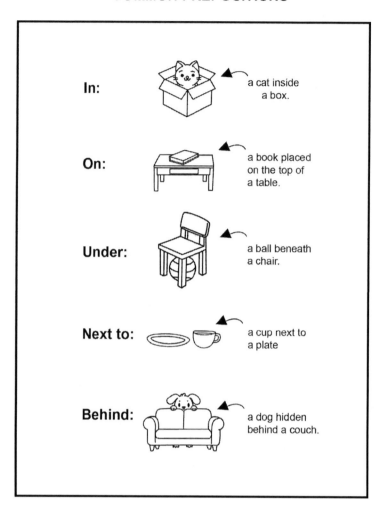

Prepositions of Place

Prepositions of place describe where something is located. They are some of the most commonly used prepositions in English and are essential for describing physical locations and spatial relationships.

1. "In"

"In" is used to describe something that is inside an enclosed space or within boundaries.

Examples:

Usage	Sentence Example
Inside a room or building	"She is in the kitchen."
Inside a country or city	"He lives in New York."

Within a specific area	"The keys are in my bag."

Explanation:

- "In" is used when something is enclosed or surrounded by boundaries, whether physical or conceptual.

2. "On"

"On" is used to describe something that is on a surface or in contact with a surface.

Examples:

Usage	Sentence Example
On a surface	"The laptop is on the desk."
On a horizontal line	"There are pictures on the wall."
Used with streets or roads	"The café is on Main Street."

Explanation:

- "On" is used when something is physically resting on or attached to a surface.

3. "At"

"At" is used to describe a specific point or location, often a particular place or time.

Examples:

Usage	Sentence Example
Specific location or address	"We will meet at the station."
Events or gatherings	"She is at the concert."
General location (e.g., home, work)	"He is at work."

Explanation:

- "At" is used for more precise locations, often specific points rather than broader areas.

Table: Prepositions of Place

Preposition	Function	Example
"in"	Inside a space	"She is in the car."
"on"	On a surface	"The picture is on the wall."
"at"	Specific point	"He is at the airport."

Prepositions of Direction

Prepositions of direction show the movement or path from one place to another. These words are important for explaining how things move or where they are in relation to other objects.

1. "To"

"To" is used to indicate movement towards a specific destination or direction.

Examples:

Usage	Sentence Example
Movement towards a place	"He is going to the store."
Indicating direction	"She walked to the park."
Giving something to someone	"Please give this to your teacher."

Explanation:

"To" is used when movement occurs from one place to another, indicating the destination or recipient.

2. "From"

"From" is used to indicate the starting point of a movement or action.

Examples:

Usage	Sentence Example
Starting point	"She traveled from Paris to London."
Origin	"This package is from my friend."

Explanation:

"From" indicates where something starts, whether it's a physical movement or the origin of an item.

3. "Into"

"Into" is used to describe movement from outside to a space within.

Examples:

Usage	Sentence Example
Entering a space	"He walked into the room."
Movement towards the inside	"The cat jumped into the box."

Explanation:

"Into" describes the action of entering a place or moving towards the inside of something.

BOOK 2

Building Vocabulary

Expand Your Vocabulary with Essential Words and Phrases for Everyday Use

Explore to Win

Chapter 1: Introduction to Vocabulary Building

"Without words, we would be a vague, shapeless mass of thoughts."

— Virginia Woolf

Building a strong vocabulary is important for good communication. In this chapter, we'll explain why growing your vocabulary is helpful and how it can make you more confident when you speak and write. You'll learn simple ways to learn and remember new words, tips for using them in your daily life, and how having a rich vocabulary can help you understand more and have better conversations. Whether you're just starting or looking to improve your language skills, this chapter will guide you on your journey to building a better vocabulary.

Importance of a Strong Vocabulary

Having a strong vocabulary is like having a set of tools that help you express your thoughts, ideas, and feelings clearly. A good vocabulary not only improves your communication but also opens up more opportunities in your personal and work life. Whether you're just starting to learn English or want to improve your skills, building a strong vocabulary is vital for mastering the language.

Why Vocabulary Matters

Vocabulary is the foundation of language. Every time we speak or write, we use words, and the more words we know, the better we can express ourselves. But vocabulary isn't just about knowing a lot of words—it's also about knowing how to use them correctly in different situations.

1. Enhances Communication

A strong vocabulary helps you say what you mean clearly and correctly. Whether you're describing something, sharing your ideas, or asking for help, using the right words can make a big difference. With a good vocabulary, people can easily understand what you're trying to say, which helps avoid misunderstandings.

Examples:

Situation	With Limited Vocabulary	
Describing a feeling	"I feel bad."	"I feel disappointed and frustrated."
Explaining a concept	"This is good."	"This solution is effective and efficient."

Explanation:

In the examples above, the sentences with a stronger vocabulary provide more detail and clarity, making the communication more effective.

2. Improves Reading Comprehension

Having a strong vocabulary is important for understanding what you read. When you know more words, it's easier to understand books, articles, and other writings. This makes reading more enjoyable and helps you learn new things more quickly.

Examples:

Text	With Limited Vocabulary	
"The situation was dire."	Might not understand the word "dire."	Understands that "dire" means very serious or urgent.

Explanation:

- If you understand the word "dire," you can better comprehend the gravity of the situation being described in the text.

3. Expands Expressive Abilities

A strong vocabulary helps you express yourself in more detailed and interesting ways. Instead of using simple words, you can choose more specific and descriptive ones to clearly share your message. This makes your communication more engaging and enjoyable for others.

Examples:

Basic Expression	Enhanced Expression
"The food was good."	"The food was exquisite and flavorful."
"She is happy."	"She is elated and overjoyed."

Explanation:

- The enhanced expressions provide more vivid and precise descriptions, making the communication richer and more engaging.

Visualizing the Impact of Vocabulary:

Think of your vocabulary like a box of colors. With only a few colors, your picture might look simple and plain. But with many colors, you can create bright and detailed pictures. In the same way, a strong vocabulary helps you "paint" your thoughts with more detail and meaning.

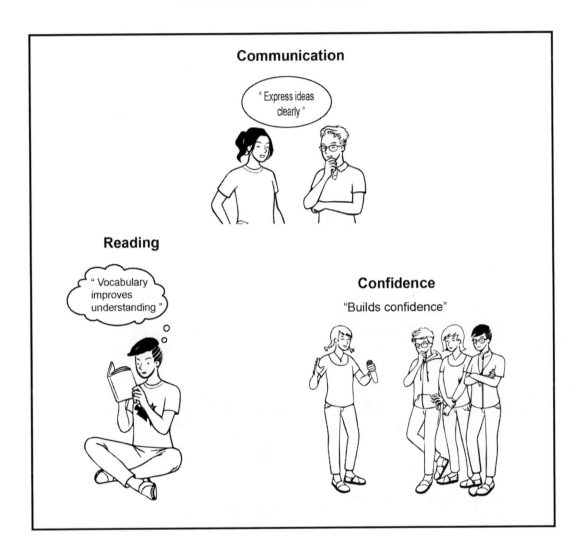

The Benefits of a Strong Vocabulary

Building a strong vocabulary has many benefits that extend beyond just communication. Let's explore some of the key advantages of having a rich and varied vocabulary.

1. Boosts Confidence

When you have a strong vocabulary, you feel more sure of yourself when you speak or write. You know you have the right words to share your thoughts and ideas, which can make you feel less nervous in conversations, presentations, or writing. This confidence can help you do well in social situations, at school, and at work.

Examples:

Situation	With Limited Vocabulary	
Giving a presentation	Nervous about finding the right words	Confident in expressing ideas clearly
Writing an essay	Struggles to convey ideas effectively	Writes clearly with varied vocabulary

Explanation:

- A strong vocabulary equips you with the tools you need to communicate confidently, whether speaking or writing.

2. Enhances Critical Thinking

Having a strong vocabulary helps you think more clearly and understand things better. When you know many words, it's easier to understand complex ideas, link different thoughts, and explain yourself more accurately. This is especially important in school and work, where careful thinking is very important.

Examples:

Task	With Limited Vocabulary	
Analyzing a text	Struggles with complex words and ideas	Understands nuances and makes connections
Debating an issue	Lacks the words to articulate points	Clearly presents and supports arguments

Explanation:

A rich vocabulary allows you to engage with complex ideas more effectively, improving your critical thinking skills.

3. Facilitates Learning

Learning new subjects or skills often involves understanding special words or ideas. A strong vocabulary makes it easier to understand new things, whether you're studying language, science, history, or any other topic. It also helps you explain what you've learned to others.

Examples:

Subject	With Limited Vocabulary	
Learning English	Struggles with new words and phrases	Quickly learns and uses new vocabulary
Studying science	Difficulty understanding technical terms	Easily grasps and uses scientific terminology

Explanation:

A strong vocabulary accelerates learning by making it easier to understand and retain new information.

4. Expands Career Opportunities

In many jobs, having a solid vocabulary is very important for doing well. Whether you're writing reports, giving presentations, or talking with clients, knowing the right words helps you share your ideas clearly and professionally. It can also help you stand out from others, leading to new chances and career growth.

Examples:

Profession	With Limited Vocabulary	
Sales	Struggles to persuade clients	Persuasively communicates benefits
Writing	Limited word choice in content	Creates engaging and varied content

Explanation:

- A strong vocabulary is a valuable asset in any career, helping you to communicate more effectively and achieve your professional goals.

Techniques for Learning and Retaining New Words

Learning and remembering new words is very important when learning any language, especially English. A strong vocabulary helps you speak clearly, understand others better, and have good conversations. But building your vocabulary takes regular practice and good strategies. In this section, we will explore different ways to help you learn and remember new words for a long time. These methods are simple and practical, making them easy to use, even if you are just starting to learn English.

Understanding How Memory Works

Before we start learning techniques, it's good to understand how memory works. Our brains store information in different ways, and how we learn new words can change how well we remember them.

1. Short-Term Memory vs. Long-Term Memory

- **Short-Term Memory:** This is where your brain keeps information for a short time. For example, you might remember a phone number just long enough to dial it, but then you might forget it afterward.

- **Long-Term Memory:** This is where your brain stores information for a long time. When you learn new words, the goal is to move them from short-term memory to long-term memory so you can easily remember them when you need to.

2. The Importance of Repetition

Repeating a word many times helps move it from short-term to long-term memory. The more you see and use a word, the more likely it is to stay in your memory and become a permanent part of your vocabulary.

3. Active vs. Passive Learning

- **Active Learning:** This means practicing by using new words in sentences or conversations.

- **Passive Learning:** This means taking in information without doing anything with it, like listening to someone talk or reading a text. Both ways of learning are crucial, but practicing and using what you learn usually helps you remember words better.

Techniques for Learning New Words

Now that you know a bit about how memory works, let's look at some simple techniques to help you learn new words easily. These methods are practical, easy to use, and suitable for learners at any level.

1. Flashcards

Flashcards are a simple and helpful tool for learning new words. They let you practice a word many times, which makes it easier to remember.

How to Use Flashcards:

- **Create Your Flashcards:** Write the new word on one side of a card and its definition or a sentence using the word on the other side.

- **Review Regularly:** Go through your flashcards daily, focusing on the words you find most challenging. The repetition helps move the words into your long-term memory.

- **Use Digital Flashcards:** If you prefer, use apps like Anki or Quizlet, which allow you to create and review flashcards on your phone or computer.

Example:

Front of Card	Back of Card
"Eloquent"	"Fluent or persuasive in speaking or writing"

2. Word Maps

Word maps, also called mind maps or word webs, help you see and organize information about a new word. They show how the word is connected to other ideas, making it easier to understand and remember.

How to Create a Word Map:

- **Start with the Word:** Write the new word in the center of a page.
- **Branch Out:** Draw lines from the word to related ideas, synonyms, antonyms, and example sentences. You can also include images that represent the word's meaning.
- **Review:** Regularly review your word maps to reinforce the connections in your mind.

Example:

Word	Word Map Branches
"Eloquent"	Synonyms: "articulate," "fluent" Antonyms: "inarticulate," "tongue-tied" Example: "She gave an eloquent speech."

3. Mnemonics

Mnemonics are simple tools that help you remember new words by connecting them to something you already know, like a rhyme, a short word, or a picture.

How to Use Mnemonics:

- **Create a Story or Image:** Imagine a story or picture that connects to the word and its meaning. The more colorful and unique it is, the easier it will be to remember.
- **Use Rhymes or Acronyms:** Make up a short rhyme or a simple acronym that includes the word and its meaning.
- **Practice:** Use your mnemonic device regularly until the word becomes familiar.

Example:

Word	Mnemonic
"Resilient"	"Imagine a rubber band that snaps back into shape no matter how much you

	stretch it."

4. Contextual Learning

Learning new words in context, rather than in isolation, can help you understand how they are used in real-life situations. This method involves seeing the word in sentences, paragraphs, or conversations.

How to Practice Contextual Learning:

- **Read Regularly:** Read books, articles, and other materials in English. Pay attention to how new words are used in different contexts.
- **Highlight and Note:** Highlight new words and write down the sentences they appear in. Review these sentences regularly.
- **Practice Writing:** Use new words in your writing. Try to create sentences or short paragraphs that incorporate the words you're learning.

Example:

Word in Context	Sentence Example
"Eloquent"	"The author's eloquent writing captivated the audience."

5. Spaced Repetition

Spaced repetition is a way of reviewing new words by going over them at different times, gradually spacing out the reviews. This method helps you remember words better in the long run.

How to Implement Spaced Repetition:

- Use an App: Apps like Anki or Memrise are designed to help you practice spaced repetition. They show you words at intervals based on how well you know them.
- Create a Schedule: If you prefer manual methods, create a schedule where you review words after 1 day, 3 days, 1 week, 2 weeks, and 1 month.
- Adjust Intervals: If you find certain words particularly difficult, review them more frequently.

Example:

Day	Review
Day 1	"Eloquent," "Innovative"
Day 3	"Eloquent," "Resilient"
Day 7	"Eloquent," "Articulate"
Day 14	"Innovative," "Resilient"

Techniques for Retaining New Words

Learning new words is only half the battle—you also need to retain them over time. Here are some techniques that can help you keep new vocabulary fresh in your memory.

1. Regular Review

Consistent review is essential for retaining new vocabulary. The more often you revisit a word, the more likely it is to stick in your memory.

How to Review Regularly:

- **Set a Schedule:** Dedicate a few minutes each day to reviewing your vocabulary. Consistency is key.

- **Mix Old and New Words:** During review sessions, mix older words with new ones. This helps reinforce the older words while still introducing new vocabulary.

- **Use Review Apps:** Apps like Anki or Quizlet can automate your review schedule, making it easier to stay on track.

2. Active Use

Actively using new words in your speech and writing helps reinforce your memory and understanding of them. The more you use a word, the more familiar it becomes.

How to Practice Active Use:

- **Write Daily:** Try to write something every day using the new words you've learned. This could be a diary entry, a short story, or even a social media post.

- **Speak in Conversations:** Use new words in your conversations with others. Don't be afraid to practice, even if you make mistakes—this is how you learn.

- **Join Language Groups:** Join English-speaking groups or online forums where you can practice using your vocabulary in discussions.

3. Engage with Media

Engaging with English media—such as books, movies, podcasts, and articles—exposes you to new words in context and helps reinforce the vocabulary you've already learned.

How to Engage with Media:

- **Watch Movies and TV Shows:** Choose English-language films and shows, and pay attention to how words are used. Try watching with subtitles to help with comprehension.

- **Listen to Podcasts:** Find podcasts on topics that interest you. Listening to different speakers helps you hear how words are used in various contexts.

- **Read Widely:** Read books, articles, and blogs on a variety of topics. This not only helps you learn new words but also shows you how they're used in different types of writing.

Chapter 2: Everyday Vocabulary

"The limits of my language mean the limits of my world."

— Ludwig Wittgenstein

In your everyday life, knowing common words is really important for good communication. In this chapter, we'll focus on the simple words and phrases you use in different situations, like at home, at work, and when talking to others. You'll learn useful words that will help you feel confident in daily conversations, making your interactions easier and more meaningful. Whether you're ordering food, asking for directions, or having a chat, the words you learn here will be your go-to tools.

Common Words and Phrases Used in Daily Life

Learning everyday vocabulary is a very important step in becoming good at any language. These are the words and phrases you use all the time, like when talking with friends, asking for directions, or doing simple tasks. They are the foundation of your ability to speak clearly and confidently in English. In this section, we'll go over a variety of common words and phrases that are important for daily life. We'll explain what they mean, how to use them, and give examples to help you understand how to use them in real situations.

1. Greetings and Polite Expressions

The way you greet others and use polite expressions sets the tone for your interactions. These phrases are essential for making a good impression and showing respect in any conversation.

Common Greetings:

Phrase	Usage	Example
"Hello"	General greeting, formal or informal	"Hello, how are you?"
"Hi"	Informal greeting, casual situations	"Hi! It's good to see you."
"Good morning"	Greeting in the morning	"Good morning! Did you sleep well?"
"Good afternoon"	Greeting in the afternoon	"Good afternoon, Mrs. Smith."
"Good evening"	Greeting in the evening	"Good evening, everyone."

Explanation:

"Hello" and "Hi" are the most versatile greetings, suitable for most situations. "Good morning," "Good afternoon," and "Good evening" are more formal and time-specific.

Polite Expressions:

Phrase	Usage	Example
"Please"	To make a request politely	"Can you pass the salt, please?"
"Thank you"	To express gratitude	"Thank you for your help."
"You're welcome"	To respond to "thank you"	"You're welcome. Glad to help."
"Excuse me"	To get someone's attention or to apologize	"Excuse me, can I ask you a question?"
"I'm sorry"	To apologize	"I'm sorry for being late."

Explanation:

"Please" and "Thank you" are basic words of courtesy that show respect and consideration for others. "Excuse me" and "I'm sorry" help you navigate social situations smoothly.

2. Asking for and Giving Directions

Knowing how to ask for and give directions is crucial when you're trying to find your way around a new place. These phrases will help you navigate unfamiliar areas and communicate with others when you need help.

Common Phrases for Asking Directions:

Phrase	Usage	Example
"Can you tell me how to get to...?"	To ask for directions to a specific place	"Can you tell me how to get to the train station?"
"Where is the nearest...?"	To ask for the location of the closest place	"Where is the nearest pharmacy?"
"How do I get to...?"	To ask for directions	"How do I get to the library?"
"Is it far from here?"	To ask about the distance to a place	"Is it far from here to the park?"

"Which way do I go?"	To ask for the direction	"Which way do I go to get to the bus stop?"

Explanation:

These phrases are commonly used when you need to find a location or navigate a new area. They are straightforward and easy to understand.

Common Phrases for Giving Directions:

Phrase	Usage	Example
"Go straight ahead"	To direct someone to continue in the same direction	"Go straight ahead until you see the post office."
"Turn left/right"	To instruct someone to change direction	"Turn left at the next traffic light."
"It's on your left/right"	To indicate the location of a place relative to the person	"The café is on your right."
"Take the first/second... street"	To direct someone to a specific street	"Take the second street on your left."
"You can't miss it"	To indicate that a place is easy to find	"The museum is just ahead. You can't miss it."

Explanation:

These phrases are essential for helping others find their way. They are simple and direct, making it easy for the listener to follow your instructions.

3. Shopping and Buying Things

When shopping, knowing the appropriate vocabulary can help you interact with store employees, ask for what you need, and make purchases smoothly. Here are some common phrases you might use or hear in a shopping scenario.

Common Phrases for Shopping:

Phrase	Usage	Example
"How much does this cost?"	To ask for the price of an item	"How much does this jacket cost?"

"I'm just looking"	To let a salesperson know you don't need help yet	"Thanks, I'm just looking."
"Do you have this in a different size/color?"	To ask for an alternative size or color	"Do you have this shirt in a larger size?"
"Can I try this on?"	To ask if you can try on clothing	"Can I try these shoes on?"
"Where is the fitting room?"	To ask for the location of the fitting room	"Where is the fitting room?"
"I'll take it"	To confirm a purchase	"I'll take this dress."

Explanation:

These phrases are useful in a variety of shopping situations, from browsing to making a purchase. They help you communicate your needs clearly and politely.

Common Phrases at the Checkout:

Phrase	Usage	Example
"Do you take credit cards?"	To ask if the store accepts credit cards	"Do you take credit cards, or is it cash only?"
"Can I get a receipt?"	To ask for a receipt for your purchase	"Can I get a receipt, please?"
"Would you like a bag?"	A common question from cashiers	"Would you like a bag for your items?"
"How would you like to pay?"	A common question about payment method	"How would you like to pay—cash or card?"

Explanation:

These phrases help you complete your transaction at the checkout smoothly and efficiently.

Vocabulary for Home, Work, and Social Situations

In your daily life, you go through different places—home, work, and social situations—each with its own set of words and phrases. Knowing the right words to use in each place is important for clear and easy communication. This section will focus on important vocabulary for these three main areas, helping you feel more confident in your conversations.

Vocabulary for Home

Home is where you spend a lot of your time, so it's important to know the words used in this place. Whether you're talking about chores, family members, or describing your home, these words and phrases will be very useful.

Common Household Items:

Item	Definition	Example Sentence
"Sofa"	A comfortable seat with cushions, typically for two or more people	"We bought a new sofa for the living room."
"Refrigerator"	A large appliance used to keep food and drinks cold	"Please put the milk in the refrigerator."
"Microwave"	An appliance used to heat food quickly	"I'll warm up the leftovers in the microwave."
"Lamp"	A device that provides light, typically with a shade	"Turn on the lamp if you need more light."
"Curtains"	Fabric panels that cover windows to block light or provide privacy	"I need to close the curtains before it gets dark."

Explanation:

These are common items found in most homes. Knowing their names helps you talk about your home environment more easily.

Household Chores:

Chore	Definition	Example Sentence
"Vacuuming"	The act of cleaning floors using a vacuum cleaner	"I need to do some vacuuming in the living room."
"Dusting"	The process of removing dust from surfaces	"She spends the morning dusting the furniture."
"Doing the dishes"	Washing plates, cups, and other kitchenware	"I'll do the dishes after dinner."
"Laundry"	The process of washing, drying, and folding clothes	"It's laundry day, so I'll be busy for a while."
"Mopping"	Cleaning the floor with a wet mop	"I need to mop the kitchen floor after cooking."

Explanation:

These chores are common in most households. Being able to talk about them is essential for discussing daily routines and responsibilities.

Family Members:

Family Member	Definition	Example Sentence
"Mother"	The female parent of a child	"My mother is an excellent cook."
"Father"	The male parent of a child	"My father works in the city."
"Sibling"	A brother or sister	"I have two siblings, one brother and one sister."
"Spouse"	A husband or wife	"My spouse and I enjoy traveling together."
"Cousin"	A child of your uncle or aunt	"My cousin is visiting us this weekend."

Explanation:

Understanding the names of family members is important for discussing your relationships and family dynamics.

Vocabulary for Work

The workplace has its own special words that are important for talking with colleagues, supervisors, and clients. Knowing these words and phrases will help you feel more confident at work.

Common Workplace Items:

Item	Definition	Example Sentence
"Desk"	A piece of furniture where you work, typically with a flat surface	"I keep my computer and documents on my desk."
"Computer"	An electronic device used for work, communication, and entertainment	"I use a computer to complete most of my tasks."
"Printer"	A machine that prints documents onto paper	"Could you print the report for me?"
"Meeting room"	A space where people gather to discuss work-related topics	"The meeting room is reserved for our afternoon discussion."
"Office	Items used in the workplace, such as	"We need to order more office supplies."

supplies"	pens, paper, and staplers	

Explanation:

These items are commonly found in offices and workplaces. Knowing their names is essential for discussing your work environment.

Workplace Actions:

Action	Definition	Example Sentence
"Emailing"	Sending messages through electronic mail	"I'll email you the details later today."
"Scheduling"	Planning events or meetings	"I'm scheduling a meeting for next Monday."
"Presenting"	Giving a presentation to share information or ideas	"She will be presenting her project tomorrow."
"Collaborating"	Working together with others on a task or project	"We are collaborating on a new marketing strategy."
"Networking"	Building professional relationships	"Networking is important for career growth."

Explanation:

These actions are typical in many workplaces. Understanding them helps you describe what you do at work and how you interact with colleagues.

Job Titles and Roles:

Phrase	Usage	Example Sentence
"I'm in a meeting"	To inform someone that you are currently in a meeting	"I can't talk right now; I'm in a meeting."
"Let's touch base"	To suggest following up or checking in on a topic	"Let's touch base later this week about the project."
"Deadline"	The time or date by which something must be completed	"The deadline for the report is Friday."
"I'm working on it"	To indicate that you are in the process of completing a task	"I'm working on the presentation now."
"Can you clarify?"	To ask for more information or	"Can you clarify what you meant by

	explanation	that?"

Explanation:

These phrases are commonly used in professional settings. They help you communicate more effectively about your tasks and responsibilities.

Vocabulary for Social Situations

Social interactions are an important part of life; knowing the right words helps you make friends and have good conversations. Whether you're at a party, talking with friends, or meeting new people, these words and phrases will be beneficial.

Visualizing Daily Life Vocabulary:

Think of daily life vocabulary as the toolkit you carry around every day. Just like a toolkit contains essential tools to handle routine tasks and unexpected situations, daily life words equip you to navigate the world—whether you're ordering food, giving directions, or having a conversation. These everyday words help you communicate effectively, making sure you're prepared for all the little moments that make up your day.

Chapter 3: Vocabulary for Specific Situations

"The right word may be effective, but no word was ever as effective as a rightly timed pause."

— Mark Twain

Every situation needs specific words; having the right ones can make a big difference. In this chapter, we'll talk about essential words and phrases for different situations you might face, like traveling, shopping, and emergencies. You'll learn the words that will help you feel confident and communicate clearly, no matter where you are or what you're doing. Whether you're booking a hotel, asking for directions, or dealing with an urgent problem, this chapter will give you the language skills you need.

Words and Phrases for Travel, Shopping, and Emergencies

Traveling, shopping, and handling emergencies require specific words to help you manage these situations well. Knowing the right words can make these experiences easier, more enjoyable, and safer. In this section, we'll learn the important words you need for these situations, with simple explanations, examples, and helpful tips. This guide is easy to follow, so even if you're just starting to learn English, you'll be able to communicate clearly in these situations.

1. Travel Vocabulary

When you travel, whether for fun or work, you often need to use services like transportation, hotels, and restaurants. Knowing the right words and phrases can help you get around, ask for what you need, and enjoy your trip.

Booking and Accommodation:

When planning a trip, you'll likely need to book accommodation and other services. Here are some common words and phrases you'll encounter:

Phrase	Usage	Example Sentence
"Reservation"	An arrangement made in advance to secure accommodation, a table, etc.	"I'd like to make a reservation for a double room."
"Check-in"	The process of registering upon arrival at a hotel or airport	"What time is check-in at the hotel?"
"Check-out"	The process of leaving and settling your bill	"Check-out is at 11 AM."

	at a hotel	
"Confirmation"	Proof that your booking has been accepted	"I received a confirmation email for my flight."
"Amenities"	Additional services or features offered at a hotel, such as a gym or pool	"Does the hotel offer any amenities?"
"Single room/Double room"	Types of hotel rooms based on the number of beds	"I'd like to book a double room with a sea view."

Explanation:

Understanding these terms is essential when booking and staying at hotels or other accommodations. They help you clearly communicate your needs.

At the Airport:

Navigating an airport can be challenging, especially in a foreign country. Here are key phrases that will help you manage your travel experience:

Phrase	Usage	Example Sentence
"Boarding pass"	A document that allows you to board a flight	"Where can I print my boarding pass?"
"Gate"	The designated area where passengers board the plane	"Your flight departs from Gate 22."
"Baggage claim"	The area where you collect your luggage after a flight	"Where is the baggage claim area?"
"Layover"	A stop between connecting flights	"I have a two-hour layover in Chicago."
"Customs"	The place where your belongings are checked upon entering a country	"You need to go through customs after you land."
"Departure/Arrival"	The scheduled times when flights leave and arrive	"What time is the departure for my flight?"

Explanation:

These terms are crucial for understanding the various steps and processes involved in air travel, ensuring you get to your destination smoothly.

Getting Around:

Once you've arrived at your destination, you'll need to know how to get around. Here are some useful words and phrases for using public transportation or renting a vehicle:

Phrase	Usage	Example Sentence
"Taxi"	A car service that transports you to your destination	"Can you call a taxi for me?"
"Bus stop"	A designated place where buses pick up and drop off passengers	"Where is the nearest bus stop?"
"Subway/Metro"	An underground train system used for city transportation	"Is there a subway station nearby?"
"Ticket"	A pass that allows you to travel on public transportation	"Where can I buy a subway ticket?"
"Fare"	The cost of a ride on public transportation	"How much is the fare for the bus?"
"Rental car"	A car that you rent for a short period	"I need to rent a car for the weekend."

Explanation:

These phrases help you navigate your new environment, ensuring you can easily travel from place to place.

2. Shopping Vocabulary

We all shop, whether we're buying things we need or gifts to take home. Knowing the right words can help you ask for what you want, understand prices, and pay easily.

At the Store:

When shopping in a store, these phrases will help you communicate with the staff and find what you're looking for:

Phrase	Usage	Example Sentence
"Do you have this in stock?"	To ask if a particular item is available	"Do you have this sweater in stock?"
"On sale"	Items being sold at a reduced price	"Are these shoes on sale?"

"How much does this cost?"	To ask for the price of an item	"How much does this jacket cost?"
"Can I try this on?"	To ask if you can try on clothing before buying	"Can I try this dress on?"
"Receipt"	A document that shows proof of purchase	"Can I get a receipt, please?"
"Refund"	Returning an item for a money-back guarantee	"Can I get a refund for this item?"

Explanation:

These phrases are essential for a smooth shopping experience, helping you interact with salespeople and make informed purchasing decisions.

Payment Methods:

Understanding payment options is crucial when shopping. Here are some common phrases related to payments:

Phrase	Usage	Example Sentence
"Credit card"	A card that allows you to buy items on credit	"Can I pay with a credit card?"
"Debit card"	A card that deducts money directly from your bank account	"Do you accept debit cards?"
"Cash"	Physical money in the form of coins or bills	"Do you have change for cash?"
"Contactless payment"	Paying by tapping a card or device without inserting it	"Can I use contactless payment here?"
"Installments"	Payments made over a period of time for large purchases	"Can I pay for this in installments?"
"Total amount"	The full price that you need to pay	"What's the total amount for these items?"

Explanation:

These phrases help you complete transactions using various payment methods, ensuring you're prepared for any payment situation.

3. Emergency Vocabulary

Emergencies can happen anytime, so knowing the right words can help you act quickly and stay safe. Whether it's a medical emergency, a fire, or another urgent situation, these words and phrases are very important.

Medical Emergencies:

In a medical emergency, clear communication can save lives. Here are some key phrases to know:

Phrase	Usage	Example Sentence
"Call an ambulance"	To request emergency medical services	"Someone is hurt! Call an ambulance!"
"I need a doctor"	To request medical attention	"I think I need a doctor, I'm not feeling well."
"What's your emergency?"	A common question asked by emergency responders	"What's your emergency?"
"Allergic reaction"	A severe response to an allergen	"She's having an allergic reaction to peanuts!"
"Heart attack"	A serious medical condition involving the heart	"I think he's having a heart attack!"
"First aid"	Basic medical care given before professional help arrives	"Does anyone know first aid?"

Explanation:

These phrases are critical for getting help quickly in a medical emergency, ensuring you can clearly communicate the situation.

Fire Emergencies:

If there's a fire, knowing the right vocabulary can help you stay safe and get the help you need:

Phrase	Usage	Example Sentence
"Fire extinguisher"	A device used to put out small fires	"Where is the fire extinguisher?"
"Evacuate"	To leave a building or area quickly due to danger	"We need to evacuate the building immediately!"
"Smoke alarm"	A device that detects smoke and sounds	"The smoke alarm is going off!"

	an alarm	
"Fire escape"	A special exit used in case of fire	"Take the fire escape, it's safer."
"Emergency exit"	A designated door for use in emergencies	"Where is the nearest emergency exit?"
"Call the fire department"	To request help from firefighters	"There's a fire! Call the fire department!"

Explanation:

These terms are essential for ensuring your safety and the safety of others during a fire emergency.

General Emergency Phrases:

In any emergency, these general phrases will help you get the assistance you need:

Phrase	Usage	Example Sentence
"Help!"	A cry for immediate assistance	"Help! I need help!"
"Stay calm"	A reminder to keep calm during a crisis	"Stay calm, help is on the way."
"I'm lost"	To ask for help when you don't know where you are	"I'm lost, can you help me find my way?"
"Can you call the police?"	To request police assistance	"There's been an accident, can you call the police?"
"What's happening?"	To ask about the nature of an emergency	"There's a lot of noise outside, what's happening?"
"Where is the nearest hospital?"	To find medical care quickly	"Where is the nearest hospital?"

Explanation:

These phrases are crucial for quickly communicating the need for help in various emergency situations.

Cultural Vocabulary and Idioms

Cultural words and idioms are unique to each language and culture. They help you understand how people think, feel, and express themselves. In English, idioms and culture-specific words can be confusing because they don't always make sense when translated directly. However, learning these expressions will help you speak English more smoothly and connect better with people from English-speaking cultures.

Understanding Cultural Vocabulary

Cultural vocabulary includes words and phrases that are connected to the traditions, customs, and social habits of a culture. These words often have meanings beyond what you find in a dictionary because they reflect the values and beliefs of the people who use them.

Common Cultural Vocabulary:

Word/Phrase	Meaning	Cultural Context
"Thanksgiving"	A holiday celebrated primarily in the United States and Canada, marked by a feast with family and friends	Reflects the tradition of giving thanks for the harvest and blessings of the past year.
"Siesta"	A short nap taken in the early afternoon, common in Spanish-speaking countries	Reflects the cultural practice of taking a break during the hottest part of the day.
"Hygge" (pronounced "hoo-gah")	A Danish concept that describes a cozy, comfortable atmosphere that fosters well-being	Reflects the importance of coziness and contentment in Danish culture.
"Carnival"	A festive season that occurs before Lent, featuring parades, music, and dancing, particularly in Latin America and Europe	Reflects the celebration of life and community before a period of religious observance.
"Tea time"	A light meal or snack, usually including tea, typically served in the afternoon in the U.K.	Reflects the British cultural tradition of taking a break with tea and snacks.

Explanation:

These words and phrases are associated with specific cultural practices and holidays. Knowing them can help you talk more easily about cultural events and traditions.

Idioms: The Heart of Cultural Expression

Idioms are phrases that mean something different from the actual words. They are common in everyday conversation and can confuse learners because you can't understand them by translating each word. However, learning idioms is important for improving your English and making your speech sound more natural.

Common English Idioms:

Idiom	Literal Meaning	Figurative Meaning	
"Break the ice"	To physically break ice	To initiate a conversation in a social situation, making people feel more comfortable	"He told a joke to break the ice at the party."
"Piece of cake"	A literal piece of cake	Something very easy to do	"The exam was a piece of cake."
"Spill the beans"	To literally spill beans	To reveal a secret	"Who spilled the beans about the surprise party?"
"Bite the bullet"	To literally bite a bullet	To endure a painful or unpleasant situation	"I'll have to bite the bullet and get that tooth pulled."
"Hit the nail on the head"	To literally hit a nail with a hammer	To describe exactly what is causing a situation or problem	"You hit the nail on the head with your analysis."

Explanation:

These idioms are often used in daily conversations. Learning what they mean will help you understand conversations better and use these expressions confidently.

Cultural Significance of Idioms

Idioms often reveal a culture's history, values, and beliefs. By learning the meaning behind these idioms, you can better understand how people from different backgrounds think and talk.

Cultural Themes in Idioms:

1. **Work and Productivity:**
   - Work-related idioms like "burn the midnight oil" (working late) or "hit the ground running" (starting a task with energy) show that hard work and being efficient are important in many English-speaking cultures.

2. **Nature and Animals:**
   - Many idioms use animals or nature, like "barking up the wrong tree" (going in the wrong direction) or "a storm in a teacup" (making a big deal out of something small). These sayings often show how language is connected to nature.

3. Food and Drink:

- Food-related idioms like "piece of cake" (something easy) or "spill the beans" (reveal a secret) show how food influences the way we talk. In many cultures, food is a big part of social life, and this is reflected in the language we use.

4. Emotions and Relationships:

- Idioms about feelings or relationships, like "wear your heart on your sleeve" (showing your feelings openly) or "in hot water" (being in trouble), show how important emotions and relationships are in communication.

Explanation:

- Understanding the cultural meanings behind idioms helps you see how language reflects the values of those who use it. This can improve your communication and make you more aware of different cultures.

Visualizing Vocabulary for Specific Situations:

Think of vocabulary for specific situations as a specialized set of keys. Just like each key is designed to open a particular lock, these words are tailored for specific contexts—whether it's at the doctor's office, in a business meeting, or while traveling. Using the right vocabulary in the right situation unlocks clearer communication, helping you handle unique environments with confidence and precision.

ESSENTIAL VOCABULARY FOR TRAVEL, SHOPPING, AND EMERGENCIES

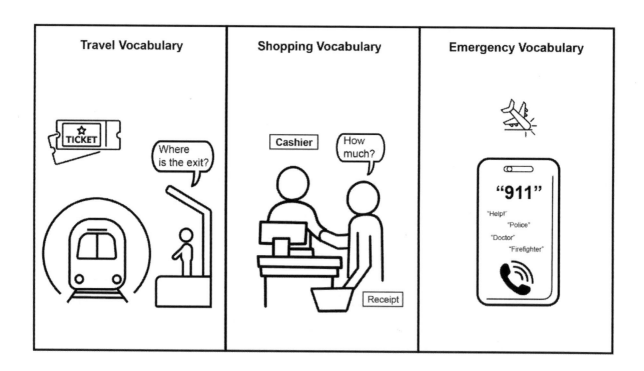

Chapter 4: Synonyms and Antonyms

"To broaden your vocabulary is to broaden your thinking."

— Bertrand Russell

Words are powerful, and having a strong vocabulary helps you express yourself clearly and with more variety. In this chapter, we will learn about synonyms and antonyms—words that have similar or opposite meanings. Using synonyms can help you avoid repeating the same words, making your language more interesting. Understanding antonyms will help you see the full meaning of words in different situations. This chapter will show you easy ways to learn more words by using these word pairs, helping you communicate better and making your speech and writing more lively.

Expanding Vocabulary Through Synonyms and Antonyms

Having a strong and varied vocabulary is important for clear communication. It helps you share your ideas more accurately. Learning about synonyms and antonyms is a good way to grow your vocabulary. Synonyms are words that mean the same or almost the same thing, while antonyms are words that mean the opposite. Knowing these words can help you avoid saying the same thing repeatedly, improve your writing and understand what you read better.

In this section, we will explore synonyms and antonyms. You will see how these words can make your language more interesting and help you communicate more clearly. This chapter has simple examples, exercises, and tips designed for beginners, so you can easily understand and use these ideas in your daily English.

Understanding Synonyms

What Are Synonyms?

Synonyms are words with the same or nearly the same meaning as another word. For example, "happy" and "joyful" are synonyms because both words describe the feeling of being pleased. Using synonyms helps you avoid repeating the same word, making your speaking and writing more interesting and clear.

Examples of Common Synonyms:

Word	Synonyms	Example Sentences
"Happy"	Joyful, Cheerful, Content, Delighted	"She felt happy/joyful/content after receiving the news."

"Big"	Large, Huge, Enormous, Gigantic	"They bought a big/large/enormous house."
"Smart"	Intelligent, Clever, Bright, Brainy	"He is a smart/intelligent student."
"Fast"	Quick, Rapid, Speedy, Swift	"The cheetah is a fast/quick animal."
"Beautiful"	Attractive, Pretty, Lovely, Gorgeous	"The garden is beautiful/attractive in spring.

Explanation:

Using synonyms allows you to choose the word that best fits the context of your sentence. It also adds variety to your language, making your writing and speaking more interesting.

Understanding Antonyms

What Are Antonyms?

Antonyms are words that mean the opposite of each other. For example, "hot" and "cold" are antonyms because they describe opposite temperatures. Knowing and using antonyms can help you clarify your meaning, show differences, and express a wider range of ideas.

Examples of Common Antonyms:

Word	Antonyms	Example Sentences
"Hot"	Cold, Cool	"The soup is too hot/cold to eat."
"Big"	Small, Tiny	"He lives in a big/small apartment."
"Fast"	Slow	"The car is fast/slow on the highway."
"Happy"	Sad, Unhappy	"She felt happy/sad after the movie ended."
"Rich"	Poor	"He became rich/poor after winning/losing the lottery."

Explanation:

- Antonyms are helpful for showing differences or opposite ideas. They can make your communication clearer and more interesting by highlighting contrasts.

Visualizing Synonyms and Antonyms in Context:

Imagine a word tree where the root word branches out into synonyms, and opposite branches represent antonyms. This tree shows how different words are connected and how they can be used to enrich your language.

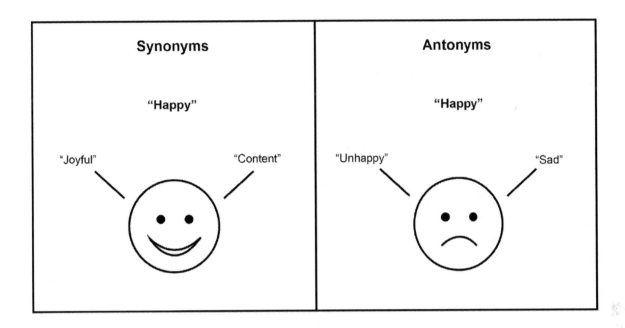

Using Thesauruses and Other Resources

Expanding your vocabulary by learning synonyms and antonyms can greatly improve your language skills, making your speech and writing more lively and clear. A thesaurus is a helpful tool for finding synonyms and antonyms, as it groups words by their meanings and offers other words with similar or opposite meanings. Besides using a thesaurus, you can use other ways and tools to grow your vocabulary and pick the right words for every situation.

In this section, we will learn how to use a thesaurus and other helpful tools like online resources, dictionaries, and vocabulary apps. We will also discuss choosing the best synonyms and antonyms depending on the situation. By the end of this chapter, you will know how to use these tools to grow your vocabulary, making your communication clearer and more interesting.

Understanding the Thesaurus

What is a Thesaurus?

A thesaurus is a book or online tool that groups words with similar meanings (synonyms) and sometimes opposite meanings (antonyms). It is a helpful resource for anyone who wants to use different words and find the best word to express what they mean.

Types of Thesauruses:

1. Print Thesaurus:

- Traditional thesauruses, like "Roget's Thesaurus," have been used for many years to help writers find synonyms and antonyms. These books are organized by alphabet or by topic, providing lists of similar words.

2. Online Thesaurus:

- Online thesauruses, like Thesaurus.com or Merriam-Webster's online thesaurus, give you quick access to many synonyms and antonyms. These tools also often offer extra features, such as word suggestions, examples of how to use the words, and related words.

3. Built-in Thesaurus Tools:

- Many word processing programs, like Microsoft Word, have a built-in thesaurus. You can right-click on a word to see synonyms instantly. This feature is helpful when you need a quick reference while writing.

Example of Using a Thesaurus:

Let's say you're writing a paragraph and you've used the word "happy" multiple times. To add variety, you might consult a thesaurus.

- **Original Sentence:** "She was happy with the happy news."
- **Using a Thesaurus:** "She was delighted with the joyful news."

Explanation:

- By using the thesaurus, you found synonyms for "happy" ("delighted" and "joyful"), which makes your sentence more engaging and less repetitive.

Exploring Other Resources for Vocabulary Expansion

In addition to the thesaurus, there are several other resources that can help you expand your vocabulary and find the right words for any situation. These resources include dictionaries, online tools, vocabulary apps, and more.

1. Dictionaries:

Dictionaries are essential for understanding the meanings, pronunciations, and proper usage of words. They often include information about word origins, part of speech, and example sentences.

- **Types of Dictionaries:**
  - **Standard Dictionaries:** Offer definitions, pronunciations, and basic information about words. Examples include Merriam-Webster and Oxford English Dictionary.

- **Learner's Dictionaries:** Designed specifically for non-native speakers, these dictionaries provide simplified definitions and examples. Examples include Cambridge Learner's Dictionary and Longman Dictionary of Contemporary English.
- **Bilingual Dictionaries:** Provide translations between two languages, which can be useful for learners who are not yet fully comfortable with English.

Example of Using a Dictionary:

If you come across the word "exuberant" and aren't sure what it means, a dictionary can provide the definition and examples.

- **Definition:** "Full of energy, excitement, and cheerfulness."
- **Example Sentence:** "The children were exuberant as they ran through the park."

Explanation:

Using a dictionary helps you understand the exact meaning of a word and how to use it correctly in a sentence.

2. Online Tools and Websites:

There are many online tools and websites designed to help you expand your vocabulary and find the right words. These tools often offer features like word suggestions, usage examples, and interactive exercises.

- **Examples of Online Tools:**
  - **Thesaurus.com:** An online thesaurus that provides synonyms, antonyms, and word suggestions.
  - **WordHippo:** A versatile tool that offers synonyms, antonyms, translations, and more.
  - **Merriam-Webster:** An online dictionary and thesaurus with additional resources like quizzes and word games.

Example of Using an Online Tool:

If you're looking for synonyms for the word "important," you might use Thesaurus.com to find alternatives like "crucial," "vital," and "significant."

Explanation:

- Online tools provide quick access to a wealth of vocabulary resources, making it easy to find the right word when you need it.

3. Vocabulary Apps:

Vocabulary apps are a convenient way to learn new words and practice using them. These apps often include interactive exercises, flashcards, and quizzes to help you build your vocabulary over time.

- **Examples of Vocabulary Apps:**
    - **Quizlet:** A popular app that allows you to create and study flashcards with vocabulary words.
    - **Vocabulary.com:** An app that offers personalized vocabulary quizzes and tracks your progress.
    - **Duolingo:** A language-learning app that includes vocabulary practice as part of its lessons.

Example of Using a Vocabulary App:

Using Quizlet, you can create a set of flashcards with synonyms and antonyms. You can then practice matching the words to their meanings and using them in sentences.

Explanation:

- Vocabulary apps offer a fun and engaging way to learn new words and reinforce your understanding through regular practice.

4. Word of the Day Features:

Many websites, apps, and even email subscriptions offer a "Word of the Day" feature. This is a great way to gradually expand your vocabulary by learning one new word each day.

- **Example of a Word of the Day:**
    - **Word:** "Ebullient"
    - **Definition:** "Cheerful and full of energy."
    - **Example Sentence:** "Her ebullient personality made her the life of the party."

Explanation:

- Learning a new word each day helps you steadily build your vocabulary, making it easier to remember and use new words over time.

Chapter 5: Root Words and Affixes

"Words are the keys to the heart."

— Ahmed Deedat

Learning about the roots of words, along with prefixes and suffixes, is like cracking a secret code. In this chapter, we'll explore the basic parts of English words—root words, prefixes, and suffixes. By understanding how these parts fit together, you'll be able to figure out the meanings of new words, grow your vocabulary faster, and understand English better. This chapter will walk you through common roots and word parts, with easy examples and exercises to help you practice and learn.

Understanding Root Words, Prefixes, and Suffixes

The English language can seem big and complicated, but knowing the basic parts of words—root words, prefixes, and suffixes—can make it easier to understand. By breaking words into these smaller parts, you can often figure out what they mean, even if you've never seen them before. This skill is very helpful for learning new words and understanding what you read.

In this section, we will learn what root words, prefixes, and suffixes are, how they work together to create new words, and how you can use this knowledge to understand words you don't know. We'll give you clear explanations, simple examples, and exercises to help you use these ideas in your everyday English.

What Are Root Words?

Definition of Root Words

A root word is the main part of a word that gives it its basic meaning. It's like the core of the word, and you can add prefixes (at the beginning) or suffixes (at the end) to make new words. Knowing root words helps you understand and recognize many related words.

For example, the root word "ject" comes from the Latin word "jacere," which means "to throw." This root is found in many English words, like "eject" (to throw out), "project" (to throw forward), and "reject" (to throw back).

Examples of Common Root Words:

Root Word	Meaning	Examples	Explanation
"port"	To carry	Transport, Export, Import, Portable	The root "port" relates to carrying or moving something.
"scrib/script"	To write	Describe, Manuscript, Inscription, Prescription	The root "scrib/script" is related to writing.
"spect"	To see, watch	Inspect, Spectator, Perspective, Spectacle	The root "spect" relates to seeing or observing.
"struct"	To build	Construct, Structure, Instruction, Destruction	The root "struct" is connected to building or forming something.
"dict"	To say, speak	Dictate, Dictionary, Predict, Contradict	The root "dict" involves speaking or saying something.

Explanation:

- By recognizing the root word, you can often infer the meaning of a word, even if you've never seen it before. For instance, if you know "spect" means to see, you can guess that a "spectator" is someone who watches something.

What Are Prefixes?

Definition of Prefixes

A prefix is a group of letters that you add to the beginning of a root word to change its meaning. Prefixes can make the word mean something different, like its opposite or a stronger version of the word.

For example, the prefix "un-" means "not" or "the opposite of." When you add "un-" to the word "happy," it becomes "unhappy," which means "not happy."

Examples of Common Prefixes:

Prefix	Meaning	Examples	Explanation
"un-"	Not, opposite of	Unhappy, Unkind, Unusual, Uncertain	The prefix "un-" negates or reverses the meaning of the root word.
"re-"	Again, back	Rewrite, Rebuild, Return, Replay	The prefix "re-" indicates doing something again or going back.
"pre-"	Before	Preview, Predict, Prehistoric, Preschool	The prefix "pre-" indicates something that happens before.

"dis-"	Not, opposite of, apart	Disagree, Disappear, Disconnect, Disapprove	The prefix "dis-" often reverses or negates the meaning of the root word.
"mis-"	Wrongly, badly	Misunderstand, Misplace, Mislead, Mistake	The prefix "mis-" indicates something done incorrectly or badly.

Explanation:

- Prefixes change the meaning of the root word, helping you make new words with similar but different meanings. For example, "appear" means to come into view, while "disappear" means to go out of view.

What Are Suffixes?

Definition of Suffixes

A suffix is a group of letters added to the end of a root word. It changes the word's meaning or how it is used. Suffixes can show if a word is a noun, verb, adjective, or adverb, and can also change the word's meaning.

For example, the suffix "-ness" turns an adjective into a noun. Adding "-ness" to the root word "happy" makes "happiness," which means the state of being happy.

Examples of Common Suffixes:

Suffix	Meaning	Examples	Explanation
"-ness"	State or quality of	Happiness, Sadness, Kindness, Darkness	The suffix "-ness" turns adjectives into nouns.
"-ful"	Full of, characterized by	Joyful, Hopeful, Careful, Wonderful	The suffix "-ful" turns nouns or verbs into adjectives.
"-less"	Without, lacking	Hopeless, Careless, Fearless, Useless	The suffix "-less" indicates the absence of something.
"-ly"	In a certain way	Quickly, Happily, Slowly, Carelessly	The suffix "-ly" turns adjectives into adverbs.
"-ment"	Action or result of	Payment, Employment, Development, Enjoyment	The suffix "-ment" turns verbs into nouns.

Explanation:

- Suffixes change a word's meaning and show how it is used in a sentence. For example, "careful" means "full of care," while "careless" means "without care."

Combining Root Words, Prefixes, and Suffixes

Learning how root words, prefixes, and suffixes work helps you understand complex words. You can break them into parts to figure out their meanings. Let's see how these parts fit together:

Example 1:

- **Word:** "Unhappiness"
- **Root Word:** "happy" (feeling pleasure or contentment)
- **Prefix:** "un-" (not)
- **Suffix:** "-ness" (state of)
- **Meaning:** The state of not feeling pleasure or contentment.

Example 2:

- **Word:** "Misunderstanding"
- **Root Word:** "understand" (grasp the meaning of something)
- **Prefix:** "mis-" (wrongly)
- **Suffix:** "-ing" (indicates an ongoing action)
- **Meaning:** The act of grasping the meaning of something incorrectly.

Example 3:

- **Word:** "Reconstruction"
- **Root Word:** "construct" (to build)
- **Prefix:** "re-" (again)
- **Suffix:** "-ion" (action or process)
- **Meaning:** The process of building something again.

Explanation:

By looking at the root word, prefix, and suffix, you can often understand difficult words, even if you've never seen them before. This helps you learn new words and understand what you read better.

Visualizing Root Words and Affixes:

Think of root words and affixes as the roots and branches of a tree. The root word is the core foundation, like the trunk of a tree, carrying the essential meaning. Affixes—prefixes and suffixes—are like the branches and leaves that grow from the trunk, modifying and expanding the meaning. Just as branches can stretch in different directions, affixes change the root's meaning or function, helping create a variety of new words from a single base.

BREAKING DOWN ROOT WORDS, PREFIXES, AND SUFFIXES

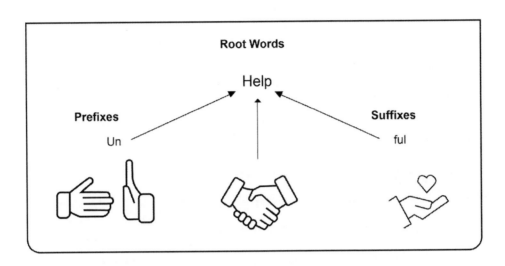

Building New Words From Roots

Language changes and grows, and one way this happens is by making new words. Knowing how to build words from root words helps you learn more vocabulary and understand English better. By adding prefixes and suffixes to root words, you can create many new words, each with its own meaning.

In this section, we will learn how to build new words from roots. We will see how different prefixes and suffixes can change root words to make new words with specific meanings. This chapter will give you easy explanations, examples, and exercises to help you understand word-making better. The goal is to make this process simple and clear, especially for those who are just starting to learn English.

The Process of Building New Words

Understanding Word Formation

Word formation is how we make new words by adding prefixes and suffixes to root words. This helps us create new words that can describe things, actions, or ideas. By learning how to form words, you can understand and make new words even if you haven't seen them before.

Key Components of Word Formation:

1. **Root Words:**

   The core part of a word that carries the fundamental meaning. For example, "struct" is a root that means "to build."

2. Prefixes:

Elements added to the beginning of a root word to modify its meaning. For example, the prefix "re-" means "again," so adding it to "struct" forms "reconstruct," which means "to build again."

3. Suffixes:

Elements added to the end of a root word to change its grammatical function or meaning. For example, adding the suffix "-ion" to "construct" forms "construction," which refers to the process of building.

Example of Word Formation:

Let's take the root word "scribe," which means "to write." By adding different prefixes and suffixes, we can create new words with related but distinct meanings:

- **Inscription:** The act of writing or engraving words.
- **Describe:** To write down or explain something in detail.
- **Manuscript:** A handwritten or typed document.
- **Subscription:** An agreement to receive or participate in something regularly.

Explanation:

By recognizing the root word and understanding the meanings of prefixes and suffixes, you can build and comprehend a variety of words related to writing.

Chapter 6: Advanced Vocabulary Building Techniques

"The limits of my language mean the limits of my world."

— Ludwig Wittgenstein

Learning new words takes time, but you can make it easier with good methods. In this chapter, we'll look at ways to build your word bank. We'll use tools like flashcards, practice over time, and learning words in sentences. These methods will help you remember and use new words better and keep learning.

Using Flashcards and Spaced Repetition

Knowing a lot of words is important for learning English. It's not just about learning new words but also about remembering and using them well. Flashcards and spaced repetition are great tools to help with this. They are especially helpful for beginners and those who want to get better at using new words.

In this section, we'll learn how to use flashcards and spaced repetition to grow your vocabulary. We'll talk about why these tools are useful, how to make and use flashcards, and how spaced repetition helps you remember words. By the end, you'll know how to use these methods to improve your English.

What Are Flashcards?

Definition of Flashcards

Flashcards are a simple and helpful way to learn new words. Each flashcard has a word or phrase on one side and its meaning or an example sentence on the other side. You can use flashcards to study not just words but also grammar rules, idioms, and phrases.

Benefits of Using Flashcards:

1. **Active Recall:**

   Flashcards promote active recall, which is the process of actively retrieving information from memory. This strengthens neural connections and improves long-term retention of vocabulary.

2. **Portability:**

   Flashcards are portable and can be used anywhere, whether you're commuting, waiting in line, or taking a break. This makes it easy to incorporate vocabulary practice into your daily routine.

3. **Customization:**

   Flashcards can be customized to suit your learning style. You can create your own flashcards with words that are relevant to your goals, or use pre-made flashcards from apps and websites.

4. **Gamification:**

   Many learners find flashcards fun and engaging, especially when combined with games or quizzes. This can increase motivation and make learning more enjoyable.

Example of a Flashcard:

Let's take the word "benevolent."

- **Front of the Flashcard:** "Benevolent"
- **Back of the Flashcard:** "Meaning: Kind and generous. Example Sentence: The benevolent teacher always helped students after class."

Explanation:

- The front of the card prompts you to recall the word's meaning, while the back provides the answer along with an example sentence to reinforce understanding.

What Is Spaced Repetition?

Definition of Spaced Repetition

Spaced repetition is a way to help you remember things better. You review a word or fact more often at first, and then less often as you start to remember it. This helps you keep the information in your memory for a longer time. It's a great way to learn new words and make sure you don't forget them.

How Spaced Repetition Works:

1. **Initial Learning:**

   When you first learn a new word, review it shortly after to reinforce your memory.

2. **First Interval:**

   If you recall the word correctly, wait a little longer before reviewing it again (e.g., the next day).

3. **Subsequent Intervals:**

   Continue to review the word at longer intervals (e.g., after two days, a week, two weeks, etc.). If you forget the word, reset the interval and review it more frequently until it sticks.

Example of Spaced Repetition Schedule:

Let's say you're learning the word "benevolent."

- **Day 1:** First review
- **Day 2:** Second review

- **Day 4:** Third review
- **Day 8:** Fourth review
- **Day 15:** Fifth review

Explanation:

- The idea is to review the word just before you forget it. Over time, the intervals become longer, and the word becomes ingrained in your long-term memory.

Benefits of Spaced Repetition:

1. **Maximized Retention:**

   Spaced repetition helps you retain information for longer periods by reinforcing memory just as it begins to fade.

2. **Efficient Learning:**

   Instead of cramming, spaced repetition allows for efficient use of study time by focusing on words that need reinforcement while reducing review frequency for words already mastered.

3. **Personalization:**

   Many spaced repetition systems (SRS) are adaptive, meaning they adjust the intervals based on your performance, focusing more on words that are difficult for you to remember.

Visualizing Advanced Vocabulary Building Techniques

Think of advanced vocabulary building techniques like planting seeds in a garden. Flashcards are the seeds, helping you plant new words into your memory by focusing on one word at a time.

Spaced repetition is like regularly watering those seeds—it strengthens your recall by reviewing words at carefully timed intervals, allowing them to take root and grow in your long-term memory.

Together, these techniques cultivate a thriving vocabulary over time, ensuring your new words flourish and stick.

Reading and Contextual Learning

Reading is a fun and easy way to learn new words. When you read, you see words used in sentences, which helps you understand their meanings and how to use them. This helps you learn words better and remember them longer.

In this section, we will talk about why reading is great for learning new words. We'll also cover how to pick books or articles that match your level and ways to learn words from what you read. We'll give you tips and exercises to help you make reading a regular part of your learning. By the end, you will know how to use reading to build a strong vocabulary.

The Importance of Reading for Vocabulary Building

Why Reading is Crucial

Reading is a fun and great way to learn new words. When you read, you see how new words are used in sentences. This helps you understand what they mean and how they work with other words. Reading helps you learn words naturally and remember them better.

Benefits of Reading for Vocabulary Acquisition:

1. **Contextual Understanding:**

   When you read, you see words in sentences or stories. This helps you understand what the words mean. The sentences give you clues about how the word is used and how it connects with other words.

2. **Exposure to Natural Language:**

   Reading helps you learn real, everyday language. You will see idioms, phrasal verbs, and casual phrases that aren't always in textbooks but are important for speaking well.

3. **Reinforcement Through Repetition:**

   When you read a text, you see words and phrases many times. This helps you remember them better. Seeing a word in different places shows you how it can be used in different ways.

4. **Cultural and Conceptual Learning:**

   Reading different materials shows you how language is used in different cultures. This helps you understand more about the language and its background, not just the words.

Example of Contextual Learning:

Let's take the word "intricate."

- **Sentence Example 1:** "The artist created an intricate design with hundreds of tiny details."
- **Sentence Example 2:** "The plot of the novel was so intricate that it kept me guessing until the very end."

Explanation:

- In the first sentence, "intricate" means something that is very detailed and complex, like a design. In the second sentence, "intricate" means a story that is complicated and has many twists. By seeing "intricate" used in different ways, you learn more about how the word can be used.

Choosing the Right Reading Materials

Selecting Materials Based on Your Level

To build your vocabulary by reading, pick books or texts that are right for your level. If the material is too hard, you might not understand it and could get frustrated. If it's too easy, you won't find many new words to learn.

Types of Reading Materials:

1. Beginner Level:

- **Graded Readers:** These are special books made for people learning a new language. They use simple words and sentences. They are great for beginners because they start with easy language and slowly use more difficult words as you get better.

- **Children's Books:** Books for children use simple words and lots of pictures. These books help you learn new words and understand their meanings better.

Example of Graded Reader:

- **Book Title:** "The Adventures of Tom Sawyer" (simplified version)

- **Explanation:** This version of the classic novel has been adapted with simpler language, making it accessible for beginners while still offering exposure to new vocabulary.

2. Intermediate Level:

- **Young Adult (YA) Novels:** These books are written for teenagers and often use more complex language than children's books, but they are still accessible to learners with an intermediate level of English.

- **Short Stories:** Short stories are a great way to practice reading without committing to a long text. They often focus on specific themes or emotions, providing rich context for vocabulary learning.

Example of YA Novel:

- **Book Title:** "The Hunger Games" by Suzanne Collins

- **Explanation:**This book has interesting language and a great story. It's perfect for people who want to learn new words while enjoying a good read.

3. Advanced Level:

- **Novels:** Long novels use lots of different words and phrases. They help advanced learners practice and understand more difficult language and ideas.

- **Non-Fiction Books:** Books about topics you like, like history, science, or self-help, teach you new words and show how people talk about different subjects.

Example of Advanced Novel:

- **Book Title:** "To Kill a Mockingbird" by Harper Lee
- **Explanation:** This classic book uses complex words and talks about deep ideas. It is good for advanced learners who want to improve their vocabulary and understand English better.

How to Gauge the Difficulty of a Text:

- **Vocabulary Density:** Count how many words you don't know on a single page. If there are more than 5-10 unfamiliar words, the text might be too difficult.
- **Comprehension:** If you keep having to read the same sentences or parts again to understand them, the text might be too hard for you right now.

Strategies for Learning Vocabulary Through Context

Using Context Clues

Context clues are hints in a sentence or paragraph that help you understand a new word. By looking at the words around it, you can often guess what the new word means without a dictionary.

Types of Context Clues:

1. **Definition Clues:**

   The meaning of the word is directly stated in the sentence, often following words like "is," "means," or "refers to."

   Example:

   - "The arboretum, a place where trees are grown and studied, was a peaceful retreat."
   - **Explanation:** The phrase "a place where trees are grown and studied" directly defines the word "arboretum."

2. **Synonym Clues:**

   A synonym or a word with a similar meaning is used in the sentence to clarify the unfamiliar word.

   Example:

   - "The child was very aloof, or distant, from the others in the group."
   - **Explanation:** The word "distant" is a synonym for "aloof," helping you understand its meaning.

3. **Antonym Clues:**

   An antonym or a word with an opposite meaning is used in the sentence to provide contrast.

Example:

- "Unlike his boisterous friends, who were always loud and active, John was quite reticent."

- **Explanation:** The contrast between "boisterous" and "reticent" helps you infer that "reticent" means quiet or reserved.

4. **Inference Clues:**

The meaning of the word is not directly stated but can be inferred from the overall context of the sentence or paragraph.

Example:

- "After the marathon, she felt completely enervated, barely able to lift her legs to walk."

- **Explanation:** The context of feeling exhausted after a marathon helps you infer that "enervated" means drained of energy.

Using a Dictionary for Confirmation:

While context clues help, it's also good to look up new words in a dictionary. This makes sure you know the word's meaning and can use it correctly.

- **Example:**

  - If you see the word "enervated" in a sentence about feeling very tired, you can look it up. You will find that it means "to make someone feel very weak and tired."

Explanation:

- Looking up a word in a dictionary helps you understand it better and avoid confusion.

Combining Reading with Vocabulary Practice:

When you read, write down new words in your flashcards or vocabulary journal. Review these words often to remember them better.

- **Example:**

  - If you find the word "precipice" while reading, write it down with its meaning and a sample sentence. Later, put it on your flashcards to study.

Explanation:

- Combining reading with other vocabulary-building techniques reinforces your learning and helps you retain new words.

Daily Practice Routines for Continued Improvement

Learning new words is something you need to keep doing, not just once. It takes regular practice to build a strong vocabulary. Doing a little each day helps you learn and remember new words better.

In this part, we will look at different ways to practice your vocabulary every day. You will see ideas like using flashcards, reading books, writing, listening to English, and speaking in English. We will give you simple tips and examples to help you fit these activities into your daily life. Our goal is to make learning new words easy and fun, so you keep getting better over time.

The Importance of Consistent Daily Practice

Why Daily Practice Matters

Practicing every day is very important to remember and learn new words. Just like learning any skill, you need to keep practicing to get better. If you don't practice regularly, it's easy to forget new words or use them wrong. Daily practice helps keep the words you learn fresh in your mind and makes using them in your speech and writing easier.

Benefits of Daily Vocabulary Practice:

1. **Steady Progress:**

   Daily practice allows you to make continuous improvements, even if they are small. Over time, these small gains add up to significant progress.

2. **Reinforcement of Learning:**

   Repeated exposure to words through various activities strengthens your memory and helps move vocabulary from short-term to long-term memory.

3. **Increased Fluency:**

   Regular practice in speaking, writing, and listening helps you become more comfortable and fluent in using new vocabulary in different contexts.

4. **Habit Formation:**

   By making vocabulary practice a daily routine, you develop a habit that supports your long-term language learning goals.

Example of Daily Practice:

Let's take a daily routine that includes different activities:

- **Morning:** Spend 10 minutes reviewing flashcards.
- **Afternoon:** Read a short article or chapter of a book.
- **Evening:** Write a journal entry using new vocabulary words.
- **Before Bed:** Listen to an English podcast or watch a short video in English.

Explanation:

- Using vocabulary practice throughout your day helps you remember and use new words better. This means you will keep improving and speaking more smoothly.

Morning Routine: Kickstart Your Day with Vocabulary Review

Flashcards and Spaced Repetition

Starting your day with a quick review of vocabulary helps wake up your memory and get you ready to use English. Using flashcards and reviewing them regularly helps you remember words better.

Example Morning Flashcard Session:

- **Flashcard 1:** "Gregarious" (Recall: "Sociable, enjoys being with others")
- **Flashcard 2:** "Loquacious" (Recall: "Very talkative")
- **Flashcard 3:** "Ephemeral" (Recall: "Lasting a very short time")

Explanation:

- Looking at vocabulary in the morning helps get your brain ready for the day. It makes it easier to see and use these words correctly.

Afternoon Routine: Expand Your Vocabulary Through Reading

Reading for Vocabulary Building

In the afternoon, it's a great time to read. Reading helps you see new words used in sentences and makes it easier to learn them. Pick books that are a bit challenging but not too hard, so you keep learning new words without getting frustrated.

Example Afternoon Reading Session:

- **Book:** "The Alchemist" by Paulo Coelho (an accessible yet meaningful novel for intermediate learners)
- **New Word:** "Omens" (Meaning: Signs of what will happen in the future)
- **Example Sentence:** "The boy learned to read the omens that guided him on his journey."

Explanation:

- Reading in the afternoon allows you to immerse yourself in the language, exposing you to new vocabulary and reinforcing the words you've already learned.

Evening Routine: Reinforce Learning Through Writing

Writing Practice for Vocabulary Retention

Writing helps you remember new words better. When you use new words in your writing, you practice using them in sentences. This helps you remember and understand the words more.

Example Evening Writing Session:

- **Journal Entry:**

  "Today, I felt particularly gregarious, as I spent the afternoon with a loquacious friend who loves to share stories. Despite our lively conversation, I noticed how ephemeral time can feel when you're deeply engaged in a dialogue."

Explanation:

- Writing in the evening helps consolidate the vocabulary you've learned throughout the day, ensuring that it becomes a part of your active language skills.

Before Bed Routine: Enhance Learning Through Listening

Listening to English

Listening to English is very important for learning. It helps you understand, speak better, and use words more easily. Listening to English before bed can be both relaxing and helpful. It helps you learn new words in a natural way.

Example Before Bed Listening Session:

- **Podcast:** "Stuff You Should Know" (an informative podcast that covers a wide range of topics, suitable for intermediate to advanced learners)

- **New Word:** "Conundrum" (Meaning: A confusing or difficult problem or question)

- **Example Sentence from the Podcast:** "The conundrum of how to reduce waste while increasing productivity is one that many companies face."

Explanation:

- Listening to English before bed helps you learn new words and get better at listening. It's a calm way to practice and remember what you've learned.

BOOK 3

Mastering Sentence Structure

Learn to Build Simple, Compound, and Complex Sentences with Confidence

Explore to Win

Chapter 1: Sentence Formation Basics

"A sentence is both the opportunity and limit of thought—what we have to think with, and what we have to think in."

— Stanley Fish

Understanding sentence structure is key to speaking and writing clearly in English. In this chapter, we'll look at the basic parts of sentences: subjects, verbs, and objects. You'll see how these parts fit together to make simple sentences. Learning these basics will help you create sentences that clearly show your ideas.

Subject-Verb-Object (SVO) Structure

To speak and write well in English, you need to understand how sentences are built. The basic structure of most English sentences is Subject-Verb-Object (SVO). This means you start with the subject (who or what the sentence is about), then add the verb (the action), and finish with the object (who or what the action is done to). In this section, we will explain this SVO structure, give examples, and provide practice exercises to help you learn it well.

What is the Subject-Verb-Object (SVO) Structure?

Definition of SVO Structure

1. **The SVO** structure is the most basic and common sentence pattern in English. It consists of three main components:

2. **Subject (S):** The subject is the person, place, thing, or idea that performs the action in the sentence. It is what the sentence is about.

3. **Verb (V):** The verb expresses the action performed by the subject or describes the state of being. It is the heart of the sentence.

Object (O): The object receives the action of the verb. It is the entity that is affected by the action.

Example of SVO Structure:

- **Sentence:** "The cat (Subject) chased (Verb) the mouse (Object)."

- **Explanation:** In this sentence, "The cat" is the subject (who is doing something), "chased" is the verb (what the subject is doing), and "the mouse" is the object (who or what the action is done to). This sentence uses the SVO structure, which helps show who is doing the action and who is receiving it.

Why is the SVO Structure Important?

The SVO structure is important because it helps you build clear and easy-to-understand sentences. It shows who is doing something, what they are doing, and who or what is receiving the action. Learning SVO makes it easier to create more complex sentences and express your ideas clearly.

Breaking Down the Components: Subject, Verb, and Object

1. Understanding the Subject

The subject of a sentence is the person, place, thing, or idea that is doing or being something. The subject typically appears at the beginning of the sentence and answers the question "Who?" or "What?"

Types of Subjects:

- **Nouns:** A noun is a word that names a person, place, thing, or idea. In the SVO structure, nouns often serve as the subject.
  - **Example:** "The dog (Subject) barked loudly."
- **Pronouns:** Pronouns are words that replace nouns to avoid repetition. Common pronouns include "he," "she," "it," "they," etc.
  - **Example:** "She (Subject) reads a book every night."
- **Proper Nouns:** Proper nouns are specific names of people, places, or organizations and are always capitalized.
  - **Example:** "Alice (Subject) loves to dance."

Explanation:

- The subject is the main part of the sentence. It tells us who or what the sentence is about. Knowing the subject helps make the sentence clear and easy to understand.

2. Understanding the Verb

The verb is the action word or the word that describes the state of being. In the SVO structure, the verb follows the subject and tells what the subject is doing or what is happening to the subject.

Types of Verbs:

- **Action Verbs:** Action verbs describe physical or mental actions.
  - **Example:** "The teacher (Subject) explains (Verb) the lesson."
- **Linking Verbs:** Linking verbs connect the subject to additional information about the subject, often an adjective or a noun.
  - **Example:** "The sky (Subject) is (Verb) blue."
- **Helping Verbs:** Helping verbs assist the main verb in a sentence by providing additional meaning, such as tense or mood.

- **Example:** "She (Subject) has (Helping Verb) finished (Main Verb) her homework."

Explanation:

The verb is the key to understanding what the subject is doing or experiencing. It is essential for conveying the action or state in the sentence.

3. Understanding the Object

The object of a sentence is the noun or pronoun that receives the action of the verb. It answers the question "Whom?" or "What?" after the verb.

Types of Objects:

- **Direct Object:** The direct object directly receives the action of the verb.
  - **Example:** "The chef (Subject) cooked (Verb) the meal (Direct Object)."
- **Indirect Object:** The indirect object is the recipient of the direct object and usually comes before the direct object in the sentence.
  - **Example:** "She (Subject) gave (Verb) him (Indirect Object) a gift (Direct Object)."

Explanation:

- The object completes the action in the sentence, providing a target or recipient for the verb's action. Without the object, the sentence might feel incomplete or unclear.

Importance of Word Order in English Sentences

In English, the order of words in a sentence is very important for making your meaning clear. Unlike some languages that change word endings to change meaning, English depends on word order. In this chapter, we will look at why word order matters in English. We will explain the basic rules, give examples, and provide exercises to help you use word order correctly and communicate better.

Why Word Order is Crucial in English

Understanding the Role of Word Order

In English, the order of words is the main way to show their meaning. Some languages change word endings to show how words work in a sentence, but English uses word order instead. This is why it is very important to get the word order right to make your message clear.

How Word Order Affects Meaning:

The order in which words are placed in a sentence can completely change its meaning. For example, consider the following sentences:

1. **"The dog bit the man."**
   - **Explanation:** The word order indicates that the dog is the one doing the biting, and the man is the one being bitten.

2. **"The man bit the dog."**

   - **Explanation:** By simply switching the subject and object, the meaning of the sentence changes dramatically. Now, it's the man who is biting the dog.

Consequences of Incorrect Word Order:

Using the wrong word order can lead to confusion or even miscommunication. For non-native speakers, this can result in sentences that sound unnatural or are difficult to understand.

Example of Miscommunication:

- **Incorrect Word Order:** "A cake is eaten by John every day."

  - **Explanation:** While this sentence is grammatically correct in a passive voice, it's less natural than the active voice version.

- **Correct Word Order:** "John eats a cake every day."

  - **Explanation:** This version is clearer and more direct, making it easier for the listener to understand who is doing the action and what is being acted upon.

Basic Word Order in English Sentences

The Standard Word Order: Subject-Verb-Object (SVO)

As discussed in the previous section, the most common and basic word order in English is Subject-Verb-Object (SVO). This structure ensures that sentences are clear and that the relationships between the different parts of the sentence are easy to understand.

Components of the SVO Structure:

1. **Subject (S):** The person, place, thing, or idea that is performing the action.

   - **Example:** "The cat (Subject) sleeps."

2. **Verb (V):** The action or state of being.

   - **Example:** "The cat sleeps (Verb)."

3. **Object (O):** The entity that is affected by the action.

   - **Example:** "The cat chased (Verb) the mouse (Object)."

Examples of Simple SVO Sentences:

- **"The student (Subject) studies (Verb) the book (Object)."**

  - **Explanation:** The subject "student" performs the action "studies" on the object "book."

- **"She (Subject) plays (Verb) the piano (Object)."**

  - **Explanation:** The subject "She" performs the action "plays" on the object "piano."

Understanding the Flexibility of Word Order:

While SVO is the standard word order, English sentences can sometimes be rearranged for emphasis, especially in questions or passive constructions. However, the basic relationship between the subject, verb, and object usually remains clear.

Example of Rearranged Word Order:

- **Question:** "Does the cat (Subject) chase (Verb) the mouse (Object)?"
  - **Explanation:** In a question, the auxiliary verb "does" comes before the subject, but the relationship between the subject, verb, and object remains intact.

Visualizing Standard Word Order:

Imagine a train where each car represents a part of the sentence: the first car is the subject, the second is the verb, and the third is the object. When arranged correctly, the train moves smoothly, just like a well-ordered sentence.

UNDERSTANDING SUBJECT-VERB-OBJECT (SVO) STRUCTURE

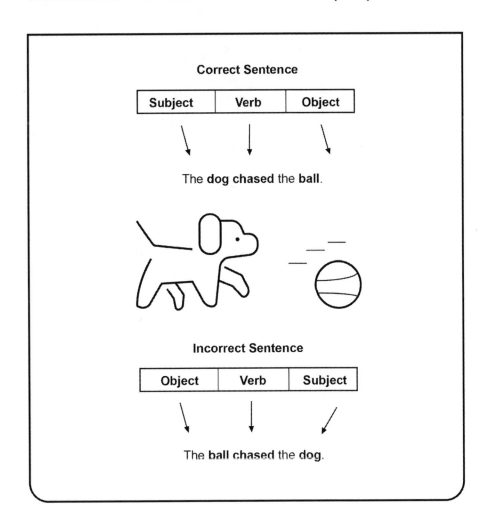

Variations in Word Order: Questions, Negatives, and Passive Voice

1. Word Order in Questions

In English, forming questions often involves changing the standard SVO word order. This is usually done by moving an auxiliary verb (a helping verb like "do," "have," or "be") to the beginning of the sentence.

2. Word Order in Negative Sentences

In negative sentences, we add "not" or "n't" after a helping verb. This changes the sentence a bit but the main order of words (subject-verb-object) stays the same.

3. Word Order in Passive Voice

The passive voice emphasizes the action or the object of the action rather than the subject. This often involves a rearrangement of the usual word order.

Chapter 2: Simple Sentences

"The art of simplicity is a puzzle of complexity."

— Douglas Horton

In this chapter, we will learn about simple sentences. Simple sentences are basic but very useful for clear communication. We will see how to make simple sentences using the Subject-Verb-Object (SVO) order and why it is important to get good at these before learning more complex sentences. By the end, you will know how to make clear and strong sentences.

Definition and Structure of Simple Sentences

A simple sentence is a basic part of speaking and writing in English. It might seem easy, but it helps you share clear and direct messages. Learning about simple sentences, how they are built, and how they work is very important for learning English. In this chapter, we will explain simple sentences, show examples, and give you practice to help you understand them well.

What is a Simple Sentence?

Definition of a Simple Sentence

A simple sentence is a sentence that contains only one independent clause. An independent clause is a group of words that has a subject and a verb and expresses a complete thought. In other words, a simple sentence can stand alone as a complete sentence without needing any additional information.

Key Characteristics of a Simple Sentence:

1. **One Independent Clause:**

   A simple sentence consists of a single independent clause. This means it has only one subject and one predicate (verb) and expresses a complete idea.

2. **No Dependent Clauses:**

   A simple sentence does not contain any dependent clauses. Dependent clauses cannot stand alone and need to be connected to an independent clause to form a complete sentence.

3. **Can Include Modifiers:**

   While a simple sentence is basic, it can still include modifiers such as adjectives, adverbs, and prepositional phrases to add detail and depth.

Why Simple Sentences Matter:

Simple sentences are very important for clear communication. They are easy to understand and give clear information. Learning to make simple sentences well helps you build more complex sentences and talk or write effectively in English.

Visualizing Simple Sentences:

Imagine a single brick representing a simple sentence. Just as a brick is a fundamental unit of construction, a simple sentence is a fundamental unit of language.

WHAT IS A SIMPLE SENTENCE?

Base Sentence

The cat sleeps.

| The cat Subject | | sleeps Verb |

The cat sleeps on the mat.

| The cat Subject | sleeps Verb | on the mat Object/Compliment |

The Structure of Simple Sentences

Basic Structure: Subject + Verb

The most basic structure of a simple sentence consists of just two parts: the subject and the verb. This structure is the simplest way to express a complete thought in English.

1. The Subject

The subject of a simple sentence is the person, place, thing, or idea that performs the action or is described in the sentence. The subject usually appears at the beginning of the sentence.

- **Examples:**
  - **"The cat (Subject) sleeps (Verb)."**
    - **Explanation:** "The cat" is the subject of the sentence, and "sleeps" is the action that the subject performs.
  - **"Water (Subject) flows (Verb)."**
    - **Explanation:** "Water" is the subject, and "flows" describes what the water does.

2. The Verb

The verb is the action word or the word that describes the state of being in the sentence. It is the most crucial part of the sentence because it tells us what the subject is doing or what is happening to the subject.

- **Examples:**
  - **"She (Subject) sings (Verb)."**
    - **Explanation:** The verb "sings" describes the action that the subject "She" is performing.
  - **"Time (Subject) flies (Verb)."**
    - **Explanation:** The verb "flies" describes the action of the subject "Time."

Identifying Subjects and Predicates

In English, every sentence needs two main parts: a subject and a predicate. The subject is who or what the sentence is about. The predicate tells us what the subject is doing or what is happening to it. In this chapter, we will learn how to find subjects and predicates in simple sentences. We will also look at the different types of subjects and predicates and how they work together. We will give easy explanations, examples, and practice exercises to help you understand this vital part of English grammar.

What is the Subject in a Sentence?

Definition of a Subject

The subject of a sentence is who or what is doing something. It is the main part of the sentence and usually comes first. To find the subject, ask "Who?" or "What?" about the action in the sentence.

Types of Subjects:

1. **Simple Subject:**

   The simple subject is the main word (or words) that tells who or what the sentence is about. It is usually a noun or pronoun.

   - **Example:** "The cat (Simple Subject) sleeps."

o **Explanation:** "The cat" is the simple subject because it is the noun that the sentence is about.

2. **Compound Subject:**

   A compound subject consists of two or more subjects that are joined by a conjunction (such as "and" or "or") and share the same verb.

   - **Example:** "John and Mary (Compound Subject) are studying."
     o **Explanation:** "John and Mary" are the compound subject because both are performing the same action.

3. **Complete Subject:**

   The complete subject includes the simple subject and any words that modify or describe it.

   - **Example:** "The large, brown dog (Complete Subject) barked."
     o **Explanation:** The complete subject includes the simple subject "dog" and the adjectives "large" and "brown" that describe it.

What is the Predicate in a Sentence?

Definition of a Predicate

The subject of a sentence is who or what is doing something. It is the main part of the sentence and usually comes first. To find the subject, ask "Who?" or "What?" about the action.

Types of Predicates:

1. **Simple Predicate:**

   The simple predicate is the main verb or verb phrase that tells what the subject does or what happens to the subject.

   - **Example:** "The cat sleeps (Simple Predicate)."
     o **Explanation:** "Sleeps" is the simple predicate because it is the main verb that tells what the subject "cat" is doing.

2. **Compound Predicate:**

   A compound predicate contains two or more verbs or verb phrases that share the same subject and are joined by a conjunction.

   - **Example:** "She sings and dances (Compound Predicate)."
     o **Explanation:** "Sings and dances" are the compound predicate because both actions are performed by the same subject "She."

3. Complete Predicate:

The complete predicate includes the verb and all the words that modify or give more information about the verb.

- **Example:** "The dog barked loudly at the stranger (Complete Predicate)."
    - ○ **Explanation:** The complete predicate includes the verb "barked" and the adverb "loudly" along with the prepositional phrase "at the stranger" that modifies the verb.

Identifying Subjects and Predicates in Different Types of Sentences

1. Simple Sentences

In a simple sentence, there is one subject and one predicate. Identifying the subject and predicate is usually straightforward.

- **Example:**
    - **Sentence:** "The cat (Subject) purrs (Predicate)."
    - **Explanation:** "The cat" is the subject, and "purrs" is the predicate, forming a complete thought.

2. Questions

In questions, the subject and predicate may not follow the typical order, but they are still present. The subject often comes after the auxiliary verb in a question.

- **Example:**
    - **Question:** "Does the dog (Subject) bark (Predicate)?"
    - **Explanation:** "The dog" is the subject, and "bark" is the predicate, even though the verb "Does" comes first.

3. Commands

In commands, the subject is often implied rather than explicitly stated. The predicate is usually the verb that tells the action to be performed.

- **Example:**
    - **Command:** "Sit!"
    - **Explanation:** The subject "You" is implied, and "Sit" is the predicate that tells what the subject should do.

4. Complex Sentences

In complex sentences, there may be more than one subject and predicate, but each independent clause will still have its subject and predicate.

- **Example:**
  - **Sentence:** "When the rain stops, we (Subject) will go (Predicate) outside."
  - **Explanation:** The main clause "we will go outside" has its own subject "we" and predicate "will go," even though the sentence includes a dependent clause.

Chapter 3: Compound Sentences

"Good communication is as stimulating as black coffee, and just as hard to sleep after."

— Anne Morrow Lindbergh

In this chapter, we will learn about compound sentences. These sentences join two or more simple sentences into one. This helps you share more ideas in one sentence. You will see how to use words like "and," "but," and "or," along with punctuation, to link ideas smoothly. By the end, you will be able to make compound sentences that make your writing more interesting and lively.

Using Conjunctions To Combine Simple Sentences

In learning English, combining simple sentences to make compound sentences is an important step. Compound sentences help you join related ideas, make your writing more interesting, and show more complex thoughts. To do this, you need to use conjunctions, like "and," "but," and "or." In this section, we will learn what conjunctions are, how to use them to join simple sentences, and the rules to follow. We will give you lots of examples, pictures, and exercises to help you practice making compound sentences confidently.

What Are Conjunctions?

Definition of Conjunctions

Conjunctions are words that join other words, phrases, or parts of sentences. They act like bridges to connect ideas. When making compound sentences, conjunctions link two or more simple sentences into one. This helps you express more complete thoughts.

Types of Conjunctions

1. **Coordinating Conjunctions**

   Coordinating conjunctions are the most common type of conjunctions used in compound sentences. They connect words, phrases, or independent clauses of equal importance. There are seven coordinating conjunctions in English, often remembered by the acronym FANBOYS:

   - **For:** Explains a reason or purpose (similar to "because").
   - **And:** Adds one idea to another.
   - **Nor:** Presents an additional negative idea.
   - **But:** Shows contrast or exception.
   - **Or:** Offers a choice between alternatives.

- **Yet:** Introduces a contrasting idea (similar to "but").
- **So:** Indicates a result or consequence.

2. **Subordinating Conjunctions**

Subordinating conjunctions usually help connect parts of complex sentences. They join a dependent clause to an independent clause. Sometimes, they can also work with coordinating conjunctions in compound sentences.

3. **Correlative Conjunctions**

Correlative conjunctions are pairs of words that link similar parts in a sentence. For example, "either...or," "neither...nor," and "both...and." They help join two independent clauses, making compound sentences more complex.

How Conjunctions Function in Compound Sentences

The Role of Coordinating Conjunctions

In a compound sentence, coordinating conjunctions join two or more complete ideas. Each idea could be a full sentence on its own, but the conjunction helps put them together into one sentence.

Examples of Compound Sentences Using Coordinating Conjunctions:

1. Using "And":

- **Simple Sentences:**
  - "She likes to read."
  - "She enjoys painting."
- **Compound Sentence:**
  - "She likes to read, and she enjoys painting."
- **Explanation:** The conjunction "and" links the two independent clauses, showing that both activities are equally important to her.

2. Using "But":

- **Simple Sentences:**
  - "He wanted to go to the party."
  - "He had to finish his homework."
- **Compound Sentence:**
  - "He wanted to go to the party, but he had to finish his homework."
- **Explanation:** The conjunction "but" introduces a contrast, showing that his desire to go to the party is in conflict with his obligation to do homework.

3. Using "Or":

- **Simple Sentences:**
    - "We can watch a movie."
    - "We can go for a walk."
- **Compound Sentence:**
    - "We can watch a movie, or we can go for a walk."
- **Explanation:** The conjunction "or" offers a choice between two alternatives.

Punctuation in Compound Sentences

When you use coordinating conjunctions to join simple sentences, it's important to use a comma. Put the comma before the conjunction when joining two complete ideas.

- **Example:**
    - **Correct:** "She studied hard, and she passed the exam."
    - **Incorrect:** "She studied hard and she passed the exam." (Missing comma)

Visualizing Compound Sentences:

Imagine a flowchart where simple sentences are connected by coordinating conjunctions, with commas placed before the conjunctions to ensure proper punctuation.

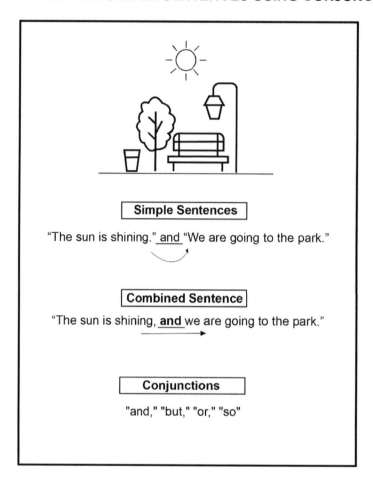

Punctuation in Compound Sentences

Punctuation is very important when writing compound sentences. It helps make your meaning clear and stops people from misunderstanding your message. When you join simple sentences together, you need to use commas, semicolons, and other punctuation marks correctly. This part of the chapter will explain how to use punctuation in compound sentences with easy examples and practice exercises. By the end, you'll know how to use punctuation well, making your writing clearer and more enjoyable.

The Role of Punctuation in Compound Sentences

Why Punctuation Matters

Punctuation marks are symbols that help us read and understand sentences better. In compound sentences, punctuation is very important. It helps to show where sentences join together and where they separate. Without the proper punctuation, compound sentences can be confusing and complicated to understand.

Common Punctuation Marks in Compound Sentences:

1. **Comma (,):** The comma is the most common punctuation mark in compound sentences. It helps to separate different parts of a sentence when you use words like "and," "but," or "or" to join them together.

2. **Semicolon (;):** A semicolon links two ideas that are closely related but don't need words like "and" or "but." It can also be used with words like "however" or "therefore" to show a connection.

3. **Colon (:):** A colon is used to add extra details that explain or list things related to the first part of a sentence. It's not used very often in compound sentences.

4. **Dash (—):** A dash can be used to add extra details or show a sudden change in a sentence.

Using Semicolons in Compound Sentences

Semicolons for Closely Related Clauses

A semicolon connects two related sentences when you don't use "and" or "but." It is stronger than a comma but not as strong as a period. It helps join ideas that are closely connected.

Examples of Semicolon Use:

1. Without a Conjunction:

- **Example:** "The storm was severe; many trees were uprooted."
- **Explanation:** The semicolon connects two related ideas without using a conjunction, showing that the events are closely linked.

2. With a Transitional Phrase:

- **Example:** "She was excited to start her new job; however, she was also nervous."
- Explanation: The semicolon is used before the transitional phrase "however," which connects the two clauses while indicating a contrast.

Rules for Using Semicolons:

- Use a semicolon to connect two independent clauses that are closely related in meaning.
- Use a semicolon before a conjunctive adverb (however, therefore, moreover, etc.) or a transitional phrase when connecting two independent clauses.
  - **Example:** "I didn't expect to win; nevertheless, I was prepared to give it my all."

Using Colons and Dashes in Compound Sentences

Colons for Introducing Explanations

The colon is less commonly used in compound sentences, but it can be effective when the second clause explains, expands on, or illustrates the first clause. It is often used for emphasis.

Examples of Colon Use:

1. Introducing an Explanation:

- Example: "He had only one goal: to win the championship."
- Explanation: The colon introduces an explanation or elaboration of the first clause.

2. Introducing a List:

- **Example:** "She brought everything she needed: a map, a flashlight, and a compass."
- **Explanation:** The colon introduces a list that explains what "everything she needed" includes.

3. Rules for Using Colons:

- Use a colon to introduce an explanation, definition, or list that follows an independent clause.
- Ensure that the clause before the colon is a complete sentence on its own.
    - Example: "The decision was clear: she had to leave immediately."

Dashes for Emphasis or Abrupt Changes

A dash is used to show extra details, add emphasis, or show a sudden change in thought. It is less formal than a semicolon or colon and makes the writing feel more conversational.

Examples of Dash Use:

1. For Emphasis:

- **Example:** "He was determined to succeed—no matter the cost."
- **Explanation:** The dash emphasizes the clause "no matter the cost," adding weight to the statement.

2. For an Abrupt Change:

- **Example:** "She was going to apologize—but then she changed her mind."
- **Explanation:** The dash introduces an abrupt shift in thought, showing a change of decision.

3. Rules for Using Dashes:

- Use a dash to add emphasis or to show a sudden change in a compound sentence.
- Don't use too many dashes. They can make your writing look messy and too casual.
    - **Example:** "The weather was perfect for a picnic—until it started raining."

Chapter 4: Complex Sentences

"The more you learn, the more you realize how much you don't know."

– Aristotle

In this chapter, we will explore complex sentences and their building blocks. You'll learn about two essential parts of complex sentences: dependent and independent clauses. We will break down what each clause is, how they work together, and how to use them in your writing. By the end of this chapter, you'll understand how to create more detailed and interesting sentences, making your writing more straightforward and engaging.

Introduction to Dependent and Independent Clauses

Understanding how to create complex sentences is an important step in mastering English. Complex sentences allow us to connect ideas and add more details to our writing, making our thoughts clearer and attractive. In this chapter, we will learn about two critical parts of complex sentences: independent clauses and dependent clauses. We will explore what these clauses are, how they work together, and how you can use them to build more advanced sentences. Let's begin by understanding the basics!

Understanding Simple Sentences First

Before we dive into complex sentences, let's quickly review simple sentences. A simple sentence has just one idea and one main part, which is called an independent clause.

Example of a Simple Sentence:

- *The cat sleeps.*

In this sentence, "The cat" is the subject, and "sleeps" is the action (predicate). It tells us one complete idea.

What Are Independent Clauses?

An independent clause is a group of words that has a subject and a predicate. It can stand alone as a complete sentence because it expresses a complete thought.

Examples of Independent Clauses:

- *She reads books.*
- *He plays football.*

Each of these can be a sentence on its own.

What Are Dependent Clauses?

A dependent clause also has a subject and a predicate, but it cannot stand alone as a complete sentence. It needs an independent clause to make sense.

Examples of Dependent Clauses:

- *Because she was tired*
- *When he finishes his homework*

These clauses leave us hanging. They need more information to complete the thought.

Combining Independent and Dependent Clauses

To make a complex sentence, you combine an independent clause with a dependent clause. The dependent clause adds extra information to the independent clause.

Example of a Complex Sentence:

- *She reads books because she loves stories.*

Here, "She reads books" is the independent clause, and "because she loves stories" is the dependent clause. Together, they make a complete and interesting sentence.

How to Use Conjunctions

To join independent and dependent clauses, we use special words called conjunctions. Some common conjunctions are:

- *Because*
- *Although*
- *If*
- *When*

Example Sentences Using Conjunctions:

- *He will go outside if it stops raining.*
- *Although she was late, she still managed to finish her work.*

These words help connect ideas and show how they relate to each other.

Visualizing Dependent and Independent Clauses:

Think of independent clauses as complete sentences that stand alone, like a solo traveler. Dependent clauses, however, need support—they can't stand alone and rely on an independent clause to make sense. Together, they form more complete thoughts, just like companions on a journey.

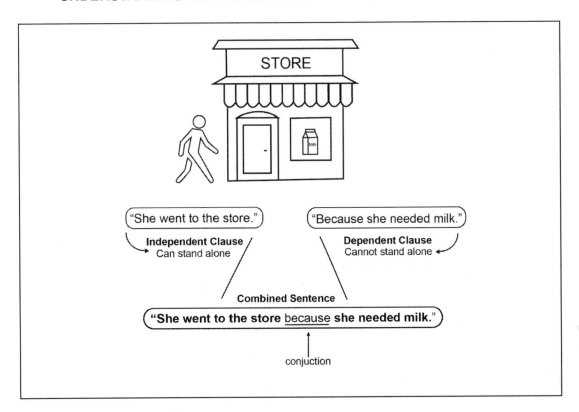

How To Create and Use Complex Sentences Effectively

Creating complex sentences can make your writing richer and more enjoyable. Complex sentences help you explain ideas more clearly and connect thoughts in a way that simple sentences alone cannot. This chapter teaches you how to build and use complex sentences effectively. We'll explore how to mix independent and dependent clauses, use different types of dependent clauses, and avoid common mistakes.

Understanding Complex Sentences

A complex sentence is made by joining an independent clause with one or more dependent clauses.

Example of a Complex Sentence:

- *The dog barked when the mailman arrived.*

Here, "The dog barked" is the independent clause, and "when the mailman arrived" is the dependent clause.

How to Create Complex Sentences

1. **Start with a Simple Sentence:**

   Begin with a basic sentence that has one independent clause. For example:

- *She went to the store.*

2. **Add a Dependent Clause:**

Choose a dependent clause to add more information. Make sure it connects with the main idea of the independent clause. For example:

- *because she needed groceries*

3. Combine Them Using a Conjunction:

Use a subordinating conjunction to link the clauses. Common subordinating conjunctions include because, although, if, and when.

Example Combined:

- *She went to the store because she needed groceries.*

Punctuation in Complex Sentences

1. **Comma Placement:**

When the dependent clause comes before the independent clause, use a comma to separate them.

Example:

- *When the rain stopped, we went outside.*

When the independent clause comes before the dependent clause, you usually do not need a comma.

Example:

- *We went outside when the rain stopped.*

2. **No Comma Needed:**

If the dependent clause is very short or closely related to the main clause, you may not need a comma.

Example:

- *She left because she was late.*

Chapter 5: Compound-Complex Sentences

"Writing is a journey, and sentences are the roads we travel. Mastering different types of sentences helps us explore new ideas more clearly and effectively."

– Melvin

In this chapter, we will learn about compound-complex sentences. These are sentences that combine compound and complex sentence features. We'll explain how to use these sentences to express more complicated ideas clearly. You'll learn what makes up a compound-complex sentence, how to put one together, and tips for using them effectively in your writing.

Combining Compound and Complex Sentence Structures

In this chapter, we will explore compound-complex sentences. These sentences combine both compound and complex sentence structures. They help us express more complicated ideas by connecting multiple thoughts in one sentence. Understanding how to create and use compound-complex sentences will make your English more interesting and fluent. Let's learn how to use these sentences effectively!

1. What Is a Compound-Complex Sentence?

A **compound-complex** sentence is a type of sentence that has at least two independent clauses and at least one dependent clause. This sentence structure allows us to connect multiple ideas and add more detail to our writing.

Independent Clause: A group of words with a subject and verb that can stand alone as a complete sentence.

Dependent Clause: A group of words with a subject and verb that cannot stand alone as a complete sentence. It needs an independent clause to make sense.

Examples of Compound-Complex Sentences:

1. "I wanted to go for a walk, but it started raining because the weather changed suddenly."

   - Independent Clause 1: "I wanted to go for a walk"

   - Independent Clause 2: "it started raining"

   - Dependent Clause: "because the weather changed suddenly"

2. "She stayed up late because she had to study, and she was tired the next morning."

   - Independent Clause 1: "She stayed up late"

- Independent Clause 2: "she was tired the next morning"
- Dependent Clause: "because she had to study"

2. Breaking Down Compound-Complex Sentences

To understand compound-complex sentences, let's break them down into smaller parts.

1. **Independent Clauses:** These are complete thoughts. Each one can be its own sentence.
   - Example: "She likes to read." and "He went to the park."
2. **Dependent Clauses:** These add extra information to the sentence but cannot stand alone.
   - Example: "because she was bored" or "after he finished his homework."
3. **Combining Clauses:** To form a compound-complex sentence, combine at least two independent clauses and one dependent clause.
   - Example: "She likes to read, but she often gets distracted because she was bored."

3. How to Create Compound-Complex Sentences

Step-by-Step Guide:

1. **Start with Two Independent Clauses:**
   - Example: "I finished my homework." and "I watched a movie."
2. **Add a Dependent Clause:**
   - Example: "because I had some free time."
3. **Combine the Clauses:**
   - Example: "I finished my homework, and I watched a movie because I had some free time."

4. Using Coordinating and Subordinating Conjunctions

To form compound-complex sentences, we use two types of conjunctions:

- **Coordinating Conjunctions:** These connect two independent clauses. Examples: **and, but, or, nor, for, so, yet.**
  - Example: "I wanted to stay home, **but** I had to go to work."
- **Subordinating Conjunctions:** These introduce dependent clauses. Examples: **because, although, since, when, while, if, unless.**
  - Example: "She was happy **because** she passed her exam."

Table: Conjunctions Used in Compound-Complex Sentences

Type of Conjunction	Examples	
Coordinating Conjunctions	and, but, or, nor, for, so, yet	"He studied hard, but he didn't pass the test."
Subordinating Conjunctions	because, although, since, when, while, if, unless	"She left early because she had a meeting."

5. Punctuation Rules for Compound-Complex Sentences

When writing compound-complex sentences, it's important to use the correct punctuation to make your meaning clear.

- **Commas:** Use a comma before a coordinating conjunction (like "and," "but," "or") that connects two independent clauses.
  - Example: "I wanted to read, **but** I was too tired."
- **No Comma Needed:** Do not use a comma when the dependent clause comes after the independent clause.
  - Example: "She was excited **because** she got a new book."
- **Comma Needed:** Use a comma when the dependent clause comes before the independent clause.
  - Example: "**Because** she got a new book, she was excited."

6. Why Use Compound-Complex Sentences?

Compound-complex sentences are useful because they:

1. **Show Relationships Between Ideas:** They help to explain why something happened or under what conditions.
   - Example: "He didn't go to the party because he was tired, but he still had a good time at home."
2. **Add Variety to Writing:** Using different sentence types makes writing more interesting.
   - Example: "I enjoy reading books, and my sister likes watching movies, but we both enjoy spending time together."
3. **Make Writing Clearer:** They help combine related ideas into one sentence, making writing more concise.
   - Example: "She finished her work early because she wanted to relax, and she went for a walk."

7. Visual Aid: Sentence Structure Diagram

To help you visualize how compound-complex sentences are structured, here is a simple diagram:

[Independent Clause 1] + [Coordinating Conjunction] + [Independent Clause 2] + [Subordinating Conjunction + Dependent Clause] = Compound-Complex Sentence

Example:

[He went to the gym] + [and] + [he worked out] + [because it was his routine] = "He went to the gym and worked out because it was his routine."

Transforming Simple Sentences Into Compound-Complex Sentences

In this chapter, we will learn how to transform simple sentences into compound-complex sentences. This process will help us create more detailed and engaging sentences in English. By combining ideas from simple sentences, we can express more complex thoughts and show how different ideas relate to each other. Let's explore how to make these transformations step by step!

1. Understanding Simple Sentences

Before transforming simple sentences into compound-complex sentences, let's understand what a simple sentence is.

A **simple sentence** contains one independent clause. It has a subject (who or what the sentence is about) and a predicate (what the subject is doing). It expresses a complete thought.

Examples of Simple Sentences:

1. "The dog barked."
   - Subject: "The dog"
   - Predicate: "barked"
2. "She reads books."
   - Subject: "She"
   - Predicate: "reads books"

Simple sentences are easy to understand and use, but sometimes, we want to connect more ideas to make our writing more interesting. This is where compound-complex sentences come in!

2. What Are Compound-Complex Sentences?

A compound-complex sentence combines both compound and complex sentences. It has at least two independent clauses and at least one dependent clause.

- **Independent Clause:** A group of words with a subject and verb that can stand alone as a complete sentence.
- **Dependent Clause:** A group of words with a subject and verb that cannot stand alone. It adds more information to the sentence.

Example of a Compound-Complex Sentence:

"I finished my homework, but I didn't understand the last question because it was very hard."

- Independent Clause 1: "I finished my homework"
- Independent Clause 2: "I didn't understand the last question"
- Dependent Clause: "because it was very hard"

3. Transforming Simple Sentences

Let's learn how to transform simple sentences into compound-complex sentences step by step.

Step 1: Start with Simple Sentences

First, we need to combine two simple sentences. Here are two examples:

1. "The cat sat on the mat."
2. "The dog barked loudly."

Step 2: Identify Relationships Between Ideas

Think about how these ideas are connected. Ask yourself questions like:

- Why did something happen?
- When did it happen?
- How are the ideas related?

Example Questions:

- Why did the dog bark?
- What happened when the cat sat on the mat?

Step 3: Introduce a Dependent Clause

A dependent clause adds more detail to the simple sentences. It explains why, when, or how something happened.

Example Dependent Clauses:

- "because it saw a stranger"
- "when it heard a noise"

Step 4: Combine Sentences Using Conjunctions

Use coordinating conjunctions (for, and, nor, but, or, yet, so) to join independent clauses. Use subordinating conjunctions (because, although, since, when, if, etc.) to add dependent clauses.

Example Transformations:

1. Original Sentences:

   - "The cat sat on the mat."
   - "The dog barked loudly."

2. Transformed into a Compound-Complex Sentence:

   - "The cat sat on the mat, and the dog barked loudly because it saw a stranger."

In this example:

- **Independent Clause 1:** "The cat sat on the mat."
- **Independent Clause 2:** "The dog barked loudly."
- **Dependent Clause:** "because it saw a stranger."

4. Visualizing the Structure

To help you understand how to build compound-complex sentences, let's use a simple table to show how we can combine clauses.

Independent Clause 1	Coordinating Conjunction	Independent Clause 2	Subordinating Conjunction	
"The cat sat on the mat"	and	"the dog barked loudly"	because	"it saw a stranger."
"Maria went to the market"	but	"she forgot to buy bread"	because	"she was in a hurry."
"John loves to play soccer"	and	"he practices every day"	because	"he wants to become better."

5. Benefits of Using Compound-Complex Sentences

Compound-complex sentences make your writing more:

1. **Detailed:** They help you provide more information in a single sentence.

2. **Engaging:** They make your writing more interesting by connecting different ideas.

3. **Clear:** They help explain the relationship between different ideas.

Example:

"I wanted to go to the park, but it started raining because the weather changed suddenly."

This sentence clearly shows:

- What the person wanted to do (go to the park)
- What stopped them (it started raining)
- Why it happened (because the weather changed)

6. Tips for Mastering Compound-Complex Sentences

1. **Read Regularly:** Look for compound-complex sentences in the books you read.
2. **Write Daily:** Practice writing your own sentences to get comfortable with different structures.
3. **Ask for Feedback:** Share your sentences with a friend or teacher to get feedback and improve.

7. Using Visual Aids and Diagrams

Here is a simple diagram to show how a compound-complex sentence is structured:

[Independent Clause 1] + [Coordinating Conjunction] + [Independent Clause 2] + [Subordinating Conjunction + Dependent Clause] = Compound-Complex Sentence

Example:

[She enjoys swimming] + [and] + [she goes to the pool] + [because it helps her relax] = "She enjoys swimming, and she goes to the pool because it helps her relax."

Visualizing Compound-Complex Sentences:

Think of compound-complex sentences as a multi-level bridge. Each independent clause represents a separate span that can stand alone, while the dependent clauses act like supporting arches, adding depth and connection. Together, they create a sturdy structure that conveys more complex ideas and relationships, allowing for richer expression in writing.

WHAT IS A COMPOUND-COMPLEX SENTENCE?

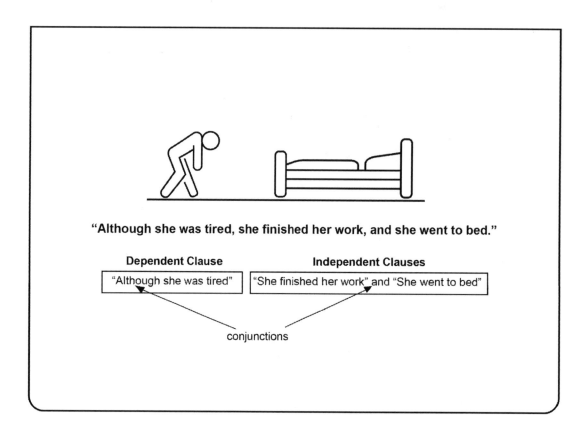

"Although she was tired, she finished her work, and she went to bed."

Dependent Clause	Independent Clauses
"Although she was tired"	"She finished her work" and "She went to bed"

conjunctions

Chapter 6: Sentence Variety and Flow

"Good writing needs variety.

– William Faulkner

In this chapter, we will explore how using different types of sentences can make your writing more exciting and clear. Just like in a dance, where various steps make the performance lively, using a mix of sentence types helps your writing flow better and keeps readers engaged. We will look at simple sentences, compound sentences, and complex sentences. You will learn how to combine these different types to create variety in your writing. We will also cover how to organize sentences so that your ideas connect smoothly. By the end of this chapter, you'll be able to use various sentence structures to make your writing more effective and enjoyable to read.

Using Different Sentence Types for Better Communication

In this chapter, we will learn about the importance of using different types of sentences to improve our writing. Just like a well-made dish needs a variety of ingredients to taste good, good writing needs different types of sentences to keep it interesting and clear.

1. The Importance of Sentence Variety

When you speak or write, you want to keep your audience interested. If you use the same type of sentence over and over again, your writing can become dull and repetitive. Sentence variety helps you keep your reader's attention by mixing different sentence types, lengths, and structures.

Example:

- **Without Variety:** "The dog barked. The cat ran. The bird flew."
- **With Variety:** "The dog barked loudly, making the cat run away, while the bird flew quietly above them."

In the second example, the sentences are more engaging because they vary in length and structure.

2. Types of Sentences

There are four main types of sentences: declarative, interrogative, imperative, and exclamatory. Each type serves a different purpose and adds variety to your writing.

2.1 Declarative Sentences

Declarative sentences make a statement or express an idea. They are the most common type of sentence and usually end with a period.

Example:

- "The sun sets in the west."
- "She enjoys reading books."

2.2 Interrogative Sentences

Interrogative sentences ask a question. They usually begin with words like who, what, where, when, why, or how and end with a question mark.

Example:

- "Where are you going?"
- "What is your favorite color?"

2.3 Imperative Sentences

Imperative sentences give a command or make a request. They often begin with a verb and can end with a period or an exclamation point, depending on the tone.

Example:

- "Please close the door."
- "Stop talking!"

2.4 Exclamatory Sentences

Exclamatory sentences express strong emotion or surprise. They always end with an exclamation point.

Example:

- "What a beautiful day!"
- "I can't believe we won!"

3. Combining Sentence Types for Better Flow

Using a mix of these sentence types can make your writing more dynamic and interesting. Let's explore how to combine them effectively.

3.1 Creating a Natural Flow

When you combine different sentence types, your writing feels more natural and conversational. This keeps the reader engaged and helps convey your message more effectively.

Example:

- **Declarative:** "I love chocolate."
- **Interrogative:** "Don't you love chocolate too?"
- **Exclamatory:** "It's the best thing ever!"

In this example, the writer starts with a simple statement, follows up with a question to engage the reader, and finishes with an exclamation to express strong emotion.

3.2 Avoiding Monotony

Using only one type of sentence can make your writing sound monotonous. Varying sentence types keeps the reader interested and helps maintain a smooth flow.

Example of Monotony:

- "He was late. He missed the bus. He had to walk."

Example with Variety:

- "He was late because he missed the bus. Did you know he had to walk all the way to school? What a rough start to the day!"

4. Sentence Length and Structure

In addition to sentence type, sentence length and structure also play a key role in creating variety and flow in your writing.

4.1 Varying Sentence Length

Mixing short and long sentences creates a rhythm that keeps the reader engaged. Short sentences are great for emphasis, while longer sentences can provide more detail.

Example:

- **Short Sentence:** "It was cold."
- **Long Sentence:** "The wind howled through the trees, sending shivers down my spine as I pulled my coat tighter around me."

By combining these two sentences, the writer creates a more vivid and engaging picture for the reader.

4.2 Simple, Compound, Complex, and Compound-Complex Sentences

Using different sentence structures can add depth and clarity to your writing. Let's review these sentence types:

- Simple Sentence: Contains one independent clause.
  - Example: "She laughed."
- Compound Sentence: Contains two or more independent clauses joined by a coordinating conjunction (for, and, nor, but, or, yet, so).
  - Example: "She laughed, and he smiled."
- Complex Sentence: Contains one independent clause and at least one dependent clause.
  - Example: "She laughed because he told a funny joke."

- Compound-Complex Sentence: Contains at least two independent clauses and at least one dependent clause.
  - Example: "She laughed because he told a funny joke, and everyone else joined in."

By using a mix of these structures, you can make your writing more varied and interesting.

5. Using Sentence Variety to Emphasize Key Points

Sometimes, the way you structure your sentences can help emphasize important points in your writing.

5.1 Emphasizing with Short Sentences

Short sentences can be powerful when used to highlight key information. They stand out and grab the reader's attention.

Example:

- "He was wrong. Very wrong."

The short sentence "Very wrong" emphasizes the mistake and leaves a strong impression on the reader.

5.2 Emphasizing with Complex Sentences

Complex sentences can show the relationship between ideas and emphasize how different factors are connected.

Example:

- "Although it was raining, we decided to go hiking because we had been planning the trip for weeks."

This complex sentence emphasizes the decision to hike despite the rain, showing determination and commitment.

6. Transition Words and Phrases

Transition words and phrases are essential for creating a smooth flow between sentences and ideas. They help guide the reader from one thought to the next.

6.1 Common Transition Words

- **Addition:** "and," "also," "furthermore"
- **Contrast:** "but," "however," "on the other hand"
- **Cause and Effect:** "because," "therefore," "as a result"
- **Time:** "before," "after," "then"

6.2 Using Transitions for Clarity

Using transitions effectively can make your writing clearer and easier to follow.

Example:

- Without Transitions: "She was tired. She went to bed."

- With Transitions: "She was tired, so she went to bed."

In the second example, the transition word "so" connects the cause and effect, making the relationship between the ideas clear.

7. Using Visual Aids and Tables

Here is a simple table to help you remember the different sentence types and when to use them:

Sentence Type	Purpose	Example
Declarative Sentence	Makes a statement or expresses an idea	"The sky is blue."
Interrogative Sentence	Asks a question	"What time is it?"
Imperative Sentence	Gives a command or makes a request	"Please sit down."
Exclamatory Sentence	Expresses strong emotion	"Wow, that's amazing!"

Techniques for Improving Sentence Flow in Writing

When we read or write, we want our words to flow smoothly, like a gentle river. Sentence flow makes writing easy to read and understand. In this chapter, we will learn techniques to improve the flow of our sentences. These techniques will help you make your writing clearer and more enjoyable for readers. We will look at different ways to connect ideas, use transition words, and vary sentence lengths. By the end of this chapter, you will know how to make your writing flow like a smooth conversation.

Understanding Sentence Flow

What is Sentence Flow?

Sentence flow is how well sentences fit together in a paragraph or a piece of writing. Good flow makes reading easy and enjoyable. When sentences flow well, they lead naturally from one idea to the next. Poor flow, on the other hand, can make writing feel choppy or confusing.

Imagine a row of dominoes. If you line them up perfectly and push the first one, they all fall smoothly. But if they are not lined up well, they stop and do not flow. Sentences work the same way in writing.

Using Transition Words

What Are Transition Words?

Transition words are words or phrases that link ideas together. They help guide the reader from one thought to another, making writing more coherent. Some common transition words include and, but, because, also, next, first, second, finally, however, therefore, and for example.

Types of Transition Words:

1. **Addition:** Adds information.

    - Examples: **also, and, in addition, furthermore**

2. **Contrast:** Shows a difference.

    - Examples: **but, however, on the other hand, yet**

3. **Cause and Effect:** Shows a reason and its result.

    - Examples: **because, therefore, as a result, consequently**

4. **Order:** Shows the order of ideas or steps.

    - Examples: **first, second, next, finally**

5. **Example:** Provides an example to clarify an idea.

    - **Examples:** for example, such as, like, for instance

Using Transition Words Effectively:

Use transition words to connect sentences and ideas smoothly. This makes it easier for readers to follow your thoughts.

Examples:

1. **Without Transition Words:**

    - "She studied hard for the test. She didn't pass."

2. **With Transition Words:**

    - "She studied hard for the test; however, she didn't pass."

In the second example, "however" contrasts the two ideas.

Varying Sentence Length

Why Vary Sentence Length?

Using sentences of different lengths helps keep writing interesting. If all sentences are short, the writing can feel choppy. If all are long, it can feel boring or hard to follow. Mixing short and long sentences makes writing feel more natural.

Examples:

1. **Short Sentence:** "Birds sing."

2. **Long Sentence:** "Birds sing in the morning when the sun rises, filling the air with their sweet melodies."

Combining Short and Long Sentences:

"Birds sing. Their melodies fill the morning air as the sun rises, creating a beautiful start to the day."

By combining short and long sentences, the writing becomes more engaging.

Using Different Sentence Structures

Types of Sentence Structures:

1. **Simple Sentences:** One independent clause.

   - Example: "The dog barks."

2. **Compound Sentences:** Two independent clauses joined by a coordinating conjunction.

   - Example: "The dog barks, and the cat meows."

3. **Complex Sentences:** One independent clause and one or more dependent clauses.

   - Example: "The dog barks because it sees a stranger."

4. **Compound-Complex Sentences:** At least two independent clauses and one or more dependent clauses.

   - Example: "The dog barks because it sees a stranger, but the cat remains calm."

Why Use Different Sentence Structures?

Using different types of sentences helps keep the reader's attention. It makes writing more dynamic.

Examples:

1. **Only Simple Sentences:**

   - "The sun set. The sky turned orange. The birds flew home."

2. **Mixed Sentence Structures:**

   - "As the sun set, the sky turned orange, and the birds flew home."

The second example flows better because it mixes different types of sentences.

Creating Rhythm with Pacing

What is Pacing?

Pacing is the speed at which a story or a piece of writing moves. Good pacing keeps the reader engaged and interested. If the writing moves too fast, the reader might miss important details. If it moves too slowly, the reader might get bored.

How to Control Pacing:

1. **Short Sentences:** Use short sentences to create a fast pace. This is good for action or excitement.

   - Example: "He ran. He jumped. He fell."

2. **Long Sentences:** Use long sentences to slow down the pace. This is good for description or reflection.

   - Example: "He ran through the forest, his feet pounding the ground, his heart racing with every step."

3. **Combining Both:** Mix short and long sentences to create a balanced pace.

   - Example: "He ran. Trees blurred past him as he sprinted through the forest, his breath quick and shallow."

Avoiding Repetition for Better Flow

Why Avoid Repetition?

Repeating the same words or ideas can make writing dull and repetitive. It can also confuse the reader. Using different words and expressions gives your writing clarity.

Examples:

1. **Repetitive Writing:**

   - "She was happy because she got a gift. The gift made her happy."

2. **Improved Writing:**

   - "She was happy because she received a gift. It brightened her day."

Using Pronouns to Avoid Repetition

What Are Pronouns?

Pronouns are words that replace nouns to avoid repetition. Common pronouns include he, she, it, they, we, and them.

Examples:

1. **Without Pronouns:**

- "John went to John's room. John picked up John's book."

2. **With Pronouns:**

   - "John went to his room. He picked up his book."

Using pronouns makes the sentences flow better and sound less repetitive.

Using Consistent Verb Tenses

Why Is Consistency Important?

Using the same verb tense throughout a sentence or paragraph helps clarify the writing. Switching tenses can confuse the reader.

Examples:

1. **Inconsistent Tense:**

- "She walks to the store and bought milk."

2. **Consistent Tense:**

- "She walked to the store and bought milk."

Keeping the verb tense consistent helps the sentence flow smoothly.

Using Parallel Structure

What is Parallel Structure?

Parallel structure means using the same pattern of words to show that two or more ideas have the same level of importance. It helps sentences flow more smoothly.

Examples:

1. **Incorrect Parallel Structure:**

   - "She likes to swim, running, and bike."

2. **Correct Parallel Structure:**

   - "She likes swimming, running, and biking."

   Or:

   - "She likes to swim, run, and bike."

Example Flowchart:

Sentence Type	Example
Simple Sentence	"The cat sleeps."

Compound Sentence	"The cat sleeps, and the dog barks."
Complex Sentence	"The cat sleeps because it is tired."
Compound-Complex Sentence	"The cat sleeps, and the dog barks because it is hungry."

Visualizing Sentence Variety and Flow:

Think of sentence variety and flow as a well-composed piece of music. Different sentence structures are like various notes and rhythms that create a dynamic melody. Just as a song needs a mix of tempos and harmonies to keep the listener engaged, varied sentence lengths and types enhance writing, making it more interesting and smooth to read. Together, they ensure that the ideas flow seamlessly, capturing the reader's attention.

ENHANCING COMMUNICATION WITH DIFFERENT SENTENCE TYPES

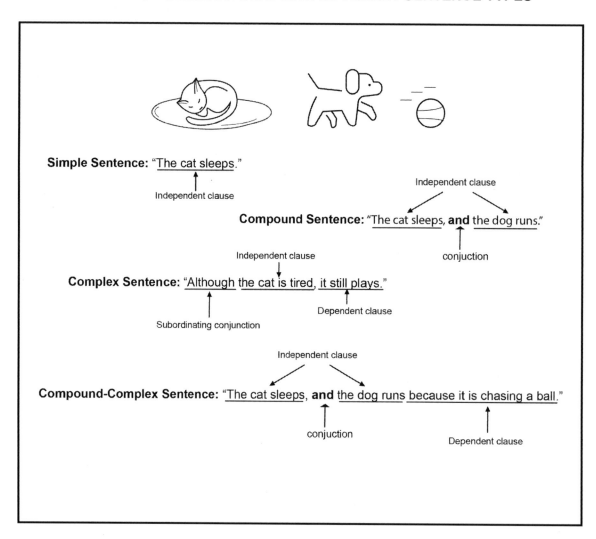

Chapter 7: Avoiding Common Sentence Errors

"Writing is easy. All you have to do is cross out the wrong words."

– Mark Twain

In this chapter, we will learn about common sentence mistakes like run-on sentences and sentence fragments. We'll discuss these errors, why they are a problem, and how to fix them. By the end, you will know how to spot and correct these mistakes, making your writing clear and easy to read.

Recognizing and Correcting Run-On Sentences and Fragments

Writing clear sentences is very important for good communication. Sometimes, we make mistakes like creating run-on sentences or sentence fragments. These mistakes can make our writing hard to understand. In this chapter, we will learn what run-on sentences and fragments are, why they are problems, and how to fix them. We will practice recognizing and correcting these errors so our writing is clear and correct.

Understanding Run-On Sentences

1. What is a Run-On Sentence?

A run-on sentence is when two or more complete thoughts (independent clauses) are joined incorrectly. This usually happens when there is no punctuation or connecting word (like "and," "but," or "because") between the thoughts.

Examples of Run-On Sentences:

1. **Incorrect:** "I went to the store I bought milk."
2. **Incorrect:** "She loves pizza she eats it every day."

In these examples, each sentence has two complete thoughts that are not separated correctly.

Why are Run-On Sentences a Problem?

Run-on sentences can confuse readers. They don't show where one idea ends and the next one begins, making it hard to understand the writer's message.

2. Types of Run-On Sentences

There are two main types of run-on sentences: fused sentences and comma splices.

1. **Fused Sentences:**

   A fused sentence is when two independent clauses are joined with no punctuation.

- **Example:** "The sun is hot it is shining brightly."

2. **Comma Splices:**

A comma splice is when two independent clauses are joined by a comma but without a coordinating conjunction.

- **Example:** "The sun is hot, it is shining brightly."

3. How to Fix Run-On Sentences

There are several ways to fix run-on sentences. Here are four simple methods:

1. **Use a Period:**

You can split the run-on into two sentences by adding a period.

- Example: "The sun is hot. It is shining brightly."

2. **Use a Comma and a Coordinating Conjunction:**

Use a comma followed by a coordinating conjunction (like "and," "but," or "or") to connect the thoughts correctly.

- Example: "The sun is hot, and it is shining brightly."

3. **Use a Semicolon:**

A semicolon can connect two related independent clauses.

- Example: "The sun is hot; it is shining brightly."

4. **Use a Subordinating Conjunction:**

You can use a subordinating conjunction (like "because," "since," "although") to connect the clauses properly.

- Example: "The sun is hot because it is shining brightly."

4. Practice: Fixing Run-On Sentences

Let's practice fixing run-on sentences. Here are some run-on sentences for you to correct:

1. **Run-On:** "I love to read books I read every night."
2. **Run-On:** "She wanted to go shopping she didn't have enough money."

Corrected Sentences:

1. "I love to read books, and I read every night."
2. "She wanted to go shopping, but she didn't have enough money."

5. Understanding Sentence Fragments

What is a Sentence Fragment?

A sentence fragment is a group of words that does not express a complete thought. It is not a full sentence because it lacks a subject, a verb, or both.

Examples of Sentence Fragments:

1. **Fragment:** "Because I was late."

2. **Fragment:** "Running through the park."

These examples are fragments because they do not form a complete idea. They leave the reader asking, "What happened because you were late?" or "Who was running through the park?"

Why are Fragments a Problem?

Fragments can make writing unclear and leave the reader confused. Every sentence needs to have a subject (who or what the sentence is about) and a predicate (what the subject is doing).

6. Common Causes of Sentence Fragments

There are several reasons why sentence fragments happen:

1. **Missing Subject or Verb:**

    *   **Fragment:** "Running to the store."

    *   **Fixed:** "She was running to the store."

2. **Dependent Clause Posing as a Sentence:**

    *   **Fragment:** "Although it was raining."

    *   **Fixed:** "Although it was raining, we went outside."

3. **Phrase Standing Alone:**

    *   **Fragment:** "On the kitchen table."

    *   **Fixed:** "The book is on the kitchen table."

7. How to Fix Sentence Fragments

To fix a fragment, you need to add the missing parts to make it a complete sentence.

1. **Add the Missing Subject or Verb:**

    *   **Fragment:** "Running late."

    *   **Fixed:** "She is running late."

2. **Complete the Thought:**
   - **Fragment:** "Because he forgot his keys."
   - **Fixed:** "He was late because he forgot his keys."

8. Practice: Fixing Sentence Fragments

Let's practice fixing sentence fragments. Here are some fragments for you to correct:

1. **Fragment:** "After the party ended."
2. **Fragment:** "Walking down the street."

Corrected Sentences:

1. "After the party ended, we went home."
2. "She was walking down the street."

9. Visualizing Run-On Sentences and Fragments

To help you understand better, here is a table that shows the difference between correct sentences, run-on sentences, and fragments:

Type	Example	Explanation
Correct Sentence	"The cat sleeps on the mat."	Complete thought with a subject and a verb.
Run-On Sentence	"The cat sleeps on the mat she is tired."	Two complete thoughts without proper punctuation or a connecting word.
Fragment	"Because the cat is tired."	Incomplete thought. Missing independent clause.

Visualizing How to Fix Run-On Sentences and Fragments:

Think of run-on sentences as a tangled ball of yarn—too many threads make it confusing. Breaking them into shorter sentences untangles the mess. Fragments are like incomplete puzzle pieces; they need additional pieces to form a complete picture. Fixing them creates clear, cohesive writing that's easy to follow.

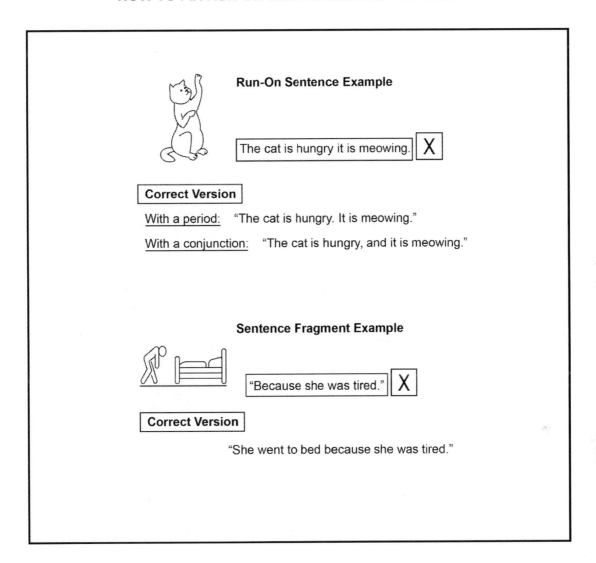

10. Tips for Avoiding Run-On Sentences and Fragments

1. **Read Aloud:** Reading your writing out loud can help you hear where a sentence might be too long or missing something.

2. **Look for Key Parts:** Make sure each sentence has a subject and a verb. Check that every sentence expresses a complete thought.

3. **Use Simple Sentences:** Start with simple sentences before combining them into more complex ones.

4. **Ask Questions:** After writing a sentence, ask yourself, "Does this make sense by itself?" If not, it might be a fragment.

11. Review: Key Points to Remember

- **Run-On Sentences** occur when two independent clauses are not properly connected.

- **Fragments** are incomplete sentences that do not express a complete thought.

- To avoid these errors, make sure every sentence has a subject and a verb and expresses a complete idea.

- Use punctuation and connecting words to link ideas properly.

BOOK 4

Increasing Comprehension

Improve Reading Comprehension with Strategies for Understanding and Interpretation

Explore to Win

Chapter 1: Introduction to Reading Comprehension

"Reading is to the mind what exercise is to the body."

– Joseph Addison

Reading comprehension helps us make sense of the words we read. It is not just about recognizing words but understanding their meaning. In this chapter, we will explore why reading comprehension is crucial for learning a language. We will discuss how being able to understand what you read helps you learn better, makes learning more fun, and improves your ability to communicate. You will also learn simple tips to practice reading comprehension and how it can help you in everyday life.

Importance of Comprehension in Language Learning

Reading comprehension is a key part of learning any language. It helps us understand and use language effectively. In this chapter, we will explore why reading comprehension is important, what it means to understand text, and how improving these skills can make learning easier and more enjoyable. We will also discuss different techniques to help you better understand what you read.

1. What is Reading Comprehension?

Definition

Reading comprehension means understanding the meaning of words and sentences when you read. It is more than just recognizing words; it's about knowing what those words and sentences mean together.

Simple Explanation:

When you read a book or a story, reading comprehension helps you understand what is happening in the story, who the characters are, and what they are doing.

Example:

1. **Without Comprehension:** Reading the sentence "The cat sat on the mat" without knowing what it means or why the cat is on the mat.

2. **With Comprehension:** Knowing that the cat is resting on the mat and understanding why the cat might be there.

2. Why is Reading Comprehension Important?

Helps You Learn

Reading comprehension is essential because it helps you learn new things. When you understand what you read, you can learn new words, ideas, and facts.

- **Example:** Reading about dinosaurs helps you learn about their names and what they look like.

Improves School Performance

In school, reading comprehension helps with all subjects, not just reading. When you understand reading passages, you do better on tests and in writing.

- **Example:** Understanding a history lesson helps you do well on a history test.

Makes Reading Enjoyable

When you understand what you read, you enjoy it more. You can follow stories, discover what happens next, and share stories with friends.

- **Example:** Reading a fun book and being able to tell your friends about it.

3. How Does Reading Comprehension Work?

Understanding Words and Sentences

To understand what you read, you need to know the meanings of words and how they fit together in sentences. This means knowing what each word means and how it helps to tell a story or give information.

Using Context Clues

Sometimes, you may not know every word, but you can use clues from the sentences around it to understand its meaning.

- Example: If you read "The penguin slid on the icy surface," you can guess that "icy" means something very cold because penguins live in cold places.

Making Connections

Good readers connect new information with what they already know. This helps them understand and remember what they read.

- **Example:** If you know about cars and you read about how a car engine works, you can connect this new information with what you already know about cars.

4. Techniques for Improving Reading Comprehension

Active Reading

Active reading means engaging with the text. This involves asking questions, making predictions, and summarizing what you read.

- **Example:** Before reading a story, you might guess what will happen based on the title and pictures.

Highlighting Key Points

Marking important parts of the text helps you remember and understand the main ideas.

- **Example:** Highlighting the main idea in a paragraph so you can easily find it later.

Taking Notes

Writing down important details helps you remember and understand what you read.

- **Example:** Taking notes about the main events in a story.

Summarizing

After reading, try to summarize the text in your own words. This shows that you understand it.

- **Example:** After reading a chapter, you might write a few sentences about what happened in the chapter.

5. How Reading Comprehension Helps in Real Life

Everyday Tasks

Understanding instructions and reading labels is easier with good reading comprehension. For example, reading a recipe helps you cook correctly.

- **Example:** Following a recipe to make cookies requires understanding each step.

Work and Career

In jobs, reading comprehension helps understand reports, emails, and instructions.

- **Example:** Reading and understanding a work report helps you make better decisions at work.

Social Interactions

Good reading comprehension helps you understand and respond to letters, texts, and social media posts.

- **Example:** Reading and understanding a friend's message helps you reply appropriately.

6. Challenges in Reading Comprehension

Difficult Vocabulary

Sometimes, new or difficult words can make reading hard. Using a dictionary or asking for help can make it easier.

- **Example:** If you don't understand the word "caterpillar," you can look it up to find out it's a kind of insect.

Complex Sentences

Long or complicated sentences can be tricky. Breaking them down into smaller parts can help.

- **Example:** The sentence "The cat, who was very tired after a long day of exploring, finally found a cozy spot to rest" can be broken into "The cat was very tired. After a long day of exploring, it found a cozy spot to rest."

7. Improving Reading Comprehension Skills

Practice Regularly

Reading regularly helps improve comprehension skills. Choose books or articles that interest you.

- **Example:** Reading your favorite storybook helps you get better at understanding text.

Ask Questions

Asking questions about the text helps deepen your understanding.

- **Example:** Asking, "What is the main character trying to achieve?" helps you focus on the story's purpose.

Read Aloud

Reading aloud helps with understanding because you can hear the words and sentences.

- **Example:** Reading a book out loud to yourself or someone else can make it easier to understand.

Discuss What You Read

Talking about what you read with others helps you understand and remember it better.

- **Example:** Discussing a book with friends can help you understand different viewpoints and details.

Visual Aids

Table: Common Reading Comprehension Strategies

Strategy	Description	Example
Active Reading	Engaging with the text by asking questions	Predicting what will happen next
Highlighting Key Points	Marking important parts of the text	Highlighting the main idea
Taking Notes	Writing down important details	Noting the main events in a story
Summarizing	Writing a summary in your own words	Summarizing a chapter

Techniques for Improving Comprehension Skills

In this chapter, we will look at easy-to-use techniques to boost your reading comprehension. You will learn how to find the main idea of a text, notice important details, and use helpful strategies to remember what you read. By the end of this chapter, you will have practical tips to make reading and understanding texts much easier.

1. Preview the Text

What is Previewing?

Previewing means looking at the text before you start reading it carefully. This helps you get an idea of what the text is about.

How to Preview:

- **Look at the Title:** The title tells you what the text is about.
    - **Example:** A book called "The Adventures of Peter Rabbit" is about the adventures of a rabbit.
- **Check the Pictures:** Pictures help you understand the story or information.
    - **Example:** A picture of a rabbit in a garden helps you guess that the story might be about a rabbit in a garden.
- **Read the Headings and Subheadings:** These tell you what different parts of the text are about.
    - **Example:** A heading like "How Rabbits Live" will tell you that the text will explain how rabbits live.

2. Make Predictions

What is Making Predictions?

Making predictions means guessing what will happen next in the text based on what you have read so far.

How to Make Predictions:

- **Think About What You Know:** Use what you already know to guess what might happen.
  - **Example:** If you read about a rabbit finding a carrot, you might guess that the rabbit will eat the carrot.
- **Ask Questions:** Think about questions like "What happens next?" or "Why did this happen?"
  - **Example:** If the rabbit is in a garden, you might wonder if it will meet other animals.

Table Example:

What You Know	Prediction
Rabbit finds a carrot	Rabbit will eat the carrot
Rabbit is in a garden	Rabbit might meet other animals

3. Take Notes While Reading

Why Take Notes?

Taking notes helps you remember important parts of the text and makes it easier to understand.

How to Take Notes:

- **Highlight Important Information:** Use a highlighter to mark key points.
  - **Example:** Highlight the main events in a story or key facts in a textbook.
- **Write Down Main Ideas:** Jot down the main ideas of each section.
  - **Example:** Write "Peter Rabbit finds a garden" as the main idea for that part of the story.

4. Summarize the Text

What is Summarizing?

Summarizing means putting the main ideas of the text into your own words. It helps you remember and understand the text better.

How to Summarize:

- **Find the Main Points:** Identify the most important parts of the text.

- **Example:** The main points of a story about a rabbit might be: "The rabbit finds a garden, meets new friends, and learns about gardening."
- **Write a Short Summary:** Write a few sentences that cover the main ideas.
  - **Example:** "Peter Rabbit finds a garden, makes new friends, and learns how to grow carrots."

Table Example:

Main Idea	Summary
Rabbit finds a garden	Peter Rabbit discovers a new garden
Rabbit meets new friends	Rabbit makes new animal friends
Rabbit learns about gardening	Rabbit learns how to grow carrots

5. Reread Difficult Parts

Why Reread?

Rereading helps you understand parts of the text that are hard to understand the first time.

How to Reread:

- **Read Slowly:** Take your time with the difficult parts.
  - **Example:** If a sentence is complex, read it slowly and carefully.
- **Break It Down:** Read small parts of the text and try to understand each part.
  - **Example:** Break a long sentence into smaller pieces to understand it better.

6. Discuss What You Read

Why Discuss?

Talking about what you read with others helps you understand it better and see different points of view.

How to Discuss:

- **Talk with Friends or Family:** Share what you read and ask others what they think.
  - **Example:** Discuss a story with a friend and talk about your favorite parts.
- **Join a Book Club:** Join a group where people talk about books and stories.
  - **Example:** A book club helps you understand and enjoy books more.

Table Example:

Discussion Topic	Example Questions
Main Characters	Who is your favorite character?
Plot of the Story	What did you think of the ending?
Important Events	What was the most exciting part?

7. Use Context Clues

What are Context Clues?

Context clues are hints in the text that help you understand new words or phrases.

How to Use Context Clues:

- **Look at the Sentence:** Read the sentence to find hints about the meaning.
  - **Example:** If the sentence says, "The rabbit was very nimble and quick," you can guess that "nimble" means "quick."
- **Check Nearby Sentences:** Look at sentences before and after to find more hints.
  - **Example:** If other sentences talk about running fast, "nimble" might mean "fast."

8. Practice Regularly

Why Practice?

Practicing reading and comprehension regularly helps you get better over time.

How to Practice:

- **Read Different Types of Texts:** Try books, stories, and articles.
  - **Example:** Read a mix of fiction and non-fiction to improve different skills.
- **Do Comprehension Exercises:** Use worksheets or online exercises to practice.
  - **Example:** Complete exercises that ask you to summarize or answer questions about what you read.

Table Example:

Type of Text	
Fiction (Stories)	Read a story and summarize it
Non-Fiction (Articles)	Read an article and answer questions

Poems	Read a poem and discuss its meaning

Visualizing Why Comprehension Matters:

Think of comprehension as the foundation of a house. A strong foundation supports the entire structure, just as comprehension enables you to understand and connect ideas. Without it, knowledge can collapse into confusion. Good comprehension skills build a sturdy base for effective communication and lifelong learning.

WHY COMPREHENSION MATTERS IN LANGUAGE LEARNING

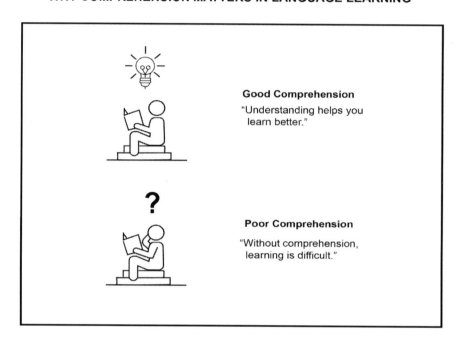

Chapter 2: Understanding Context

"Context is the key to understanding the meaning of words and ideas."

– Mary Balogh

This chapter will show you how to use context clues to guess the meaning of unfamiliar words. You will learn different types of clues that can help you, like looking at the sentences before and after the word or finding hints in the same paragraph. We will also practice using these techniques with simple examples to make learning easier.

Using Context Clues To Infer Meaning

Understanding new words can be challenging, but context clues can help you figure out what they mean. Context clues are hints or information around a word that give you a better idea of what the word means. This chapter will explain how to use these clues to understand difficult words and improve your reading skills.

1. What Are Context Clues?

Definition

Context clues are words, phrases, or sentences around an unfamiliar word that give hints about its meaning.

Why They Are Important

Context clues help you guess the meaning of a word without having to look it up in a dictionary. This makes reading easier and more enjoyable.

2. Types of Context Clues

1. Definition Clues

Sometimes, the meaning of a word is explained in the same sentence or in a nearby sentence.

How to Find Definition Clues:

- **Look for Phrases:** Words like "means," "is," or "refers to" often introduce a definition.
  - **Example:** "The rabbit was very timid, which means it was shy and scared."

Table Example:

Unfamiliar Word	Definition Clue	Meaning
Timid	means it was shy and scared	Shy and scared

2. Synonym Clues

A synonym is a word that has the same or similar meaning as the unfamiliar word.

How to Find Synonym Clues:

- **Look for Words with Similar Meanings:** Words like "also called" or "similar to" may help.
  - **Example:** "The rabbit was very timid, or shy, in new places."

Table Example:

Unfamiliar Word	Synonym Clue	Meaning
Timid	shy	Shy

3. Antonym Clues

An antonym is a word that means the opposite of the unfamiliar word. Sometimes, the text will use antonyms to help you understand.

How to Find Antonym Clues:

- **Look for Opposite Words:** Words like "but" or "however" may show contrast.
  - **Example:** "The rabbit was timid, unlike the brave lion."

Table Example:

Unfamiliar Word	Antonym Clue	Meaning
Timid	unlike the brave lion	Shy

4. Example Clues

Examples in the text can give you hints about the meaning of a word.

How to Find Example Clues:

- **Look for Examples:** Words like "for example" or "such as" introduce examples.
  - **Example:** "The rabbit was timid, such as when it hid from loud noises."

Table Example:

Unfamiliar Word	Example Clue	Meaning
Timid	such as when it hid from loud noises	Shy

3. Practice Using Context Clues

Example 1:

Read the sentence and use context clues to understand the word "arduous."

- **Sentence:** "The hike was very arduous, requiring long hours of walking up steep hills."
- **Clue:** The hike required long hours of walking up steep hills.

How to Use the Clue:

- The word "arduous" means "difficult" or "hard" because the hike was very challenging.

Example 2:

Read the sentence and use context clues to understand the word "generous."

- **Sentence:** "The generous teacher gave extra help to students who needed it."
- **Clue:** The teacher gave extra help to students.

How to Use the Clue:

The word "generous" means "kind" or "giving" because the teacher was kind in helping students.

Practice Exercise:

Read the following sentences and use context clues to figure out the meanings of the underlined words.

1. "The weather was so mild that we decided to have a picnic."
   - **Clue:** The weather was nice for a picnic.
   - **Meaning:** Mild means "pleasant" or "not extreme."
2. "The children felt elation when they saw the presents."
   - **Clue:** The children felt very happy seeing the presents.
   - **Meaning:** Elation means "great happiness."

Table Example:

Sentence	Unfamiliar Word	Context Clue	Meaning
The weather was so mild that we decided to have a picnic.	Mild	Weather was nice for a picnic	Pleasant

The children felt elation when they saw the presents.	Elation	Felt very happy seeing the presents	Great happiness

4. Tips for Using Context Clues

1. **Read Around the Word:**

   - Always read the sentences before and after the unfamiliar word to gather clues.

2. **Look for Signal Words:**

   - Words like "or," "but," "for example," and "however" can help you find clues.

3. **Practice Regularly:**

   - The more you practice using context clues, the better you will understand new words.

4. **Ask for Help:**

   - If you are unsure, ask someone for help or look up the word in a dictionary to confirm your guess.

Recognizing and Interpreting Figurative Language

Figurative language makes writing more interesting and expressive. Instead of saying things literally, figurative language uses creative ways to describe feelings and ideas. This chapter will help you understand different types of figurative language and how to interpret them correctly.

1. What Is Figurative Language?

Definition

Figurative language uses words and phrases in non-literal ways to create effects and meaning. Instead of saying something directly, it uses comparisons and other creative methods.

Why It Matters

Figurative language adds color and depth to writing. It helps us to visualize ideas and understand feelings more deeply.

2. Types of Figurative Language

1. Simile

A simile compares two different things using the words "like" or "as."

How to Recognize Similes:

- **Look for Comparison Words:** Words such as "like" or "as" show a simile.
  - **Example:** "Her smile was as bright as the sun."

Table Example:

Simile Example	Comparison Words	Meaning
"Her smile was as bright as the sun."	as bright as	Her smile was very bright.

2. Metaphor

A metaphor describes something as if it were something else without using "like" or "as."

How to Recognize Metaphors:

- **Look for Direct Comparisons: Metaphors say one thing is another.**
  - **Example:** "Time is a thief."

Table Example:

Metaphor Example	Comparison	Meaning
"Time is a thief."	Time is a thief	Time passes quickly.

3. Personification

Personification gives human qualities to animals or objects.

How to Recognize Personification:

- **Look for Human Traits: If an animal or object is described with human actions or feelings.**
  - **Example:** "The leaves danced in the wind."

Table Example:

Personification Example	Human Trait	Meaning
"The leaves danced in the wind."	danced	The leaves moved with the wind.

4. Hyperbole

A hyperbole is an exaggeration used for emphasis or effect.

How to Recognize Hyperbole:

- **Look for Over-the-Top Descriptions: Hyperboles are not meant to be taken literally.**
  - **Example:** "I'm so hungry I could eat a horse."

Table Example:

Hyperbole Example	Exaggeration	Meaning
"I'm so hungry I could eat a horse."	could eat a horse	Very hungry.

5. Idioms

An idiom is a phrase that has a meaning different from the meanings of the individual words.

How to Recognize Idioms:

- **Look for Non-Literal Meanings: The phrase doesn't mean what the words say.**
    - **Example:** "It's raining cats and dogs."

Table Example:

Idiom Example	Literal Meaning	Idiomatic Meaning
"It's raining cats and dogs."	cats and dogs are falling from the sky.	It's raining very heavily.

3. How to Interpret Figurative Language

1. Look at the Context

Figurative language often relies on the context to make sense. Look at the surrounding words and sentences to understand the meaning.

How to Use Context:

- **Read the Entire Passage:** Understand the general idea before focusing on specific phrases.
- **Check for Clues:** Words and sentences around the figurative language can help you understand its meaning.

2. Think About the Effect

Figurative language is used to create an effect or feeling. Ask yourself what the writer is trying to achieve with the language.

How to Consider Effect:

- **Ask Why the Writer Used It:** Think about how the figurative language adds to the meaning or emotion of the text.
- **Visualize the Description:** Imagine the scene or feeling being described.

Table Example:

Figurative Language	Effect	How to Interpret

| "The classroom was a zoo." | chaotic and noisy | The classroom was very noisy. |

3. Practice with Examples

Reading and practicing with different examples will help you better understand figurative language.

How to Practice:

- **Read Stories and Poems:** Look for figurative language in books, poems, and other writings.
- **Discuss with Others:** Talk about figurative language with friends or teachers to deepen your understanding.

Visualizing Understanding Context:

Think of understanding context as a map for navigating ideas. Just as a map shows relationships between locations, context provides background that clarifies meaning. Without it, messages can be misleading, making context essential for accurate interpretation and appreciation of information.

USING CONTEXT CLUES TO INFER MEANING

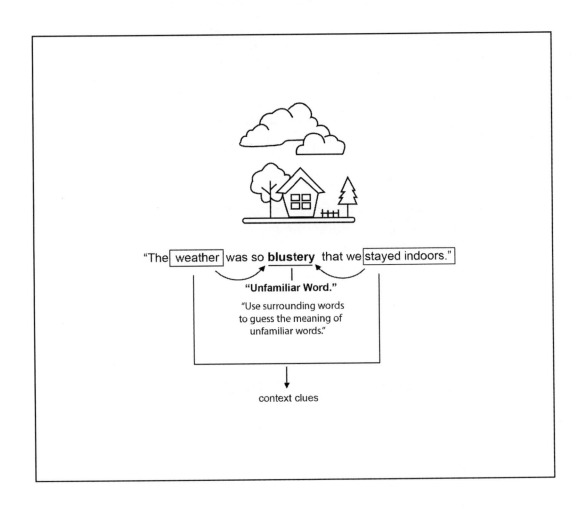

Chapter 3: Identifying Main Ideas and Details

"Reading is to the mind what exercise is to the body."

– Joseph Addison

In this chapter, you will learn what the main idea is and why it is important. We will explore different techniques for finding the main idea in a passage, whether it's in a short paragraph or a long article. You'll also discover how to spot key details that support the main idea, making your reading clearer and more meaningful.

Techniques for Finding the Main Idea in a Passage

Finding the main idea in a passage is like discovering the heart of what the writer wants to say. The main idea tells you the most important point the author is making. Everything else in the passage is there to support this main idea. Let's learn how to find the main idea and the details that help explain it.

1. What Is a Main Idea?

Definition

The main idea is the most important point or message in a passage. It tells you what the text is mostly about. Think of it as the "big idea" the author wants you to remember.

Why It Matters

Knowing the main idea helps you understand the text better and remember the key information. It helps you focus on the most critical parts and ignore less important details.

2. How to Find the Main Idea

1. Look at the Title

The title often gives clues about the main idea.

How to Use This Technique:

- **Read the Title:** The title often hints at the main idea.
  - **Example:** For a passage titled "The Importance of Exercise," the main idea is likely about why exercise is important.

Table Example:

Title Example	Possible Main Idea
"The Benefits of Reading"	Reading is good for you.
"How to Plant a Garden"	Planting a garden is explained.

2. Read the First and Last Sentences

The first and last sentences often contain important information about the main idea.

How to Use This Technique:

- **Check These Sentences:** They often introduce or summarize the main idea.
    - **Example:** In a passage, the first sentence might introduce a topic, and the last sentence might sum up the main point.

Table Example:

Sentence Position	What to Look For
First Sentence	Often introduces the main idea.
Last Sentence	Often summarizes the main idea.

3. Find the Topic Sentence

A topic sentence usually tells the main idea of a paragraph or passage.

How to Use This Technique:

- **Look for Key Sentences:** The topic sentence is often the first or last sentence in a paragraph.
    - **Example:** "Eating healthy foods is important for maintaining good health."

Table Example:

Topic Sentence Example	Main Idea
"Dogs make great pets."	Dogs are good pets.
"Reading is important."	Reading is valuable.

4. Identify Supporting Details

Supporting details help explain or give more information about the main idea.

How to Use This Technique:

- **Look for Details:** Find facts, examples, or explanations that support the main idea.

- **Example:** If the main idea is about the benefits of exercise, supporting details might include examples of exercises and their benefits.

Table Example:

Main Idea	Supporting Detail
"Exercise is healthy."	"It improves heart health."
"Reading is beneficial."	"It enhances vocabulary skills."

3. Practice Techniques

1. Practice with Short Passages

How to Do It:

- **Read a Passage:** Look for the main idea and supporting details.
  - **Example Passage:** "Cats are popular pets because they are low-maintenance and good companions. They do not require a lot of grooming and can entertain themselves."

Table Example:

Passage	Main Idea	Supporting Details
"Cats are popular pets..."	Cats are good pets.	They are low-maintenance and self-entertaining.

2. Use Graphic Organizers

Graphic organizers help you visually organize information.

How to Use Them:

- **Draw a Diagram:** Create a chart with the main idea in the center and supporting details around it.
  - **Example:** A circle in the middle with "Benefits of Exercise" and branches showing details like "Improves mood" and "Increases energy."

4. Summary and Practice

Summary

Finding the main idea involves looking at titles, first and last sentences, topic sentences, and supporting details. Practice these techniques with different passages to get better at identifying the main idea.

Practice Activities:

- **Read Different Texts:** Use the techniques to find main ideas and details.
  - **Create Your Own Graphic Organizers:** Draw diagrams to organize main ideas and supporting details.

Table Example for Practice:

Passage Example	Main Idea	Supporting Details
"The importance of teamwork..."	Teamwork is crucial.	It helps in achieving common goals and solving problems.

Distinguishing Between Main Ideas and Supporting Details

When reading a passage, it's important to know the difference between the main idea and supporting details. The main idea is the central point the author is trying to make, while supporting details help explain or back up that main idea. This chapter will guide you through how to spot both and understand their roles in a text.

1. What Is the Main Idea?

Definition

The main idea is the primary message or point that the author wants to communicate. It tells you what the passage is mostly about.

Characteristics

- **Central Focus:** The main idea is the core message of the text.
- **Summary:** It can usually be summed up in one or two sentences.
- **Example:** In a passage about the benefits of reading, the main idea might be "Reading improves knowledge and skills."

2. What Are Supporting Details?

Definition

Supporting details are pieces of information that help explain, describe, or provide evidence for the main idea. They give you more information about the main idea and make it easier to understand.

Characteristics

- **Support:** They support or elaborate on the main idea.
- **Examples:** Facts, examples, and explanations that help clarify the main idea.

- **Example:** In the passage about reading, supporting details might include "Reading enhances vocabulary" and "Reading can reduce stress."

Table Example:

Supporting Detail	How It Supports the Main Idea
"Reading enhances vocabulary"	Shows how reading helps improve language skills.
"Reading can reduce stress"	Provides a benefit of reading for mental health.

3. *How to Distinguish Between Main Ideas and Supporting Details*

1. Identify the Main Idea First

- **Look for Key Sentences:** Find the sentence that introduces the main point. This is often the topic sentence in a paragraph or the first sentence in a passage.
- **Example:** In the passage "Dogs Are Great Pets," if the first sentence is "Dogs make wonderful companions," this is likely the main idea.

2. Find Supporting Details

- **Look for Examples and Explanations:** Identify sentences that give more information about the main idea. These details explain or provide evidence for the main point.
- **Example:** In the passage about dogs, supporting details might include "Dogs are loyal and friendly" and "Dogs can be trained to help with daily tasks."

Table Example:

Passage Sentence	Type
"Dogs make wonderful companions."	Main Idea
"They are loyal and friendly."	Supporting Detail
"They can be trained to help with tasks."	Supporting Detail

3. Use the "So What?" Question

- **Ask Yourself:** After reading a sentence, ask "So what?" to determine if it's the main idea or a supporting detail.
- **Example:** For the sentence "Dogs are loyal and friendly," the answer to "So what?" is that it supports the main idea that "Dogs make wonderful companions."

Visualizing How to Find the Main Idea in a Passage:

Think of finding the main idea as searching for the core of an apple. The main idea is the seed at the center, while supporting details are the flesh and skin surrounding it. To identify the main idea, look for the key point that ties everything together, helping you understand the overall message of the passage.

HOW TO FIND THE MAIN IDEA IN A PASSAGE

"Cats are independent animals. They groom themselves, hunt alone, and enjoy solitary time."

Three techniques for finding the main idea:

- **Look at the First Sentence**
- **Summarize in One Sentence**
- **Check for Repeated Themes**

Chapter 4: Making Inferences

"Inference is the process of drawing a conclusion based on evidence and reasoning rather than from explicit statements."

— Aristotle

In this chapter, you will learn how to make inferences, which means understanding things that are not clearly stated in the text. We will start by talking about what an inference is and why it is essential. Next, you will see examples of how to find clues in the text that help you make inferences. We will also practice some exercises together to improve your skills. By the end of this chapter, you will be better at reading between the lines and understanding the hidden meanings in what you read.

Learning To Draw Conclusions Based on Text

Reading is not just about understanding the words on the page. Sometimes, the author doesn't say everything directly. Instead, they give hints and clues. To fully understand the text, you need to read between the lines. This skill is called making inferences. In this chapter, we will learn how to use these clues to figure out what the text really means.

What Is an Inference?

An inference is like a guess based on clues. When you make an inference, you use information from the text and your knowledge to understand something that is not directly stated. For example, if a story says, "Sally shivered as she stepped outside," you can infer that it is cold outside, even if the text doesn't say that directly.

Why Are Inferences Important?

Making inferences helps you understand the deeper meaning of what you read. It helps you see the bigger picture and understand characters' feelings, intentions, and the setting of the story. This skill is important for reading comprehension and helps you connect with the text better.

How to Make Inferences

1. Look for Clues: Authors often provide clues to help readers make inferences. These clues can be in the form of descriptive words, characters' actions, or what they say. For example, if a character is crying, the clue might be that they are sad.

Example:

- Text: "Tom's eyes were red, and he sniffled quietly in the corner."

- Inference: Tom might be upset or crying.

2. Use Your Knowledge: Think about what you already know about the world to help make sense of the clues. If you read that a character is wearing a heavy coat, you can infer that the weather is cold.

Example:

- Text: "Mia wore her warm winter coat and boots."
- Inference: It is winter, and it is cold outside.

3. Combine Clues: Sometimes, you must combine several clues to make an inference. Look at the whole context to understand what is happening.

Example:

- Text: "The room was dark, and the lights were out. John found a flashlight and started looking for something."
- Inference: There was a power outage, and John is looking for something in the dark.

4. Ask Questions: Think about questions like "Why did this happen?" or "What does this mean?" Asking these questions helps you focus on the clues and make better inferences.

Example:

- Text: "Sarah's parents are throwing her a big party. She is smiling and telling everyone how excited she is."
- Question: Why is Sarah excited?
- Inference: Sarah is happy because it is her birthday, and she is looking forward to the party.

Practice Making Inferences

1. **Read a Short Passage:** Practice with short texts to improve your inference skills.

Example Passage:

- "Jenny came home from school, and her mom noticed she had a big smile on her face. Jenny said she had a great day and couldn't wait to tell her about it."
- Inference: Jenny had something special happen at school that made her happy.

2. Discuss with Others: Talk about what you read with friends or family. Share your inferences and see if others agree. This helps you understand different ways to interpret the text.

3. Use Graphic Organizers: Use charts or diagrams to organize your thoughts. For example, you can use a T-chart to list clues on one side and your inferences on the other.

Graphic Organizer Example:

Clues	Inferences
"The character was sweating and fanning themselves."	"It is hot and possibly summer."
"The character is holding a cup of hot cocoa."	"It might be cold outside or they like hot drinks."

Visualizing Making Inferences:

Think of making inferences as piecing together a jigsaw puzzle. Each piece represents a clue from the text, and by examining these clues, you can form a complete picture. Just as you combine pieces to understand the whole image, you use evidence and context to draw conclusions and understand deeper meanings beyond what is explicitly stated.

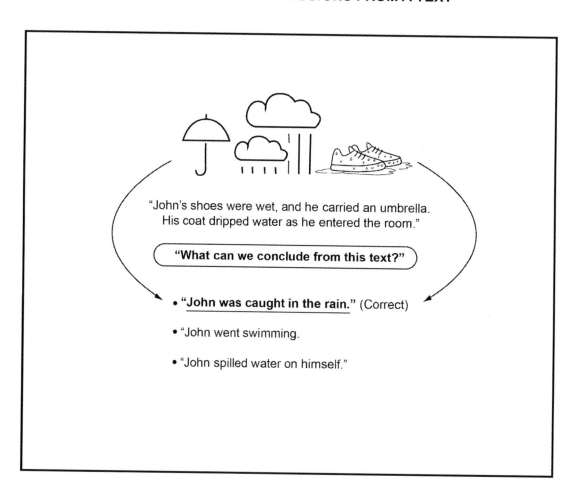

HOW TO DRAW CONCLUSIONS FROM A TEXT

"John's shoes were wet, and he carried an umbrella. His coat dripped water as he entered the room."

"What can we conclude from this text?"

- **"John was caught in the rain."** (Correct)

- "John went swimming.

- "John spilled water on himself."

Understanding Implicit Meanings and Assumptions

When we read, sometimes we need to understand more than just the words on the page. Authors often give us hints or clues about what's really happening. These hints are not always written out clearly. Instead, we need to figure out what they mean by using our own knowledge and the context of the story. This skill is called making inferences. In this chapter, we will explore how to understand these hidden meanings and assumptions to get a fuller picture of the text.

What Are Implicit Meanings?

Implicit meanings are ideas that are not directly stated but can be understood through clues. For example, if a story says, "Jenny rushed to the kitchen and started making breakfast," the implicit meaning might be that Jenny is hungry or wants to eat something quickly. The text doesn't say directly that she is hungry, but we can guess it from the context.

Why Understanding Implicit Meanings Matters

Understanding implicit meanings helps us connect better with what we are reading. It allows us to understand characters' feelings, motivations, and the situation in the story. This deeper understanding makes reading more interesting and helps us engage with the text on a higher level.

How to Find Implicit Meanings

1. Look for Contextual Clues

Authors often give us clues about what is really happening through the context of the story. Pay attention to the setting, characters' actions, and their emotions.

Example:

- Text: "The park was empty and silent. David sat on a bench and stared at the swings."
- Implicit Meaning: David might be feeling lonely or sad because the park is empty.

Table:

Clue from Text	Implicit Meaning
Empty and silent park	The character might be lonely.
David staring at swings	David is lost in thought.

2. Understand Characters' Actions

Sometimes, characters' actions give us clues about their feelings or thoughts. For instance, if a character is cleaning the house frantically, they might be anxious or trying to distract themselves from something troubling.

Example:

- Text: "Maria scrubbed the floor with extra force, wiping away every tiny spot."
- Implicit Meaning: Maria might be feeling stressed or overwhelmed.

3. Consider the Author's Tone and Style

The way an author writes can give hints about the underlying meanings. A cheerful tone might suggest that a character is happy, while a sad tone might indicate that something sad is happening.

Example:

- Text: "The sun was shining brightly as Lucy skipped through the garden, humming her favorite tune."
- Implicit Meaning: Lucy is likely feeling happy and carefree.

4. Make Assumptions Based on Known Information

Use what you already know about the world to help understand what the text implies. If you know that people often wear warm clothes in winter, you can infer that a character is likely cold if they are wearing a coat in a story set in winter.

Example:

- Text: "Tom pulled his scarf tight around his neck as he stepped outside into the snow."
- Implicit Meaning: It is very cold outside, and Tom wants to keep warm.

5. Ask Yourself Why

When reading, ask yourself questions about why a character did something or why the author included certain details. This can help you uncover hidden meanings.

Example:

- Text: "Anna received a large box with a bow on it and smiled softly as she opened it."
- Implicit Meaning: The gift is likely important or meaningful to Anna, and it makes her happy.

Table:

Text Clue	Question to Ask	
Large box with a bow	Why is the gift special?	The gift might have sentimental value.
Anna's soft smile	Why is she smiling?	The gift makes her happy or touched.

Chapter 5: Understanding Tone and Style

"Style is not just what you write, but how you write it."

– William Zinsser

In this chapter, we'll learn how to identify tone and style in writing. Tone is the feeling conveyed through words, such as happy or serious, while style is the unique way a writer uses language. We'll examine how to detect tone in various texts and explore different writing styles, including descriptive and persuasive. Through examples and exercises, we'll practice recognizing these elements and understand their impact on meaning. By the end, you'll be equipped to analyze and apply tone and style in your own writing.

Recognizing Different Writing Styles

Understanding tone and style is important for improving your reading and writing skills. Tone refers to the mood or feeling the writer wants to convey, while style is how the writer uses language to express their ideas. Recognizing different writing styles helps you understand and appreciate texts better. It also enables you to choose the right style for your own writing. In this chapter, we'll explore various writing styles and how to identify them.

What is Tone?

Definition of Tone:

Tone is the attitude or mood that a writer expresses through their writing. It can show whether the writer is happy, sad, serious, or funny. Tone is often shown through word choice, sentence structure, and the overall way a writer writes.

Examples of Tone:

1. **Happy Tone:** "The sun is shining, and the birds are singing. It's a beautiful day to go outside and play!"

    - This tone is cheerful and positive. The words and sentences make you feel happy and excited.

2. **Sad Tone:** "The sky was gray, and the streets were empty. Everything felt quiet and lonely."

    - This tone is melancholic and reflective. The words and sentences make you feel sad or thoughtful.

How to Identify Tone:

- Look at the words used. Are they positive or negative?

- Notice the sentence structure. Is it formal or informal?

- Consider the overall mood of the text. Does it make you feel a certain way?

What is Style?

Definition of Style:

Style is the way a writer uses language to express their ideas. It includes their choice of words, sentence structure, and how they organize their writing. Different writers have different styles, just like people have various ways of speaking.

Examples of Writing Styles:

1. **Descriptive Style:** "The old house had a creaky wooden floor and dusty furniture. The walls were covered with faded, floral wallpaper, and the windows were smudged with grime."

   - This style paints a vivid picture using detailed descriptions. It helps readers imagine what the place looks like.

2. **Narrative Style:** "Once upon a time, in a small village, there lived a young girl named Lily. She dreamed of exploring far-off lands and having grand adventures."

   - This style tells a story with a clear beginning, middle, and end. It focuses on characters and events.

3. **Persuasive Style:** "You should try this new book because it is filled with exciting adventures and inspiring characters. It will make you see the world in a new way."

- This style aims to convince readers to think or act in a certain way. It uses strong arguments and persuasive language.

How to Identify Style:

- Look at the writer's word choice. Are they using simple or complex words?

- Notice the sentence length and structure. Are they short and direct or long and detailed?

- Consider how the text is organized. Is it a story, a description, or an argument?

Identifying the Author's Tone and Style

Understanding the author's tone and style helps you better connect with and interpret a text. Tone is the attitude or feeling the author conveys, while style is the unique way they use words and sentences. Recognizing these aspects can make reading more enjoyable and improve your own writing. In this chapter, we'll learn how to identify both the tone and style of an author by examining different examples.

What is Tone?

Definition of Tone:

Tone is the mood or attitude that the author expresses in their writing. It can be serious, humorous, sad, or joyful. Tone helps you understand how the author feels about the topic they are writing about.

Examples of Tone:

1. **Cheerful Tone:**

- *Example:* "The sun was shining brightly, and the park was full of laughter and joy. Children played happily on the swings while parents chatted in the warm breeze."

- *Analysis:* The words "shining brightly," "laughter," and "joy" show that the tone is happy and positive.

2. **Sad Tone:**

- *Example:* "The old house stood alone at the end of the street. Its paint was peeling, and the windows were broken. Silence filled the empty rooms."

- *Analysis:* Words like "alone," "peeling," and "empty" create a feeling of sadness and loneliness.

How to Identify Tone:

1. **Word Choice:** Look at the words the author uses. Are they positive or negative? For example, words like "bright" and "happy" suggest a positive tone, while words like "dark" and "gloomy" suggest a negative tone.

2. **Sentence Structure:** Notice how the sentences are put together. Short, simple sentences might make the tone feel direct or urgent, while long, descriptive sentences might create a more reflective or detailed tone.

3. **Overall Mood:** Think about how the text makes you feel. Does it make you laugh, cry, or feel inspired? The mood created by the text can give you clues about the tone.

What is Style?

Definition of Style:

Style is the unique way an author writes. It includes their choice of words, how they form sentences, and how they organize their ideas. Each writer has a different style that sets their work apart from others.

Examples of Style:

1. **Descriptive Style:**

- *Example:* "The forest was a magical place, with tall trees that reached towards the sky. The air was filled with the sweet scent of pine and the sound of birds singing melodious tunes."

- *Analysis:* This style uses detailed descriptions to create a vivid picture of the forest. The author focuses on sensory details to paint a clear image for the reader.

2. Narrative Style:

- *Example:* "Once upon a time, in a quaint village, there was a little girl named Emma. She loved exploring the fields and forests around her home, dreaming of grand adventures."

- *Analysis:* This style tells a story with a clear beginning, middle, and end. It focuses on character and plot development.

How to Identify Style:

1. **Word Choice:** Pay attention to the words the author uses. Are they formal or informal? Are they simple or complex? For example, a formal style might use sophisticated vocabulary, while an informal style might use everyday language.

2. **Sentence Structure:** Look at how sentences are constructed. Does the author use short, direct sentences or long, flowing ones? The sentence structure can affect the style and the overall feel of the text.

3. **Organization:** Notice how the text is organized. Does it follow a clear order, like chronological events, or does it jump around? The organization can show whether the style is narrative, descriptive, argumentative, or another type.

Comparing Tone and Style:

To understand a text fully, you need to look at both tone and style. Tone gives you the emotional context of the text, while style shows you the author's unique way of writing.

Activity: Identifying Tone and Style

1. **Read a Passage:** Find a short passage from a book, article, or any piece of writing.

2. **Identify the Tone:** Determine the mood or feeling of the passage. Is it happy, sad, angry, or something else?

3. **Identify the Style:** Look at the author's choice of words, sentence structure, and overall organization. How does the author's style affect your understanding of the text?

4. **Discuss Your Findings:** Share your observations with a friend or teacher. Compare your ideas about the tone and style to theirs.

Visual Aids and Tables:

- **Tone and Style Comparison Table:**

Aspect	Tone	Style
Definition	The attitude or feeling in the writing	The unique way the author writes

Focus	Mood, emotional impact	Word choice, sentence structure, organization
Example	Cheerful, sad, serious, humorous	Descriptive, narrative, persuasive, formal
How to Identify	Word choice, sentence structure, overall mood	Vocabulary, sentence construction, organization

Visualizing Understanding Tone and Style:

Think of understanding tone and style as tuning into a musical performance. The tone is like the melody, conveying emotions and attitudes, while the style is the arrangement, reflecting the artist's unique approach. Just as different melodies and arrangements create distinct musical experiences, tone and style shape the overall feeling and impact of writing, helping you connect with the author's message.

IDENTIFYING DIFFERENT WRITING STYLES

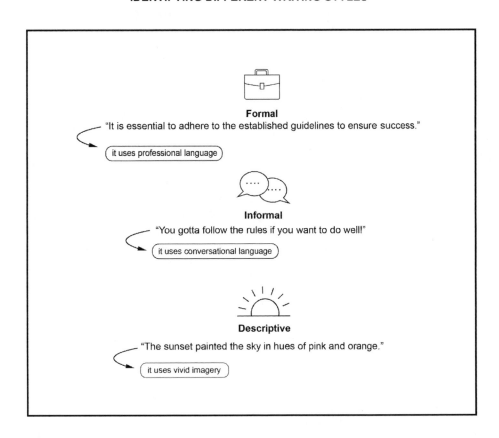

Chapter 6: Advanced Reading Techniques

"The purpose of reading is to become more intelligent and to discover new ideas."

– Mortimer Adler

In this chapter, we will explore these two essential reading strategies that help you find key details and understand texts more efficiently. Skimming allows you to get the gist of the content, while scanning helps you locate specific information. We will cover step-by-step methods for using these techniques and provide examples to practice with, so you can use skimming and scanning to enhance your reading skills.

Skimming and Scanning for Information

"Skimming and scanning are powerful tools to help you find important information quickly," says Dr. Sarah Thompson, an expert in reading strategies. In this chapter, we will explore two advanced reading techniques: skimming and scanning. These techniques help you read faster and find what you need in a text without reading every single word. We'll discuss how to use each technique, when to use them, and provide practice examples to help you improve.

What is Skimming?

Definition:

Skimming is a reading technique used to get the main ideas from a text quickly. Instead of reading every word, you look at the most important parts of the text to understand its general meaning.

How to Skim:

1. Read Titles and Headings:

- **Titles:** Start by reading the title of the text. It usually tells you what the text is about.
- **Headings and Subheadings:** Look at the headings and subheadings. These break the text into sections and help you see the main topics.

  Example:

  - *Title:* "Healthy Eating Habits"
  - *Heading:* "Benefits of a Balanced Diet"

2. Look at the First and Last Sentences:

- **First Sentences:** The first sentence of each paragraph often gives the main idea of that paragraph.
- **Last Sentences:** The last sentence can summarize the paragraph or give a conclusion.

  Example:

    - **First Sentence:** "Eating a balanced diet is essential for good health."
    - **Last Sentence:** "A balanced diet helps you stay healthy and energetic."

3. Focus on Keywords:

- Keywords: Search for important words or phrases that are bold, italicized, or underlined.

  Example:

    - Bold Keywords: "vitamins," "minerals," "fiber."

When to Use Skimming:

- **Previewing a Text:** Before reading in detail, skim to get a general idea.
- **Reviewing:** Quickly look over material to refresh your memory.
- **Finding Main Points:** When you need to get the main points without details.

What is Scanning?

Definition:

Scanning is a technique for quickly finding specific information in a text. Instead of reading the entire text, you scan for particular details like names, dates, or numbers.

How to Scan:

1. Identify What You're Looking For:

- **Specific Information:** Decide what specific detail you need, such as a name, date, or fact.

  Example:

- You need to find the publication date of a book.

2. Move Your Eyes Quickly:

- **Fast Movement:** Move your eyes quickly over the text to find the information. Don't read every word, just look for the key detail.

  Example:

- Searching for the date "2005" in a paragraph about book releases.

3. Use Markers:

- Markers: Look for visual markers like bullet points, lists, or numbers that can help you find the information faster.

  Example:

- Bullet Point: "Publication Date: 2005."

When to Use Scanning:

- **Looking Up Facts:** When you need to find a specific fact or detail.
- **Searching for Dates or Names:** Quickly finding dates, names, or other precise information.
- **Checking Lists:** Finding specific items in a list or table.

Comparing Skimming and Scanning

Technique	Purpose	Method	When to Use
Skimming	Get the general idea of a text	Read titles, headings, and first/last sentences	Previewing or understanding main points
Scanning	Find specific details	Look for specific words or phrases	Searching for specific information

Practice Exercises:

1. **Skimming Exercise:**
   - **Text:** A news article about a recent event.
   - **Task:** Skim the article to find the main event, date, and location.
2. **Scanning Exercise:**
   - **Text:** A list of book titles and authors.
   - **Task:** Scan the list to find the author of a specific book.

Speed Reading and Summarization Techniques

"Speed reading is a skill that can help you read faster without missing important information," says Dr. Emily Carter, a reading specialist. In this chapter, we will learn about speed reading and summarization techniques. Speed reading helps you read quickly while still understanding the main ideas. Summarization helps you put those ideas into a shorter form. We will go over methods to improve your reading speed and how to summarize what you read effectively.

Speed Reading

What is Speed Reading?

Speed reading is a technique for reading faster while still understanding the text. It involves using strategies to increase your reading speed and improve your comprehension.

How to Practice Speed Reading:

1. Preview the Text:

- **Overview:** Before you start reading, take a moment to look at the headings, subheadings, and any highlighted text.
- **Purpose:** This helps you get a sense of what the text is about and what to focus on.

  Example:
  - *Heading:* "How to Improve Speed Reading"
  - *Highlighted Text:* "Key Techniques," "Practice Exercises"

2. Use Your Finger or a Pointer:

- **Tracking:** Move your finger or a pointer along the lines as you read. This helps your eyes follow the text more smoothly.
- **Speed:** Try to increase the speed at which you move your finger to push your reading pace.

  Example:
  - Move your finger from left to right, following each line of text.

3. Minimize Subvocalization:

- **Subvocalization:** This is when you say the words in your head as you read. Try to reduce this to read faster.
- **Focus:** Instead, focus on understanding the meaning of groups of words.

  Example:
  - Instead of "The quick brown fox jumps over the lazy dog," think of "quick brown fox" as a unit.

4. Practice Chunking:

- **Chunking:** Break the text into small sections or "chunks" and read each chunk quickly.
- **Grouping:** Try to read several words at once instead of one word at a time.

  Example:
  - *Chunk:* "The quick brown fox / jumps over / the lazy dog."

5. Increase Your Reading Speed Gradually:

- **Pace:** Start by reading a little faster than usual and gradually increase your speed.
- **Comprehension:** Make sure you still understand what you are reading.

    Example:

    - ○ *Start Slow:* "The quick brown fox..."
    - ○ *Increase Speed:* "The quick brown fox jumps..."

When to Use Speed Reading:

- **Studying:** When you need to go through large volumes of material quickly.
- **Work:** When you have to read reports or documents efficiently.
- **Research:** When you need to get the main ideas from multiple sources.

Practice Example:

Text Excerpt: "Speed reading involves techniques to help you read faster without losing understanding. By previewing, tracking, and chunking the text, you can improve your reading speed."

Summarization Techniques

What is Summarization?

Summarization is the process of condensing a text into a shorter version that includes only the main points. This helps you focus on the essential information without the details.

How to Summarize a Text:

1. Identify the Main Idea:

- **Main Idea:** Find out what the text is mainly about. This is usually in the first or last sentence of the passage.
- **Summary Sentence:** Write a sentence that captures the main point.

    Example:

    - ○ *Main Idea:* "Exercise is important for maintaining good health."
    - ○ *Summary Sentence:* "Exercise helps keep you healthy."

2. Find Key Points:

- **Key Points:** Look for important details that support the main idea. These are often found in headings, first sentences of paragraphs, or in bold text.
- **Include:** Make sure to include these key points in your summary.

Example:

- *Key Points:* "Reduces risk of disease," "Improves mood," "Increases energy."

3. Use Your Own Words:

- **Paraphrase:** Rewrite the main idea and key points in your own words. This helps you understand the text better.
- **Avoid Copying:** Do not copy sentences directly from the text.

Example:

- *Original:* "Exercise improves physical fitness and mental well-being."
- *Paraphrased:* "Working out makes you fit and happy."

4. Write a Concise Summary:

- **Length:** Keep your summary short and to the point. Include only the most important information.
- **Clarity:** Make sure your summary is clear and easy to understand.

Example:

- *Concise Summary:* "Exercise is crucial for staying healthy. It helps prevent illnesses, boosts mood, and gives you more energy."

5. Review and Edit:

- **Check:** Review your summary to make sure it includes the main idea and key points.
- **Edit:** Correct any mistakes and make sure it flows well.

Example:

- *Review:* Ensure all key points are included.
- *Edit:* Fix any errors and improve readability.

When to Use Summarization:

- **Studying:** To review and remember important information from your notes or textbooks.
- **Work:** To create quick overviews of reports or documents.
- **Research:** To summarize findings from multiple sources.

Summary and Practice

In this chapter, you learned about speed reading and summarization techniques. Speed reading helps you read faster by using methods like previewing, tracking, and chunking. Summarization allows you to condense a text into a shorter version with just the main points. Both techniques are useful for managing large amounts of information efficiently.

Visualizing Skimming and Scanning:

Think of skimming and scanning as different techniques for fishing. Skimming is like casting a wide net over the surface to catch the bigger fish; it helps you quickly grasp the main ideas and overall themes.

HOW TO SKIM AND SCAN FOR KEY INFORMATION

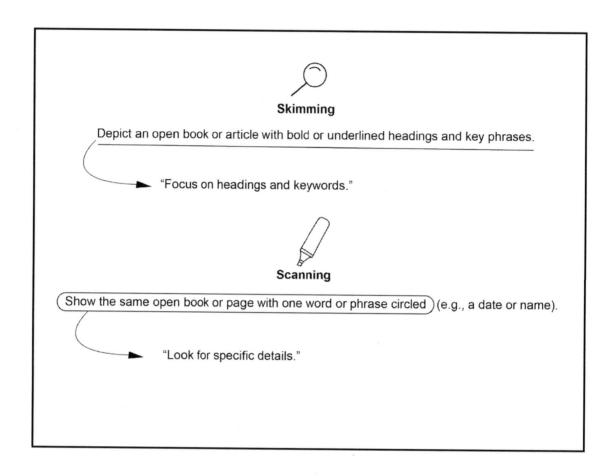

BOOK 5

Effective Communication

Develop Conversational Skills and Overcome Language Barriers in Daily Interactions

Explore to Win

Chapter 1: Introduction to Effective Communication

"Communication is the key to understanding each other."

— William James

Effective communication is vital in our everyday lives. It helps us share our thoughts and feelings with others. When we communicate well, we can build strong relationships, solve problems, and get along with people better. This chapter will explore how communication works, why it is so important, and how you can improve your own communication skills. We will look at different communication methods, such as talking, listening, and body language. By understanding these things, you will see how they can make your daily interactions more successful and meaningful.

The Role of Communication in Daily Life

Communication is an essential part of our everyday lives. It helps us share our ideas, feelings and needs with others. Whether we are talking to family, friends, or colleagues, effective communication plays a big role in how we connect and work together. In this chapter, we will explore what communication is, why it is important, and how you can improve your communication skills. We will look at different ways to communicate, including speaking, listening, writing, and using body language. Understanding these basics can help you communicate more clearly and effectively.

What is Communication?

Communication is the process of exchanging information. This can happen in several ways:

1. **Speaking:** This is when you use words to share your thoughts and ideas. For example, saying "I am going to the store" is a way to communicate what you are doing.

2. **Listening:** This is when you pay attention to what someone else is saying. Good listening helps you understand the message being shared.

3. **Writing:** Writing includes emails, texts, and notes. It allows you to share information without speaking.

4. **Body Language:** This includes gestures, facial expressions, and posture. Body language can show how you feel, even without talking.

Why Communication is Important

Communication is important for many reasons:

1. **Building Relationships:** Good communication helps you connect with others. When you talk and listen well, you build trust and friendship.

2. **Solving Problems:** Clear communication helps you explain issues and work together to find solutions.

3. **Working Together:** In group settings, like at school or work, good communication helps everyone understand their roles and work as a team.

How to Communicate Effectively

To communicate effectively, try these tips:

1. **Be Clear and Simple:** Use simple words and short sentences. This makes your message easier to understand. For example, instead of saying, "I am in need of some assistance with my homework," you can say, "I need help with my homework."

2. **Listen Actively:** Show that you are listening by nodding and asking questions. This shows respect and helps you understand better. For example, say, "Can you tell me more about that?" to show you are interested.

3. **Use Positive Body Language:** Smile, make eye contact, and use open gestures. This makes you seem friendly and approachable. For example, leaning slightly forward and smiling can show you are engaged in the conversation.

4. **Check for Understanding:** Make sure the other person understands your message. You can ask them to repeat what you said or check if they have any questions. For example, say, "Did you understand what I meant?" to ensure clarity.

Common Communication Barriers

Sometimes, communication can be difficult because of barriers. Here are some common barriers and how to overcome them:

1. **Language Differences:** If people speak different languages, it can be hard to understand each other. Using simple words and gestures can help bridge the gap.

2. **Noise and Distractions:** Background noise can make it hard to hear. Finding a quiet place to talk can improve communication.

3. **Misunderstandings:** Sometimes, people can misunderstand what you mean. Being clear and asking for feedback can help prevent confusion.

Improving Your Communication Skills

Here are some activities to help you improve your communication skills:

1. **Practice Speaking Clearly:** Try reading out loud and focusing on how you pronounce words. This can help you speak more clearly.

2. **Work on Listening:** When someone talks to you, practice listening without interrupting. Try to remember what they said and respond thoughtfully.

3. **Use Body Language:** Pay attention to your body language when talking. Practice making eye contact and using gestures to show you are engaged.

Overcoming Language Barriers

In our diverse world, people speak many different languages. This can sometimes make communication challenging. When you do not share a common language with someone, it can be hard to understand each other. This chapter will help you understand how to overcome language barriers. We will talk about why these barriers happen and how you can use different tools and strategies to make communication easier. Whether you are learning a new language or working with people from different backgrounds, these tips will help you connect better.

Understanding Language Barriers

Language barriers can make communication difficult. They happen when people speak different languages or when someone is learning a new language. These barriers can cause misunderstandings and make it hard to share ideas clearly. In this chapter, we will learn about common language barriers and how to overcome them. We will look at practical tips and strategies to help you communicate effectively, even when there are language differences.

What Are Language Barriers?

Language barriers occur when two or more people have trouble understanding each other because they speak different languages or dialects. Here are some common types:

1. **Different Languages:** When people speak different languages, they might not understand each other at all. For example, a person who speaks English might have trouble understanding someone who speaks Spanish.

2. **Different Dialects:** Even within the same language, different dialects can cause confusion. For example, British English and American English have different words and pronunciations.

3. **Limited Language Skills:** If someone is still learning a language, they might struggle with vocabulary or grammar, which can make it hard to express themselves clearly.

Why Language Barriers Matter

Language barriers can lead to:

1. **Misunderstandings:** If people don't understand each other, they might get confused or make mistakes.

2. **Frustration:** Both speakers and listeners might feel frustrated if they can't communicate clearly.

3. **Missed Opportunities:** Poor communication can lead to missed opportunities in work, school, or social situations.

Tips for Overcoming Language Barriers

Here are some practical tips to help you overcome language barriers and communicate more effectively:

1. **Use Simple Language:** Speak clearly and use simple words. Avoid using complex vocabulary or idioms. For example, instead of saying "I am ecstatic about this event," say "I am very happy about this event."

Table 1: Examples of Simple vs. Complex Language

Complex Language	Simple Language
"I am quite elated about this situation."	"I am very happy about this."
"Could you elucidate that concept for me?"	"Can you explain that idea to me?"

2. **Speak Slowly and Clearly:** Speak at a slower pace and pronounce your words clearly. This helps others understand you better. For example, say "Could you help me with this?" slowly and clearly.

3. **Use Visual Aids:** Pictures, diagrams, and gestures can help explain your message. For example, showing a picture of a bus when discussing travel can make your message clearer.

4. **Check for Understanding:** Ask questions to make sure the other person understands what you are saying. For example, ask "Do you understand what I mean?" or "Would you like me to explain that again?"

5. **Be Patient:** Understand that learning a new language takes time. Be patient and give others the chance to express themselves. Try to stay calm and avoid showing frustration.

6. **Use Translation Tools:** Technology can help bridge language gaps. Use translation apps or online dictionaries to help translate words and phrases. For example, Google Translate can be useful for translating text.

7. **Learn Basic Phrases:** If you are interacting with someone who speaks a different language, learning some basic phrases in that language can be very helpful. For example, knowing how to say "hello" and "thank you" in another language can make a big difference.

Overcoming Language Barriers in Different Settings

1. **In the Workplace:** Clear communication is important in a job. Use simple language and ask for feedback to make sure everyone understands.

2. **In School:** If you are learning in a classroom where different languages are spoken, use visual aids and ask questions to help with understanding.

3. **In Social Situations:** When meeting new people from different cultures, be respectful and use simple language. Showing kindness and patience can help build better relationships.

Visualizing Effective Communication:

Think of effective communication as a well-tuned radio. When tuned correctly, it broadcasts clear signals, allowing listeners to understand the message. Just as interference can distort sound, misunderstandings can cloud communication. By choosing the right words, tone, and body language, you ensure your message is received accurately, fostering connection and understanding.

WHY COMMUNICATION IS IMPORTANT IN DAILY LIFE

Chapter 2: Conversational English

"The art of communication is the language of leadership."

— James Humes

In daily life, we use simple phrases and expressions to talk with others. These are known as conversational English. Learning these basic phrases can help you start and continue conversations more easily. In this chapter, we will explore common phrases you can use in everyday conversations. We will also look at some easy ways to practice these phrases so you can speak confidently in English.

Basic Conversational Phrases and Expressions

Effective communication starts with knowing the correct phrases to use in everyday conversations. This chapter will introduce you to basic conversational phrases and expressions that will help you speak English with confidence. Whether you are meeting someone new, asking for directions, or simply making small talk, these phrases will be useful. We'll go over common phrases, their meanings, and how to use them in different situations.

1. Greetings and Introductions

a. Greetings

When you meet someone, it's important to start with a friendly greeting. Here are some common ways to say hello:

- **"Hello!"** — A standard way to greet someone.
- **"Hi!"** — A casual and friendly way to say hello.
- **"Good morning!"** — Used from early morning until around noon.
- **"Good afternoon!"** — Used from noon until about 6 p.m.
- **"Good evening!"** — Used from about 6 p.m. until bedtime.

b. Introducing Yourself

When you meet someone for the first time, you should introduce yourself. Use these phrases to make a good first impression:

- **"My name is [Your Name]."** — Example: "My name is John."
- **"Nice to meet you."** — A polite way to respond when introduced.
- **"I'm from [Your Country/City]."** — Example: "I'm from Canada."

2. Asking for Directions

Sometimes, you need help finding a place. Use these phrases to ask for directions:

- **"Can you help me find [place]?"** — Example: "Can you help me find the library?"
- **"Where is the nearest [place]?"** — Example: "Where is the nearest bank?"
- **"How do I get to [place]?"** — Example: "How do I get to the train station?"

3. Ordering Food

When you are at a restaurant or café, you will need to order food. Here are some useful phrases:

- **"Can I see the menu, please?"** — Ask to look at the food options.
- **"I'd like to order [dish]."** — Example: "I'd like to order a burger."
- **"Could I get the bill, please?"** — Ask for the total amount to pay.

4. Making Small Talk

Small talk helps you start conversations and build relationships. Use these phrases to talk about everyday topics:

- **"How was your day?"** — A way to ask about someone's day.
- **"What do you do for fun?"** — Ask about hobbies or interests.
- **"Have you seen any good movies lately?"** — A question to talk about recent movies.

5. Expressing Thanks and Apologies

Showing good manners is crucial. Here are phrases for expressing gratitude and apologies:

- **"Thank you!"** — To show appreciation.
- **"You're welcome."** — A polite response to "Thank you."
- **"I'm sorry."** — To apologize for a mistake.
- **"Excuse me."** — To get someone's attention or apologize for a minor mistake.

6. Practice and Application

To become comfortable using these phrases, practice regularly. Here are some tips:

a. Repetition

Repeat the phrases you learn every day. This will help you remember them better.

b. Role-Playing

Practice conversations with a friend or language partner. Act out different scenarios using the phrases.

c. Listening and Speaking

Listen to native speakers and pay attention to how they use these phrases. Try to use the phrases in your own conversations.

Visual Aids

Table of Basic Phrases

Situation	Phrase	Example
Greeting	"Hello!"	"Hello! How are you today?"
Introducing Yourself	"My name is [Your Name]."	"My name is Sarah."
Asking for Directions	"Can you help me find [place]?"	"Can you help me find the bus stop?"
Ordering Food	"Can I see the menu, please?"	"Can I see the menu, please?"
Making Small Talk	"What do you do for fun?"	"What do you do for fun?"
Expressing Thanks	"Thank you!"	"Thank you for your help!"

Visualizing Common Phrases for Everyday Conversations:

Think of common phrases for everyday conversations as the tools in a toolbox. Just as each tool serves a specific purpose—like a hammer for nails or a screwdriver for screws—these phrases help you navigate daily interactions smoothly. They provide structure and clarity, making it easier to express thoughts, ask questions, and connect with others in routine conversations.

Role-Playing Common Conversations

To become confident in speaking English, it helps to practice common conversations through role-playing. This chapter will guide you through different scenarios where you can use basic English phrases and expressions. By acting out these conversations, you will gain practical experience and feel more comfortable speaking in real-life situations. We will cover common scenarios like meeting new people, shopping, and asking for help, with simple dialogues to practice.

1. Meeting New People

When you meet someone new, it's important to introduce yourself and make a good impression. Here's how a typical conversation might go:

Scenario: At a Party

- **Person A:** "Hi, I'm Lisa. What's your name?"
- **Person B:** "Hello, Lisa. I'm Tom. Nice to meet you!"
- **Person A:** "Nice to meet you too, Tom. Where are you from?"
- **Person B:** "I'm from New York. How about you?"
- **Person A:** "I'm from Chicago. How long have you been here?"

- **Person B:** "I just arrived yesterday. How about you?"

Practice Tip: Try role-playing this scenario with a friend. Take turns being Person A and Person B to get comfortable with introducing yourself and asking questions.

2. Shopping

When you go shopping, you need to know how to ask for help and make purchases. Here's a simple dialogue for shopping:

Scenario: At a Clothing Store

- **Customer:** "Excuse me, where can I find the jackets?"
- **Store Assistant:** "They are in the back, near the fitting rooms."
- **Customer:** "Thank you! Can I try this one on?"
- **Store Assistant:** "Sure, the fitting rooms are on the right."
- **Customer:** "I'll take this jacket. How much is it?"
- **Store Assistant:** "It's $50. Would you like to pay with cash or card?"

Practice Tip: Act out this conversation with a partner. One person can be the customer and the other the store assistant. This will help you get used to asking for help and making purchases.

3. Asking for Directions

Knowing how to ask for directions is essential when you are in a new place. Here's a typical conversation:

Scenario: On the Street

- **Person A:** "Hi, can you help me? I'm looking for the nearest subway station."
- **Person B:** "Sure! Go straight ahead and take the first left. The station will be on your right."
- **Person A:** "Thank you! Is it far from here?"
- **Person B:** "No, it's about a 5-minute walk."

Practice Tip: Practice this conversation with a friend, taking turns as the person asking for directions and the person giving them.

4. Ordering Food

When you're at a restaurant or café, it's important to know how to order food. Here's how a conversation might go:

Scenario: At a Café

- **Customer:** "Hello! I'd like to order a coffee and a sandwich."

- **Barista:** "Sure, what kind of coffee would you like?"
- **Customer:** "I'd like a cappuccino, please."
- **Barista:** "And what kind of sandwich?"
- **Customer:** "A ham and cheese sandwich."
- **Barista:** "Great. That will be $8.50. Would you like to pay now or later?"
- **Customer:** "I'll pay now."

Practice Tip: Role-play this conversation with a partner, using different food items and drinks. This will help you become familiar with ordering food in English.

5. Making Small Talk

Small talk is important in many social situations. Here's a simple dialogue for making small talk:

Scenario: At a Networking Event

- **Person A:** "Hi! How are you doing today?"
- **Person B:** "I'm doing well, thank you. How about you?"
- **Person A:** "I'm good too. Have you been to this event before?"
- **Person B:** "No, it's my first time. What about you?"
- **Person A:** "I've been here a few times. It's a great place to meet new people."

Practice Tip: Try this small talk scenario with a friend. Use different questions and responses to keep the conversation interesting.

6. Asking for Help

Sometimes, you need to ask for help in various situations. Here's a common way to ask for help:

Scenario: In a Library

- **Person A:** "Excuse me, can you help me find a book about history?"
- **Librarian:** "Of course! History books are on the second floor. Is there a specific book you're looking for?"
- **Person A:** "Yes, I'm looking for 'History of Ancient Rome.'"
- **Librarian:** "I believe we have it in the history section. I'll show you where it is."

Practice Tip: Role-play this scenario to get comfortable asking for help and describing your needs.

7. Making Appointments

Setting up an appointment requires clear communication. Here's an example:

Scenario: Calling a Doctor's Office

- **Caller:** "Hello, I'd like to make an appointment with Dr. Smith."
- **Receptionist:** "Sure, when would you like to come in?"
- **Caller:** "I'm available next Monday or Tuesday."
- **Receptionist:** "Let me check the schedule. How about Tuesday at 2 p.m.?"
- **Caller:** "That works for me. Thank you!"

Practice Tip: Act out making appointments for different services, like a hairdresser or a dentist, to practice scheduling and confirming appointments.

8. Handling Complaints

If you need to express a problem or complaint, it's important to do it politely. Here's how you might handle a complaint:

Scenario: In a Restaurant

- **Customer:** "Excuse me, I ordered a vegetarian meal, but this has meat in it."
- **Waiter:** "I'm very sorry about that. I will get you a new meal right away."
- **Customer:** "Thank you. I appreciate it."

Practice Tip: Role-play different complaint scenarios to practice expressing concerns politely and effectively.

Table 1: Common Conversational Phrases

Situation	Phrase	Example
Meeting someone new	"Hello, my name is [Name]."	"Hello, my name is Alice."
Asking for directions	"Can you tell me how to get to [Place]?"	"Can you tell me how to get to the library?"
Ordering food	"I would like to order [Food]."	"I would like to order a pizza."
Making small talk	"How has your day been?"	"How has your day been?"
Asking for help	"Can you help me with [Task]?"	"Can you help me with this problem?"

By using these phrases and practicing these scenarios, you'll improve your conversational English and feel more confident in everyday interactions.

Chapter 3:
Asking Questions and Giving Answers

"The only way to get the best of an argument is to avoid it."

— Dale Carnegie

Communication is not just about talking; it is also about asking the right questions and providing clear answers. In this chapter, we will explore the basics of forming questions in English, which is a crucial skill for effective communication. We will learn different types of questions, how to form them correctly, and practice examples to make sure you feel confident in asking and answering questions in everyday conversations.

Techniques for Forming Questions in English

In this chapter, we will learn how to ask questions in English and how to give clear answers. Asking questions is important because it helps us find out information and have conversations with others. We will look at different types of questions, learn how to form them correctly, and practice examples to become better at asking and answering questions in everyday conversations.

1. Types of Questions

Questions are an important part of communication. They help us find out information, understand people better, and keep conversations going. Here are the main types of questions:

- **Yes/No Questions:** These questions can be answered with "yes" or "no." They are straightforward and usually start with an auxiliary verb (is, are, do, does, will).

Examples:

- Are you coming to the party?
- Did you finish your homework?

Table: Yes/No Questions

Question	Answer Options
Is it raining?	Yes / No
Can you swim?	Yes / No
Did you eat lunch?	Yes / No

- **Wh-Questions:** These questions ask for more detailed information. They start with words like "who," "what," "where," "when," "why," and "how."

Examples:

- *Where do you live?*
- *Why are you late?*

Table: Wh-Questions

Question	Information Asked
What is your name?	Asking for a name
When is your birthday?	Asking for a date
Where do you work?	Asking for a location
Why are you happy?	Asking for a reason

- **Choice Questions:** These questions give options for the answer. They help people choose between different things.
- **Examples:**
- *Do you want coffee or tea?*
- *Would you prefer to go to the beach or the mountains?*

Table: Choice Questions

Question	Options
Coffee or tea?	Coffee / Tea
Beach or mountains?	Beach / Mountains

2. How to Form Questions

Knowing how to form questions properly helps you get the information you need. Here's a simple guide:

- **Yes/No Questions:**
  1. Start with an auxiliary verb: *is, are, do, does, will.*
  2. Add the subject: *I, you, he, she, they.*
  3. Add the main verb (if needed).

Examples:

- *Is he coming?* (Auxiliary verb + Subject + Main verb)
- *Do you like pizza?* (Auxiliary verb + Subject + Main verb)

Table: Forming Yes/No Questions

Question	Formula	Example
Is she happy?	Is + Subject + Main verb?	Is + she + happy?
Did you see the movie?	Did + Subject + Main verb?	Did + you + see + the movie?
Can he drive?	Can + Subject + Main verb?	Can + he + drive?

- **Wh-Questions:**
  1. Start with a Wh-word: who, what, where, when, why, how.
  2. Add an auxiliary verb (if needed).
  3. Add the subject.
  4. Add the main verb (if needed).

Examples:

- *What time is it?* (Wh-word + Auxiliary verb + Subject + Main verb)
- *Where do you live?* (Wh-word + Auxiliary verb + Subject + Main verb)

Table: Forming Wh-Questions

Question	Formula	Example
What is your name?	Wh-word + Auxiliary verb + Subject + Main verb?	What + is + your name?
Where does she work?	Wh-word + Auxiliary verb + Subject + Main verb?	Where + does + she + work?
Why are they late?	Wh-word + Auxiliary verb + Subject + Main verb?	Why + are + they + late?

- **Choice Questions:**
  1. Start with a question word or auxiliary verb.
  2. Present the options clearly.

Examples:

- *Would you like tea or coffee?* (Auxiliary verb + Subject + Options)
- *Do you prefer reading or watching movies?* (Auxiliary verb + Subject + Options)

Table: Forming Choice Questions

Question	Formula	Example
Tea or coffee?	Auxiliary verb + Subject + Options	Would + you + like + tea or coffee?
Reading or movies?	Auxiliary verb + Subject + Options	Do + you + prefer + reading or watching movies?

3. Practice Examples

Practicing questions helps you get better at forming them. Try asking and answering these questions:

- *Do you like chocolate?*
- *What is your favorite color?*
- *Where are you from?*
- *Would you like to go for a walk or stay at home?*

Table: Practice Questions

Question	Answer
Do you like chocolate?	Yes / No
What is your favorite color?	[Color]
Where are you from?	[City/Country]
Would you like to go for a walk or stay at home?	Walk / Stay at home

4. Tips for Effective Questioning

- **Be Clear:** Make sure your question is easy to understand.
- **Be Polite:** Use polite phrases like "Could you please" or "Would you mind."
- **Listen Carefully:** Pay attention to the answers you get.

Table: Polite Phrases

Phrase	Use
Could you please...?	Asking for something politely
Would you mind...?	Asking for permission
Can you tell me...?	Requesting information

The Art of Open-Ended vs. Closed-Ended Questions

As the famous author and motivational speaker, Tony Robbins, once said, "The quality of your life is in direct proportion to the quality of the questions you ask." This quote highlights how asking the right questions can lead to better answers and more meaningful conversations. In this chapter, we will explore the difference between open-ended and closed-ended questions. Understanding how to use both types of questions effectively will help you gather useful information and improve your communication skills.

1. Closed-Ended Questions

Closed-ended questions are questions that can be answered with a simple "yes" or "no," or with a specific piece of information. They are straightforward and useful for getting clear, concise answers.

How to Form Closed-Ended Questions:

- Start with a verb: Often, closed-ended questions begin with verbs like "is," "are," "do," "does," "can," "will," etc.

Examples:

- *Is it raining today?*
- *Can you swim?*
- *Do you like pizza?*

When to Use Closed-Ended Questions:

- **To get quick information:** When you need a specific fact or a straightforward answer.

Examples:

- *What time does the meeting start?*
- *Did you finish the report?*
- To confirm details: When you want to check if something is true or false.

Examples:

- *Are you coming to the party?*
- *Have you completed the assignment?*

Table: Closed-Ended Questions Examples

Question	Possible Answers
Is your favorite color blue?	Yes / No
Do you have a pet?	Yes / No
Will you attend the event?	Yes / No
Does she speak Spanish?	Yes / No

2. Open-Ended Questions

Open-ended questions require more than just a "yes" or "no" answer. They encourage detailed responses and invite the person to share their thoughts, feelings, and experiences.

How to Form Open-Ended Questions:

- **Start with question words:** Use words like "what," "why," "how," "describe," "explain," etc.

  Examples:

  - *What do you enjoy doing in your free time?*
  - *How did you solve the problem?*
  - *Why did you choose this option?*

When to Use Open-Ended Questions:

- To encourage conversation: When you want to have a more detailed discussion.

  Examples:

  - *What did you like about the movie?*
  - *How do you feel about the new policy?*

- **To explore ideas:** When you are looking for detailed opinions or explanations.

  Examples:

  - *Describe your experience with the project.*
  - *Explain how you came to your decision.*

Table: Open-Ended Questions Examples

Question	Expected Response
What was the best part of your day?	Detailed description of the best part
How do you feel about the changes?	Explanation of feelings and reasons
Why did you choose this career?	Detailed reasons and motivations
Describe your favorite hobby.	Description of the hobby and why it's favorite

3. Combining Closed-Ended and Open-Ended Questions

Sometimes, using a mix of both types of questions can be effective. Start with closed-ended questions to get specific information, and then use open-ended questions to explore the topic further.

Example:

- *Closed-Ended Question: Did you like the movie? (Yes/No)*
- *Open-Ended Question: What did you like most about the movie? (Details)*

Table: Combining Questions

Closed-Ended Question	Open-Ended Question
Did you enjoy the concert?	What was your favorite part of the concert?
Are you finished with your report?	How did you approach writing the report?
Is the weather nice today?	How would you describe the weather today?

4. Tips for Effective Questioning

- **Be Clear:** Make sure your questions are easy to understand.
- **Be Specific:** Ask about specific details to get precise answers.
- **Be Open-Minded:** Be ready to listen to the answers and follow up with more questions if needed.

Using Questions To Guide a Conversation

"Conversation is an art in itself," said American author and lecturer, Dale Carnegie. This quote reminds us that asking the right questions is key to guiding and shaping a conversation. In this chapter, we will learn how to use questions effectively to keep conversations flowing and interesting. Whether you're making new friends or having a business discussion, knowing how to use questions well will help you communicate more effectively.

1. The Importance of Asking Questions

Questions are like keys that unlock new parts of a conversation. They help you learn more about the person you're talking to and keep the discussion moving forward. Good questions can make a conversation more engaging and enjoyable for everyone involved.

Why Asking Questions is Important:

- **Keeps the Conversation Going:** Helps avoid awkward silences.
- **Shows Interest:** Shows that you care about the other person's thoughts and feelings.
- **Gathers Information:** Helps you learn more about the topic or the person.

2. Techniques for Guiding a Conversation

To guide a conversation effectively, use a mix of different questions. Here are some techniques to help you manage conversations smoothly:

2.1. Balancing Question Types

Mix open-ended and closed-ended questions to keep the conversation interesting and informative. Start with open-ended questions to explore topics, and use closed-ended questions for specific details.

Examples:

- Start with an open-ended question: *What do you enjoy about your job?*
- Follow with a closed-ended question: *Do you work in an office or from home?*

2.2. Listening Actively

Listen carefully to the answers you receive. This will help you ask relevant follow-up questions and keep the conversation focused. Show that you are paying attention by nodding, making eye contact, and responding appropriately.

2.3. Being Respectful

Always be polite and respectful when asking questions. Avoid questions that may seem intrusive or uncomfortable. Make sure your questions are relevant to the conversation and the person you are talking to.

Examples:

- Respect personal boundaries: *Instead of asking about someone's income, ask about their hobbies or interests.*
- Avoid sensitive topics unless you know the person well and they are comfortable discussing them.

2.4. Using Non-Verbal Cues

Use body language and facial expressions to show interest and engagement. Smiling, nodding, and maintaining eye contact can make the conversation more pleasant and encourage the other person to share more.

Non-Verbal Cues in Conversation

Non-verbal cues play a significant role in conversations, sometimes conveying more than words themselves. By using body language, facial expressions, and gestures, you can show attentiveness and interest, encouraging the other person to feel more comfortable and engaged. Here are some key non-verbal cues to keep in mind:

- **Body Language**
  - Keep an open posture to signal that you are approachable and interested. Avoid crossing your arms, as this can come across as defensive or closed off.
- **Facial Expressions**
  - Smile to show warmth and friendliness. A slight nod while listening indicates that you are following along and interested in what the other person is saying.
- **Eye Contact**
  - Maintain appropriate eye contact, but don't stare. Regular eye contact shows that you are engaged in the conversation and paying attention to the other person's words.
- **Gestures**
  - Use natural hand gestures to emphasize points or express agreement. Be mindful of your movements so that they complement rather than distract from the conversation.

Non-verbal cues like these can help create a positive atmosphere in a conversation, making it easier for the other person to open up and feel understood.

2.5. Staying on Topic

Keep the conversation focused on the topic at hand. If the conversation strays, gently steer it back to the main subject using relevant questions.

Example:

- If the conversation shifts from work to personal topics, use a question like: *Speaking of work, what project are you working on currently?*

Visualizing Asking Questions and Giving Answers:

Think of asking questions and giving answers as a tennis match. The questions are like serves, initiating the exchange, while answers are the returns that keep the game going. This back-and-forth interaction creates a dynamic dialogue, fostering understanding and connection between people.

HOW TO FORM QUESTIONS IN ENGLISH

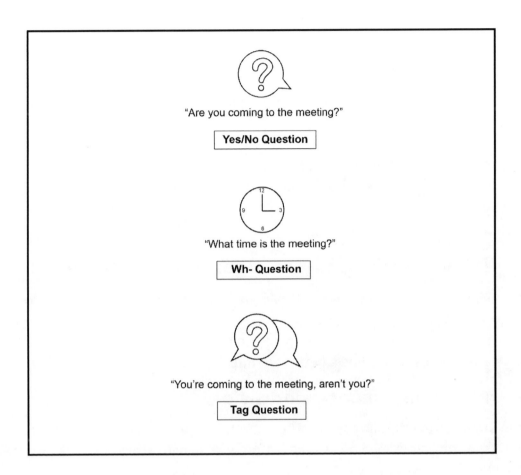

Chapter 4: Active Listening

"Most people do not listen with the intent to understand; they listen with the intent to reply,"

—Stephen R. Covey

In this chapter, we will explore the crucial role of listening in effective communication. Good listening is more than just hearing words; it's about understanding the message and responding thoughtfully. We will cover why listening is so important, how it can improve your conversations, and practical tips to become a better listener.

Importance of Listening in Communication

Listening is a crucial part of communication. It is more than just hearing the words someone says; it is about truly understanding their message and feelings. In this chapter, we will look at why listening is critical and how it affects our conversations and relationships. We will also explore practical ways to improve your listening skills to become a better communicator.

1. The Role of Listening in Communication

Listening is the key to understanding what others are trying to tell us. When we listen well, we show respect and care for the other person. Good listening can help us connect with others and solve problems more effectively. Here's why it matters:

1.1. Builds Trust

When you listen carefully, others feel valued. This trust helps build stronger and more honest relationships.

Example: If a friend shares their worries with you and you listen without interrupting, they feel supported and understood.

1.2. Reduces Misunderstandings

Active listening helps avoid confusion. By paying close attention, you can better understand what is being said and respond correctly.

Example: At work, listening carefully to instructions can prevent mistakes and improve teamwork.

1.3. Improves Relationships

Listening helps us relate better to others. It shows that we are interested in what they have to say and can lead to better connections with family, friends, and colleagues.

Example: Spending time listening to a family member's concerns can strengthen your bond and improve family harmony.

2. The Difference Between Hearing and Listening

Hearing and listening are often confused, but they are not the same. Understanding the difference can help you become a better listener.

2.1. Hearing

Hearing is the process of receiving sound through your ears. It happens automatically and does not require much effort.

Example: Hearing the sound of birds chirping outside your window.

2.2. Listening

Listening is more than just hearing sounds. It involves actively trying to understand the message behind the words. This requires effort and focus.

Example: Listening to a friend talk about their day and trying to understand their emotions and experiences.

Why Listening is More Important:

- **Grasping Feelings:** Helps you understand how others feel and what they need.
- **Giving Better Responses:** Allows you to reply in a way that is thoughtful and relevant.

3. Steps to Active Listening

Active listening is a skill that can be developed with practice. Here are some steps to help you become a better listener:

3.1. Pay Attention

- **Focus Completely:** Give your full attention to the speaker. Avoid distractions like phones or computers.
- **Show You're Listening:** Use body language like nodding and making eye contact. Say things like "I see" or "I understand."

3.2. Show You Care

- **Give Feedback:** Let the speaker know you are listening by repeating back what they said or asking clarifying questions.
- **Avoid Interrupting:** Allow the speaker to finish their thoughts before you respond.

3.3. Respond Thoughtfully

- **Provide Feedback:** Use phrases like "That sounds challenging" or "I can see why you feel that way."

- **Ask Questions:** Ask questions that help you understand better or that show you are engaged in the conversation.

3.4. Remember Key Points

- **Summarize What You Heard:** After the speaker has finished, briefly summarize the main points to confirm your understanding.

- **Follow Up:** Use what you have learned to make thoughtful responses or decisions.

4. Benefits of Active Listening

Active listening offers many benefits that can improve both personal and professional interactions:

4.1. Strengthens Relationships

When people feel heard, they are more likely to trust and respect you. This can lead to stronger and more positive relationships.

4.2. Enhances Problem-Solving

Understanding all sides of an issue through active listening can help find better solutions and make more informed decisions.

4.3. Reduces Conflict

When people feel understood, they are less likely to become defensive or angry. This can help reduce arguments and conflicts.

5. Challenges to Active Listening

Even with good intentions, active listening can be challenging. Here are some common obstacles and how to overcome them:

5.1. Distractions

- **Solution:** Find a quiet place to talk and put away distractions like phones or computers.

5.2. Prejudices

- **Solution:** Try to listen without judging or jumping to conclusions. Focus on understanding the speaker's perspective.

5.3. Interruptions

- **Solution:** Practice patience and wait for the speaker to finish before you respond. Use non-verbal signals to show you are engaged.

Table: Comparison of Hearing vs. Listening

Hearing	Listening
Automatic process	Active and intentional process
Perceiving sound	Understanding meaning
Little effort needed	Requires focus and effort
Example: Birds chirping	Example: Understanding a friend's feelings

Steps to Active Listening

- **Step 1:** Pay Attention
- **Step 2:** Show You Care
- **Step 3:** Respond Thoughtfully
- **Step 4:** Remember Key Points

Using these techniques and practicing regularly can improve your listening skills and become a more effective communicator.

Techniques for Becoming a Better Listener

Good listening is a skill that can significantly improve your relationships and communication. It's not just about hearing words but understanding and responding to them. In this chapter, we will explore simple techniques to help you become a better listener. These techniques will help you show that you care, understand better, and respond more effectively in conversations.

1. Focus on the Speaker

To listen well, you need to pay full attention to the person speaking. Here's how:

1.1. Eliminate Distractions

Turn off your phone or move to a quiet place. Make sure nothing will interrupt your listening.

Example: If you're having a conversation with a friend, put your phone away so you don't get distracted by messages or calls.

1.2. Make Eye Contact

Looking at the speaker shows that you are interested and engaged.

Example: When talking to someone, look at their face, not just their mouth. This helps you understand their emotions and feelings.

1.3. Show That You Are Listening

Use body language to show that you are paying attention. Nod your head, smile, or use short phrases like "I see" or "I understand."

Example: While your friend is talking, nod your head and make small comments to show you are following along.

2. Understand the Speaker's Message

Listening is not just about hearing words; it's about understanding the message behind them.

2.1. Listen for the Main Idea

Try to understand the main point of what the speaker is saying. What is the most important message they want to share?

Example: If someone is telling you about their day at work, focus on the main events or feelings they are describing.

2.2. Ask Clarifying Questions

If something is not clear, ask questions to get more information. This helps you understand better.

Example: If a colleague explains a project and you're confused, ask, "Can you explain what you mean by that?"

2.3. Reflect on What You Hear

Repeat back what you heard in your own words. This shows that you understand and gives the speaker a chance to clarify.

Example: If your friend says they are stressed about a test, you might say, "It sounds like you're really worried about the test."

3. Avoid Interrupting

Interrupting can make the speaker feel like you're not interested in what they are saying. Here's how to avoid it:

3.1. Wait for Them to Finish

Allow the speaker to finish their thoughts before you respond. This shows respect and gives you time to think about what they are saying.

Example: If someone is telling a story, wait until they have finished before sharing your own experiences.

3.2. Resist the Urge to Respond Immediately

Sometimes we want to respond right away, but it's better to take a moment to process the information.

Example: If a friend is sharing a problem, wait a few seconds before offering advice, so you can think about their needs.

4. Provide Feedback

Feedback helps the speaker know how their message is being received. It also shows that you are actively listening.

4.1. Use Verbal Cues

Give verbal feedback by summarizing or repeating what the speaker has said. This helps them feel heard.

Example: "So, you're saying that you're having trouble with your new job?"

4.2. Show Empathy

Express understanding and concern for the speaker's feelings. This helps build trust and connection.

Example: If someone is upset about a problem, say, "I can see why you'd feel that way. It sounds really tough."

5. Practice Active Listening

Active listening is a skill that improves with practice. Here are some ways to practice:

5.1. Practice with a Partner

Find someone to practice listening skills with. Take turns talking and listening to each other.

Example: Have a friend tell you about their day while you practice focusing and providing feedback.

5.2. Listen to Audio Clips

Listen to short audio clips or podcasts and try to summarize what you heard.

Example: Listen to a news segment and then write down the main points.

5.3. Reflect on Your Listening Skills

After conversations, think about how well you listened. What went well? What could you improve?

Example: After a meeting, review how well you understood the key points and consider ways to be a better listener next time.

6. Common Listening Challenges and How to Overcome Them

Sometimes, it's hard to listen effectively. Here's how to handle common problems:

6.1. Dealing with Distractions

If there are too many distractions, find a quiet place or ask to move the conversation to a better location.

Example: If you're in a noisy café, suggest moving to a quieter spot to have a better conversation.

6.2. Overcoming Prejudices

Try to set aside any biases or judgments you may have. Focus on understanding the speaker's point of view.

Example: If someone has a different opinion than you, listen carefully to their reasons before forming your response.

6.3. Managing Emotional Reactions

Sometimes, emotions can get in the way of listening. Try to stay calm and focus on the speaker's message.

Example: If a conversation becomes heated, take a deep breath and remind yourself to focus on understanding the other person.

Table Example:

Technique	Description	Example
Eliminate Distractions	Turn off your phone or move to a quiet place.	Put your phone away during conversations.
Make Eye Contact	Look at the speaker to show engagement.	Maintain eye contact during a discussion.
Ask Clarifying Questions	Ask questions to understand better.	"Can you explain that part again?"
Reflect on What You Hear	Repeat back what you heard to confirm your understanding.	"So, you're saying you're worried about…"

By using these techniques and practicing regularly, you can become a more effective listener and enhance your communication skills.

Visualizing Active Listening:

Think of active listening as tuning into a favorite song. Just as you focus on the lyrics and melody to fully appreciate the music, active listening requires you to concentrate on the speaker's words and emotions. This engagement allows you to understand their message deeply, respond thoughtfully, and build a stronger connection in conversations.

WHY LISTENING IS KEY IN COMMUNICATION

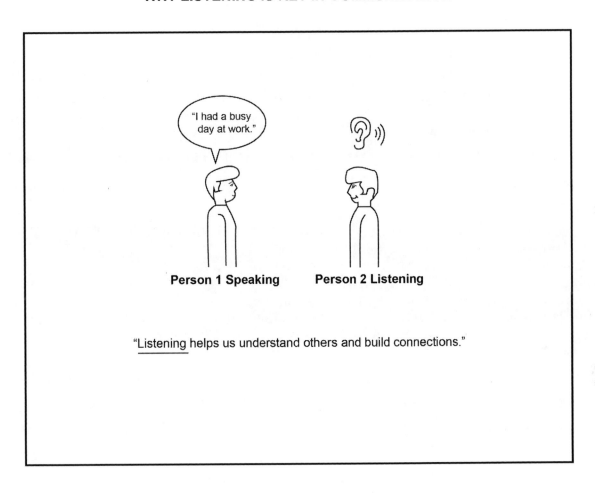

Chapter 5: Expressing Opinions and Feelings

In the world of communication, expressing our opinions and feelings clearly is essential.

—William Shakespeare

Expressing your thoughts and feelings helps others understand you better. This chapter will guide you through useful vocabulary and phrases to share your opinions and emotions clearly. By learning these words and phrases, you will be able to talk about what you think and how you feel in different situations.

Vocabulary and Phrases for Expressing Thoughts and Emotions

Understanding and sharing your thoughts and feelings is a big part of good communication. This chapter helps you learn words and phrases to express what you think and how you feel. Knowing these will help you talk clearly and connect with others better. We will cover vocabulary and phrases for giving your opinion and expressing different emotions.

1. Words for Expressing Opinions

When you want to share what you think, use these simple phrases:

1.1. Agreeing with Someone

When you agree with someone, you show that you have the same opinion as they do. Here are some phrases to use:

- "I think you're right."
- "I completely agree."
- "I feel the same way."
- "That's exactly how I feel."

Example: If a friend says they think a movie is great, you can say, "I completely agree! I loved it too."

1.2. Disagreeing with Someone

Sometimes, you might not agree with what someone says. Here are ways to show that you have a different opinion:

- "I don't think so."
- "I'm not sure about that."

- "I have a different opinion."
- "I see it differently."

Example: If someone says they don't like a certain food, you might say, "I see it differently. I actually like it a lot."

1.3. Giving Your Opinion

When you want to give your opinion, use these phrases:

- "In my opinion..."
- "I believe that..."
- "From my point of view..."
- "I think that..."

Example: If you want to share your thoughts on a new book, you could say, "In my opinion, this book is very interesting."

2. Words for Expressing Feelings

Feelings are different kinds of emotions we have. Here's how to express various feelings:

2.1. Positive Feelings

When you feel happy or good about something, you can use these phrases:

- "I'm happy about..."
- "I feel excited because..."
- "I'm really pleased with..."
- "I'm thrilled about..."

Example: If you are happy about a new game, you might say, "I'm thrilled about my new game. It's so much fun."

2.2. Negative Feelings

If you have negative feelings, like being sad or upset, use these phrases:

- "I'm sad because..."
- "I feel disappointed about..."
- "I'm upset that..."
- "I'm frustrated with..."

Example: If you are disappointed about not being able to go to a party, you can say, "I'm disappointed that I can't go to the party."

2.3. Neutral Feelings

Sometimes, you might not have strong feelings. You can use these phrases:

- "I feel okay about..."
- "I'm not sure how I feel about..."
- "I'm indifferent to..."
- "I feel neutral about..."

Example: If you don't have strong feelings about a new movie, you could say, "I'm indifferent to the new movie. It was just okay."

Visualizing Expressing Opinions and Feelings:

Think of expressing opinions and feelings as painting a canvas. Your feelings are the colors you choose, and your opinions are the brushstrokes that shape the picture. By sharing your emotions and perspectives, you create a vivid expression of your thoughts, allowing others to see the world through your eyes and fostering deeper connections in conversation.

Structuring Arguments and Supporting Opinions With Facts

When you share your opinions, it's important to explain why you feel a certain way. This helps others understand your point of view and strengthens your argument. In this chapter, we will learn how to organize our ideas and back them up with facts, making your arguments clearer and more convincing.

1. Understanding Arguments

An argument is a way of presenting your opinion and giving reasons to support it. Here's how to structure a good argument:

1.1. Start with Your Main Point

Begin by stating your main opinion or argument clearly. This is called a thesis statement. It tells others what you believe.

Example: "I think we should have longer recess at school."

1.2. Give Reasons

After stating your main point, explain why you believe this. Use clear and simple reasons. Each reason should support your main opinion.

Example: "Longer recess will help students relax and focus better in class."

1.3. Support with Facts

To make your argument stronger, use facts or evidence. Facts are pieces of information that are true and can be checked. This makes your argument more convincing.

Example: "Studies show that kids who have more playtime do better in school."

1.4. Address Counterarguments

Think about what others might say against your opinion. Address these counterarguments to show that you have thought about different sides of the issue.

Example: "Some people might say that longer recess will take time away from learning. However, research shows that more playtime can actually improve students' attention and learning."

1.5. Conclude Your Argument

Finish by summarizing your main point and reasons. Restate why your opinion is important and why others should agree with you.

Example: "In summary, longer recess will help students be happier and learn better. It is important for our schools to make this change."

2. Using Facts Effectively

Facts are very important in making a strong argument. Here's how to use them well:

2.1. Find Reliable Facts

Make sure the facts you use come from reliable sources. Reliable sources are trustworthy and provide accurate information. This could be books, scientific studies, or expert opinions.

Example: A fact from a well-known educational journal is more reliable than a random opinion online.

2.2. Use Examples

Examples help to explain facts in a way that is easy to understand. Use simple, clear examples that relate to your point.

Example: "For example, a study by the National Education Association found that students who have more time to play are more focused in class."

2.3. Show How Facts Support Your Point

Explain how each fact relates to your main point. Don't just list facts; show how they support your argument.

Example: "The fact that kids who play more often do better in school supports my argument that longer recess will help students learn better."

2.4. Avoid Misleading Information

Be careful not to use facts in a way that could mislead others. Always present facts honestly and clearly.

Example: If a study shows mixed results, don't only mention the part that supports your opinion. Share the full picture.

3. Practice Activities

3.1. Activity 1: Structuring an Argument

Choose a topic you care about. Write down your main point, reasons, and supporting facts. Practice addressing counterarguments and writing a conclusion.

Example Topic: Should schools provide free lunch to all students?

Main Point: "Schools should provide free lunch to all students."

Reasons: "Many families struggle to pay for lunch. Free lunch helps all students get nutritious food."

Facts: "According to a report by the Food Research & Action Center, free lunch programs improve student health and focus."

Counter arguments: "Some might say it's too expensive. However, investing in students' health can save money in the long run."

Conclusion: "Providing free lunch is important for ensuring that every student has access to healthy food, which supports their overall well-being and academic success."

3.2. Activity 2: Fact-checking

Find a fact related to your opinion and check its reliability. Compare it with other sources to make sure it is accurate and trustworthy.

Example: Look up a statistic about the benefits of physical exercise for kids. Compare it with information from reputable health organizations.

4. Tips for Effective Argumentation

4.1. Be Clear and Simple

Use clear and simple language. Avoid complicated words and sentences. Make sure your argument is easy to understand.

4.2. Stay Focused

Stick to your main point and reasons. Avoid going off-topic. This will strengthen and more convincingly present your argument.

4.3. Be Respectful

When addressing counter arguments, be respectful of other viewpoints. Avoid sounding confrontational or dismissive.

4.4. Practice Regularly

The more you practice making arguments and using facts, the better you will get. Practice with different topics and in various situations.

Chapter 6:
Communicating in Different Settings

"Communication is the real work of leadership."

— Nitin Nohria

In our daily lives, we communicate in many different places, like work, social events, and online. Each setting needs its own way of talking to be effective. In this chapter, we will explore how to communicate well in three important settings: at work, in social situations, and online. We will look at how to use the right words, tone, and style for each setting to make sure your message is clear and effective.

Communication at Work, in Social Settings, and Online

In today's world, how we talk to others can change depending on where we are. The way we communicate at work is different from how we talk in social settings with friends and family. And online communication has its own special rules. Understanding these different settings can help us communicate better in every situation. In this chapter, we will look at how to communicate effectively in three key places: at work, in social settings, and online. We will explore the unique features of each setting and give tips for making sure your message is clear and appropriate.

Communication at Work

1. **Importance of Professional Communication**

   At work, it's vital to communicate clearly and professionally. This means using polite language and being respectful. When we talk to our colleagues or bosses, we need to be careful about how we say things. Professional communication helps build good relationships and prevents misunderstandings.

   Example:

   - **Before:** "I need this done fast. Just get it done."

   - **After:** "Could you please complete this task by the end of the day? I would really appreciate it."

2. **Effective Meetings**

   Meetings are a common part of work. During meetings, it is important to listen carefully and participate actively. Use clear and direct language when sharing your ideas. Always stay on topic and avoid interrupting others.

Tips for Effective Meetings:

- Prepare your points ahead of time.
- Listen to others without interrupting.
- Keep your contributions brief and relevant.

Table: Common Meeting Phrases

Phrase	Use Case
"Can you clarify..."	When you need more information
"I suggest that..."	To offer a new idea or solution
"Let's summarize..."	To recap what has been discussed

3. **Written Communication**

Emails and reports are essential in the workplace. Always start with a greeting, be clear about the purpose, and end with a polite closing. Avoid using slang or informal language.

Example:

- **Before:** "Hey, need this info ASAP."
- **After:** "Hi [Name], Could you please send me the requested information by tomorrow? Thank you."

Communication in Social Settings

1. **Casual Conversations**

When talking with friends or family, you can use a more relaxed tone. It's okay to use slang or jokes, as long as everyone understands and feels comfortable.

Tips for Casual Conversations:

- Use simple and friendly language.
- Be a good listener.
- Share stories or experiences.

    Example:

- **Before:** "Let's meet after work."
- **After:** "Hey, let's grab coffee later!"

Table: Common Casual Phrases

Phrase	Use Case
"What's up?"	To ask how someone is doing
"I'm so excited!"	To show enthusiasm about something
"Let's hang out!"	To suggest spending time together

2. **Showing Empathy**

In social settings, showing empathy is important. This means understanding and sharing the feelings of others. Use phrases that show you care about their feelings and experiences.

Example:

- **Before:** "Don't worry about it."
- **After:** "I understand this is difficult for you. Let's find a way to help."

3. **Respecting Personal Space**

Remember to respect personal space and boundaries when talking to friends and family. This means being mindful of physical distance and sensitive topics.

Tips for Respecting Space:

- Avoid standing too close.
- Ask before discussing personal issues.
- Be aware of non-verbal cues.

Online Communication

1. **Email and Messaging Etiquette**

Online communication includes emails, texts, and social media messages. You ought to be clear and polite, even in short messages. Always double-check your spelling and grammar before sending.

Tips for Online Communication:

- Use proper greetings and closings.
- Be concise but clear.
- Avoid using all caps, which can seem like shouting.

Example:

- **Before:** "WHAT TIME IS THE MEETING"

- **After:** "Hi, could you please let me know the time of the meeting? Thanks!"

Table: Online Communication Dos and Don'ts

Dos	Don'ts
Use complete sentences	Avoid using slang excessively
Check for spelling mistakes	Don't use all caps
Be polite and respectful	Don't send messages when angry

2. Social Media Interactions

Social media is a place to share thoughts and connect with others. It's essential to be careful about what you post and how you interact. Always be respectful and think before you share.

Tips for Social Media:

- Think about how your post might affect others.
- Respond to comments politely.
- Avoid sharing private information.

Example:

- **Before:** Posting negative comments about someone.
- **After:** Sharing positive or neutral updates.

3. Video Calls

Video calls are a popular way to communicate online. Make sure your environment is tidy, and your internet connection is stable. Speak clearly and look at the camera when talking.

Tips for Video Calls:

- Find a quiet place with good lighting.
- Use a clear and professional background.
- Pay attention to your body language.

Example:

- **Before:** Joining a video call from a noisy or cluttered space.
- **After:** Setting up in a quiet, well-lit room with a clean background.

Table: Video Call Best Practices

Practice	Description
Check your equipment	Ensure your camera and microphone work
Dress appropriately	Wear suitable clothing for the call
Maintain eye contact	Look at the camera to appear engaged

Practice Scenarios for Various Communication Settings

Communicating well means knowing how to adapt your words to fit different situations. In this chapter, we will practice different ways to communicate in various settings. By exploring specific scenarios, you will learn how to use the right language and approach for each type of situation. This will help you feel more confident and clear in your conversations, whether you're at work, with friends, or online.

1. Communication at Work

Scenario 1: Giving Feedback to a Colleague

Situation: You need to give feedback to a coworker about their recent project.

Approach:

- **Start with a Compliment:** Begin by mentioning something positive about their work.
- **Be Specific:** Point out exactly what you think could be improved.
- **Offer Solutions:** Suggest ways to improve the work.

Example:

- **Before:** "Your report was not good. It needs changes."
- **After:** "I really liked how detailed your report was. However, I think it would be even better if you could add more data to support your conclusions. Let me know if you need help with this."

Scenario 2: Asking for Help with a Task

Situation: You need help from a team member to finish a project.

Approach:

- **Be Polite:** Ask politely if they can help.
- **Be Clear About What You Need:** Explain what the task involves.
- **Acknowledge Their Time:** Show that you appreciate their help.

Example:

- **Before:** "Can you help me with this?"
- **After:** "Hi [Name], I'm working on this project and could really use your expertise with [specific task]. Could you please help me with it? I'd appreciate it a lot."

Table: Tips for Professional Communication at Work

Tip	Description
Be Clear and Concise	Use simple and direct language.
Show Respect	Always be polite and considerate.
Focus on Solutions	Offer constructive feedback and solutions.

2. Communication in Social Settings

Scenario 1: Making a New Friend

Situation: You meet someone new at a social event.

Approach:

- **Start with a Greeting:** Begin with a friendly hello.
- **Ask Open-Ended Questions:** Encourage them to talk about themselves.
- **Share About Yourself:** Give some information about yourself to build a connection.

Example:

- **Before:** "Hi, what's your name?"
- **After:** "Hi, I'm [Your Name]. It's great to meet you! What brought you here today? I'm really interested in [related topic]."

Scenario 2: Organizing a Social Event

Situation: You're planning a party and need to invite friends.

Approach:

- **Be Friendly and Enthusiastic:** Make your invitation sound exciting.
- **Include Details:** Provide information about the time, date, and location.
- **Ask for a Response:** Let them know how to RSVP.

Example:

- **Before:** "I'm having a party next week. You should come."

- **After:** "Hey [Name]! I'm throwing a party next Saturday at 7 PM at my place. It's going to be a lot of fun with music and snacks. I really hope you can make it! Please let me know if you can come."

Table: Social Communication Tips

Tip	Description
Be Warm and Approachable	Use friendly language and a positive tone.
Provide Clear Information	Give all necessary details about the event.
Encourage Participation	Ask questions to get them involved in the conversation.

3. Communication Online

Scenario 1: Sending an Email

Situation: You need to write an email to a teacher or a professor.

Approach:

- **Use a Proper Greeting:** Start with "Dear [Title] [Last Name],".
- **Be Brief and Specific:** State your purpose clearly and quickly.
- **End Politely:** Use a formal closing.

Example:

- **Before:** "Hey, I need help with the assignment."
- **After:** "Dear Professor [Last Name], I hope this message finds you well. I am having some difficulty understanding the assignment on [specific topic]. Could you please provide some additional guidance? Thank you very much for your help. Sincerely, [Your Name]"

Scenario 2: Participating in a Forum

Situation: You're joining an online discussion about a topic you're interested in.

Approach:

- **Read the Rules:** Follow the guidelines for the forum.
- **Be Respectful:** Respect others' opinions and be polite.
- **Contribute Constructively:** Add useful information or ask thoughtful questions.

Example:

- **Before:** "I think this idea is dumb."

- **After:** "I see your point, but I have a different perspective. Could you explain more about [specific aspect]? I think it might help if we consider [alternative idea]."

Table: Online Communication Tips

Tip	Description
Follow the Rules	Respect the guidelines of the platform.
Be Respectful	Avoid negative comments and be polite.
Be Clear and Constructive	Provide valuable input and ask relevant questions.

Visualizing Communicating in Different Settings:

Think of communicating in different settings as switching outfits for various occasions. Just as you dress appropriately for a job interview, a casual gathering, or a formal event, your communication style should adapt to the context. Whether it's using formal language in a meeting or a relaxed tone with friends, adjusting your approach helps ensure your message is understood and received well in each environment.

COMMUNICATING EFFECTIVELY IN DIFFERENT SETTINGS

BOOK 6

Practical Writing Skills

Master Paragraphs, Essays, Emails, and More for Effective Written Communication

Explore to Win

Chapter 1: Introduction to Writing in English

"Writing is the painting of the voice."

– Voltaire

Writing in English is a key skill for communicating your ideas clearly and effectively. This chapter will introduce you to the basics of writing in English. We will start with simple writing techniques and gradually move to more complex ideas. You will learn about the importance of clear writing, the basic structure of sentences, and how to organize your thoughts. By the end of this chapter, you will have a solid foundation for writing well in English.

Importance of Writing in Language Learning

Writing is a key part of learning any language, including English. It helps you practice and use new words and rules you learn. Writing also enables you to organize your thoughts and communicate clearly. This chapter will explain why writing is critical and how it helps you become better at English.

1. Writing Helps You Practice English

When you write in English, you use new words and grammar rules. This helps you practice what you have learned. Just like you need to practice speaking to get better at talking, you need to practice writing to get better at it.

Example: If you learn the past tense of verbs, writing sentences using the past tense helps you remember how to use it correctly.

2. Writing Improves Your Understanding

Writing helps you understand English better. When you write, you think about how to use words and sentences correctly. This helps you see how different parts of the language work together. For example, writing a story enables you to see how to use verbs, nouns, and adjectives in a way that makes sense.

Table: Benefits of Writing

Benefit	Description
Practice	Helps you use new words and rules.
Understanding	Shows how different parts of the language work.
Organization	Helps you organize your thoughts clearly.

Communication	Improves how you share ideas with others.

3. Writing Helps You Organize Your Thoughts

When you write, you put your ideas in order. This helps you think clearly. For example, when writing a letter, you first introduce yourself, then explain your message, and finally give a closing.

Example: To write a letter to a friend, you would start with "Dear [Friend's Name]," then share news, and end with "Sincerely, [Your Name]."

4. Writing Enhances Communication Skills

Writing is an important way to share ideas. It helps you tell people what you think and feel. Good writing makes your message clear and easy to understand. For example, if you write a clear email to your teacher, it is easier for them to understand what you need help with.

5. Writing is Useful for Many Situations

Writing skills are needed in many parts of life. You use writing at school, work, and in everyday life. For example, you write essays in school, emails at work, and notes to friends. Being good at writing helps you in all these areas.

Example: Writing a job application letter helps you get a job by showing your skills and experience.

6. Writing Helps You Learn More About English

When you write, you get to know English better. You learn new words and how to use them. You also learn grammar rules and how to put sentences together. This helps you improve your English skills over time.

Table: How Writing Helps Language Learning

How It Helps	Example
Learning New Words	Writing sentences using new vocabulary.
Grammar Practice	Applying grammar rules in written work.
Sentence Structure	Creating clear and correct sentences.
Expressing Ideas	Sharing thoughts through writing.

7. Writing Builds Confidence

When you practice writing, you get better at it. As you improve, you feel more confident in your writing skills. This confidence helps you write more and use English more effectively.

Example: Writing a story or a report becomes easier with practice, and you become more comfortable with writing in general.

Basic Writing Skills for Beginners

Writing is a skill you use every day, from writing notes to sending emails. For beginners, it's important to start with the basics. This chapter will cover the essential writing skills you need to begin writing in English. We will look at simple rules, practice exercises, and tips to help you get started.

1. Understanding the Basic Parts of a Sentence

A sentence is a group of words that makes complete sense. Every sentence has three main parts:

- **Subject:** The person or thing doing the action.
- **Verb:** The action or state of being.
- **Object:** The person or thing receiving the action.

Example:

- **Subject:** "She"
- **Verb:** "eats"
- **Object:** "an apple"

Complete Sentence: "She eats an apple."

2. Using Capital Letters and Punctuation

Capital letters and punctuation marks help make your writing clear. Here are some basic rules:

- **Capitalize the First Word:** Start every sentence with a capital letter.

  Example: "My name is John."

- **Use Periods (.):** End a sentence with a period.

  Example: "I like to read."

- **Use Question Marks (?):** End a question with a question mark.

  Example: "What time is it?"

- **Use Exclamation Marks (!):** End a sentence with an exclamation mark to show strong feelings.

  Example: "Wow, that's amazing!"

Table: Punctuation Marks

Punctuation Mark	Use	Example
Period (.)	Ends a statement	"I have a cat."
Question Mark (?)	Ends a question	"Do you like pizza?"
Exclamation Mark (!)	Shows excitement or strong feeling	"Great job!"

3. Writing Simple Sentences

Start with simple sentences to practice. Here are steps to create a simple sentence:

- **Choose a Subject:** Who or what is the sentence about?

  Example: "The dog"

- **Choose a Verb:** What is the subject doing?

  Example: "barks"

- **Add an Object (optional):** What is the subject doing something to?

  Example: "at the mailman"

Complete Sentence: "The dog barks at the mailman."

4. Writing Short Paragraphs

A paragraph is a group of sentences about one main idea. Here's how to write a basic paragraph:

- **Start with a Topic Sentence:** This tells what the paragraph is about.

  Example: "I love going to the beach."

- **Add Supporting Sentences:** Give details about the topic.

  Example: "The sand feels warm under my feet. The water is cool and refreshing. I enjoy building sandcastles."

- **End with a Closing Sentence:** Summarize the main idea.

  Example: "Going to the beach is always fun and relaxing."

5. Common Mistakes to Avoid

Here are some common writing mistakes and how to avoid them:

- **Spelling Errors:** Always check your spelling. Use a dictionary or spell checker if needed.

  Example: "Recieve" should be "Receive."

- **Grammar Mistakes:** Make sure your sentences are complete and correct.

Example: "She don't like apples." should be "She doesn't like apples."

- **Run-on Sentences:** Don't put too many ideas in one sentence. Break them into shorter sentences if needed.

  Example: "I went to the store and I bought some bread and then I went home." could be "I went to the store. I bought some bread. Then I went home."

Table: Common Writing Mistakes

Mistake	Example	Correction
Spelling Error	"Recieve"	"Receive"
Grammar Error	"She don't like apples."	"She doesn't like apples."
Run-on Sentence	"I went to the store and I bought some bread and then I went home."	"I went to the store. I bought some bread. Then I went home."

6. Review and Revise

After writing, always review and revise your work. Check for mistakes, make sure your ideas are clear, and improve your sentences. Revising helps you improve your writing.

Steps to Revise:

- **Read Your Writing Aloud:** This helps you catch mistakes and see if your sentences make sense.

- **Ask Someone to Read It:** Another person can give you feedback and find mistakes you might have missed.

- **Make Changes:** Correct errors and improve your writing based on the feedback.

Visualizing Why Writing is Important for Learning English:

Think of writing as a bridge connecting thoughts and language. It allows you to organize ideas, practice vocabulary, and improve grammar skills. Just as a bridge provides a safe passage over obstacles, writing helps you overcome challenges in learning English by reinforcing comprehension and encouraging self-expression. Through writing, you gain confidence and clarity, making it essential for effective communication and mastery of the language.

WHY WRITING IS IMPORTANT FOR LEARNING ENGLISH

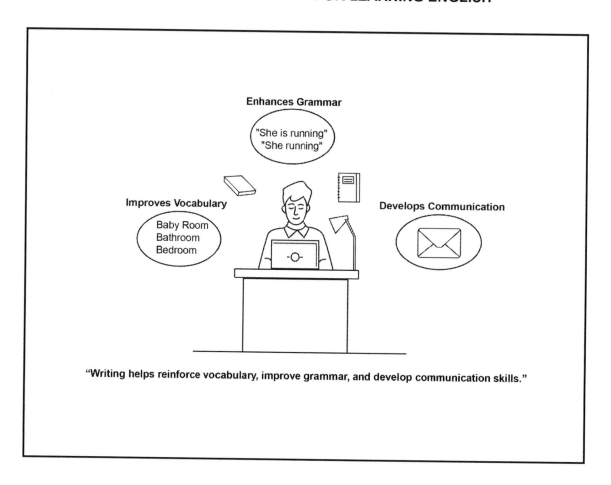

Chapter 2: Writing Paragraphs

"The most important thing about writing is to keep it simple and clear"

– William Zinsser

Understanding how to structure a paragraph is essential for effective writing. Just as a house needs a solid foundation and well-constructed walls, a good paragraph requires a clear structure. In this chapter, we will learn how to build paragraphs step-by-step. We will cover what makes a strong paragraph, how to organize your ideas, and the importance of each part of a paragraph. By the end of this chapter, you will be able to write clear and organized paragraphs, making your writing easier to understand and more enjoyable to read.

How To Structure a Paragraph

Creating a well-structured paragraph is essential for clear and effective writing. Just like building a house, a good paragraph needs a strong structure. It should have a clear beginning, middle, and end. In this chapter, we will learn how to make a paragraph from scratch. We'll explore each part of a paragraph and how to put them together. By the end, you will know how to create paragraphs that are clear, organized, and easy to understand.

1. What is a Paragraph?

A paragraph is a group of sentences that work together to discuss one main idea. Think of a paragraph as a small part of your writing that focuses on a single topic.

Parts of a Paragraph:

- **Topic Sentence:** Introduces the main idea.
- **Supporting Sentences:** Give more details and examples.
- **Closing Sentence:** Summarizes the paragraph and gives a final thought.

2. The Topic Sentence

The topic sentence is the first sentence in a paragraph. It tells the reader what the paragraph will be about. It should be clear and direct.

How to Write a Good Topic Sentence:

- **Be Specific:** Make sure it clearly states the main idea.
- **Be Interesting:** Write it in a way that grabs attention.

Examples:

- Good Topic Sentence: "Dogs are excellent pets for families with children."
- Not-So-Good Topic Sentence: "Dogs are nice."

In the good example, the topic sentence clearly tells us what the paragraph will discuss—why dogs are great pets for families with children.

3. Supporting Sentences

After the topic sentence, you need supporting sentences. These sentences help explain the main idea by providing more information.

How to Write Supporting Sentences:

- **Add Details:** Describe more about the topic.
- **Give Examples:** Provide specific examples to illustrate your point.
- **Use Descriptions:** Describe what you mean to make your idea clearer.

Examples:

- **Adding Details:** "Dogs are loyal animals that love to play with kids."
- **Giving Examples:** "For example, many dogs enjoy playing fetch with a ball."
- **Using Descriptions:** "Dogs often wag their tails and jump up when they see their favorite people."

4. The Closing Sentence

The closing sentence is the last sentence of the paragraph. It sums up the main idea and gives a final thought.

How to Write a Good Closing Sentence:

- Summarize the Main Idea: Restate the main point in a different way.
- Provide a Final Thought: Leave the reader with something to think about.

Examples:

- Good Closing Sentence: "Because of their loyalty and playful nature, dogs make wonderful companions for families with children."
- Not-So-Good Closing Sentence: "In conclusion, dogs are nice pets."

In the good example, the closing sentence restates the main idea and gives a final thought.

5. Putting It All Together

To make a strong paragraph, follow these steps:

- **Write the Topic Sentence:** Start with a clear sentence that introduces the main idea.
- **Add Supporting Sentences:** Provide details, examples, and descriptions to explain the topic.
- **End with a Closing Sentence:** Summarize the main idea and give a final thought.

Example Paragraph:

Topic Sentence: "Dogs are excellent pets for families with children."

Supporting Sentences:

- "Dogs are loyal animals that love to play with kids."
- "For example, many dogs enjoy playing fetch with a ball."
- "Dogs often wag their tails and jump up when they see their favorite people."

Closing Sentence: "Because of their loyalty and playful nature, dogs make wonderful companions for families with children."

6. Common Mistakes to Avoid

Here are some mistakes to watch out for:

- **Lack of a Clear Topic Sentence:** Without a clear topic sentence, your paragraph can be confusing.
- **Not Enough Supporting Details:** Ensure you provide enough details to explain your main idea.
- **Weak Closing Sentence:** A weak closing sentence doesn't sum up the paragraph well.

Examples of Mistakes:

- **Lack of Clear Topic Sentence:** "I like to cook. I cook different types of food. Cooking is fun. I cook on weekends."
- **Not Enough Supporting Details:** "I like pizza. It's good. Pizza is tasty."

7. Tips for Improving Your Paragraphs

- **Read Your Paragraph Out Loud:** This helps you see if it makes sense and flows well.
- **Use Transition Words:** Words like "first," "next," and "finally" help connect your ideas.
- **Revise and Edit:** Check for mistakes and make improvements.

8. Visual Aids

Table: Parts of a Paragraph

Part	Description	Example
Topic Sentence	Introduces the main idea	"Cats are great pets for people who live in small apartments."
Supporting Sentences	Provide details and examples	"They don't need as much space as dogs. Many cats enjoy sitting by a window."
Closing Sentence	Summarizes the paragraph and gives a final thought	"Because they are low-maintenance and independent, cats are perfect for apartment living."

Visualizing Structuring a Paragraph:

Think of structuring a paragraph as building a house. The topic sentence is the foundation, presenting the main idea. Supporting sentences are the walls, providing details and examples that reinforce the topic. Finally, the concluding sentence is the roof, summarizing the key points and providing closure. Together, they create a solid and coherent paragraph that effectively conveys your message.

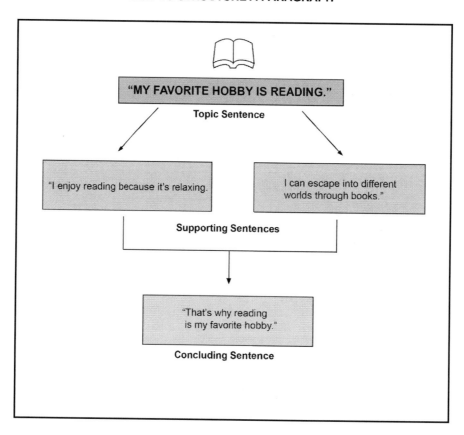

HOW TO STRUCTURE A PARAGRAPH

Writing Paragraphs on Various Topics

Writing paragraphs about different topics helps you become a better writer. It allows you to practice organizing your thoughts and clearly expressing your ideas. In this chapter, we will look at how to write paragraphs on various topics. We will use simple examples to show how you can create clear and effective paragraphs. By the end, you'll be able to write paragraphs on many different subjects with confidence.

1. Choosing a Topic

Before you start writing, you need to choose a topic. A topic is what your paragraph will be about. It can be anything that interests you or that you need to write about.

How to Choose a Good Topic:

- **Interest:** Pick something you like or care about.
- **Specificity:** Choose a topic that is clear and not too broad.
- **Relevance:** Make sure the topic fits the purpose of your writing.

Examples:

- **Good Topic:** "The benefits of eating healthy foods."
- **Too Broad:** "Food."

2. Writing a Topic Sentence

The topic sentence tells the reader what the paragraph will be about. It is usually the first sentence. A strong topic sentence will help guide your writing.

How to Write a Topic Sentence:

- **Be Clear:** Make sure it clearly states the main idea.
- **Be Focused:** Keep it specific and to the point.

Examples:

- **Good Topic Sentence:** "Eating healthy foods can improve your energy and overall health."
- **Weak Topic Sentence:** "Healthy foods are good."

3. Adding Supporting Sentences

Supporting sentences give more details about the topic. They help explain why the topic sentence is true. Use facts, examples, and descriptions to support your main idea.

How to Add Supporting Sentences:

- **Include Facts:** Provide information that supports your topic sentence.
- **Give Examples:** Use specific instances to make your point clearer.

- **Use Descriptions:** Describe details to help the reader understand.

Examples:

- **Facts:** "Eating fruits and vegetables provides important vitamins and minerals."
- **Examples:** "For instance, oranges are high in vitamin C, which boosts your immune system."
- **Descriptions:** "A colorful salad with a variety of vegetables can be both tasty and nutritious."

4. Writing a Closing Sentence

The closing sentence wraps up the paragraph. It restates the main idea in a new way and gives a final thought.

How to Write a Closing Sentence:

- **Summarize:** Restate the main idea of the paragraph.
- **Give a Final Thought:** Leave the reader with something to think about.

Examples:

- **Good Closing Sentence:** "By including more healthy foods in your diet, you can feel better and stay healthier."
- **Weak Closing Sentence:** "Healthy foods are important."

5. Using Different Paragraph Types

Different types of paragraphs can be used for various purposes. Here are a few common types:

- Descriptive Paragraphs: Describe a person, place, or thing in detail. Use sensory details to make your writing vivid.
    - Example: "The old library was filled with the smell of aged paper and the quiet rustling of pages."
- Narrative Paragraphs: Tell a story or describe an event in a sequence. Focus on the sequence of actions and events.
    - Example: "Yesterday, I went to the park. First, I played on the swings. Then, I had a picnic with my friends."
- Expository Paragraphs: Explain or inform about a topic. Provide clear facts and details.
    - Example: "Photosynthesis is the process by which plants make their own food. It uses sunlight to turn carbon dioxide and water into glucose and oxygen."
- Persuasive Paragraphs: Try to convince the reader of something. Use reasons and evidence to support your point.
    - Example: "Adopting a pet from a shelter is a great choice. Shelters have many animals that need loving homes, and adopting saves lives."

6. Reviewing and Revising Paragraphs

After writing a paragraph, it's important to review and revise it. Check for any mistakes and make sure your ideas are clear.

How to Review and Revise:

- **Check for Clarity:** Ensure each sentence supports the main idea.
- **Look for Mistakes:** Fix any spelling, grammar, or punctuation errors.
- **Read Aloud:** Reading your paragraph aloud can help you catch mistakes and improve the flow.

Table 1: Parts of a Paragraph

Part	Description	Example
Topic Sentence	Introduces the main idea	"Dogs are great pets for families."
Supporting Sentences	Provide details and examples	"Dogs are loyal and love to play."
Closing Sentence	Summarizes and gives a final thought	"Dogs make wonderful family members."

Chapter 3: Writing Emails and Letters

"Writing is an exploration. You start from nothing and learn as you go."

— E. L. Doctorow

Writing emails and letters is a crucial skill for clear and effective communication. In this chapter, we'll explore how to write emails and letters correctly. You will learn the basics of formatting and structuring these types of written communication. We will cover what to include in each part of an email and letter, how to address the recipient, and how to organize your thoughts clearly. By the end of this chapter, you will be able to write emails and letters that are well-structured and easy to understand.

Format and Structure of Emails and Letters

Writing emails and letters is an important skill for both personal and professional communication. In this chapter, we will explore how to format and structure emails and letters so that your messages are clear, polite, and effective. This will help you communicate better with others and get the results you want.

Introduction to Email and Letter Writing

When you write an email or a letter, it is vital to follow a clear format. This helps the reader easily understand your message. A well-organized email or letter shows that you are professional and that you care about how your message is received.

1. The Basic Parts of an Email

An email has several parts. Here is a simple guide to help you understand them:

1. **Subject Line**

   This is the title of your email. It should be short and give a clear idea of what your email is about. For example: "Meeting Request for Monday."

2. **Greeting**

   Start your email with a polite greeting. Use "Dear" followed by the person's name. If you don't know the person's name, you can use "Hello" or "Hi." For example:

   - "Dear Ms. Smith,"
   - "Hello John,"

3. **Body**

   The body is the main part of your email. Write your message clearly and concisely. Start with the most important information and then add details if necessary. Use short paragraphs to make it easy to read.

4. **Closing**

   End your email with a polite closing phrase. Typical closings are "Best regards," "Sincerely," or "Thank you." After the closing, write your name.

5. **Signature**

   This is where you include your contact information, like your phone number or job title, if needed.

Here is an example of an email:

Subject: Team Meeting on Monday

Dear Team,

I would like to schedule a meeting for Monday at 10 AM to discuss our project updates. Please let me know if this time works for you.

Best regards,
Jane Doe]

2. *The Basic Parts of a Letter*

Letters are more formal than emails but follow a similar structure. Here's how to format a letter:

1. **Sender's Address**

   Write your address at the top of the letter. Include your street address, city, state, and ZIP code.

2. **Date**

   Write the date below your address. Use the format "Month Day, Year." For example: "August 26, 2024."

3. **Recipient's Address**

   Write the recipient's address below the date. Include their name, street address, city, state, and ZIP code.

4. **Greeting**

   Begin with a polite greeting. Use "Dear" followed by the person's title and last name. For example:

   - "Dear Mr. Johnson,"

5. **Body**

   Write the main content of your letter here. Like an email, start with the most important information and then add details. Use paragraphs to separate different ideas.

6. **Closing**

   End with a polite closing phrase, such as "Sincerely," "Yours truly," or "Respectfully."

7. **Signature**

   Leave space for your signature and then type your name. If you are sending a printed letter, sign above your typed name.

Here is an example of a letter:

123 Main Street
Springfield, IL 62704

August 26, 2024

Ms. Laura Green
456 Elm Street
Springfield, IL 62705

Dear Ms. Green,

I am writing to inform you about our upcoming community event on September 15th. We would be honored if you could attend and speak about your work.

Sincerely,
John Smith]

Tips for Effective Email and Letter Writing

1. **Be Clear and Concise**

   Make sure your message is easy to understand. Avoid using long sentences or complicated words. Stick to one main idea per paragraph.

2. **Use Proper Grammar and Spelling**

   Check your email or letter for spelling and grammar mistakes. This makes your message look professional.

3. **Be Polite and Professional**

   Use polite language and formal titles when appropriate. This shows respect for the reader.

4. **Format Properly**

   Use paragraphs to separate different ideas. This makes your message easier to read.

5. **Proofread Before Sending**

   Always read your email or letter again before you send it. This helps you catch any mistakes and ensures your message is clear.

Visualizing How to Format Emails and Letters:

Think of formatting emails and letters as setting a dining table for a meal. The greeting is like the place setting, welcoming the recipient. The body of the message is the main course, providing the essential information. Closing remarks and your signature are like the dessert, leaving a pleasant final impression. Just as a well-set table enhances the dining experience, proper formatting ensures clarity and professionalism in your communication.

HOW TO FORMAT EMAILS AND LETTERS

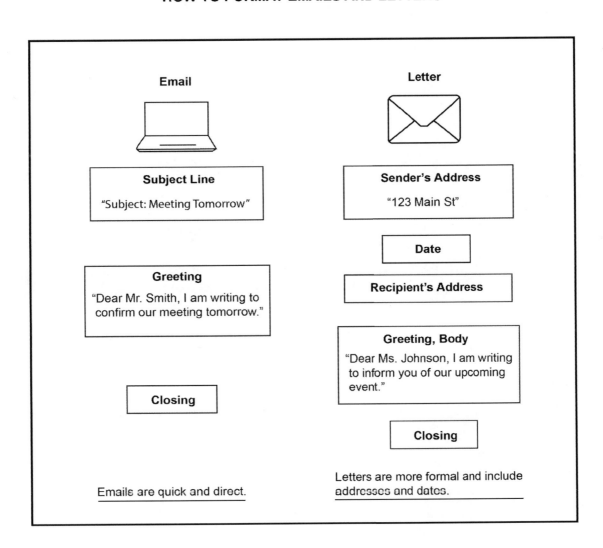

Writing Formal and Informal Communications

Writing effective emails and letters involves understanding when to use formal or informal communication. This chapter will help you learn how to write both types of messages clearly and appropriately. You will see examples and tips for each style to improve your writing skills.

Understanding Formal and Informal Communication

Formal Communication is used in professional or serious situations. It is polite and follows specific rules. **Informal Communication** is more relaxed and friendly, usually used with people you know well.

1. Writing Formal Emails and Letters

Formal emails and letters are used for professional or serious topics. They are common in business, job applications, and official communications. Here's how to write a formal email or letter:

a. Structure of a Formal Email

1. **Subject Line**

   Clearly state the purpose of your email. For example: "Application for Marketing Manager Position."

2. **Greeting**

   Use a formal greeting such as "Dear Mr. Johnson," or "Dear Dr. Lee,". If you don't know the recipient's name, use "Dear Sir/Madam,".

3. **Body**

   - **Introduction:** Start by stating the purpose of your email. For example, "I am writing to apply for the Marketing Manager position at your company."
   - **Main Content:** Provide detailed information related to your topic. For example, "I have five years of experience in marketing, and I believe my skills would be a good fit for your team."
   - **Conclusion:** End with a polite statement, such as "Thank you for considering my application."

4. **Closing**

   Use a formal closing phrase like "Sincerely," "Best regards," or "Yours faithfully," followed by your full name.

5. **Signature**

   Include your contact details, such as your phone number or job title.

Example of a Formal Email:

Subject: Request for Extension on Project Deadline

Dear Ms. Thompson,

I hope this message finds you well. I am writing to request an extension on the deadline for the XYZ project. Due to unforeseen circumstances, I will need an additional week to complete the work.

Thank you for your understanding. Please let me know if this is possible.

Best regards,
Emily Carter]

b. Structure of a Formal Letter

1. Sender's Address

Write your address at the top left corner.

2. Date

Write the date of writing the letter below your address.

3. Recipient's Address

Write the recipient's address below the date.

4. Greeting

Use "Dear Mr. Smith," or "Dear Ms. Brown,".

5. Body

- Introduction: State why you are writing.
- Main Content: Provide the necessary details.
- Conclusion: Politely end your letter.

6. Closing

Use a formal closing such as "Sincerely," or "Yours faithfully," followed by your name.

7. Signature

Sign your name above your typed name.

Example of a Formal Letter:

123 Main Street
City, State, ZIP Code

August 25, 2024

Mr. John Doe
456 Elm Street
City, State, ZIP Code

Dear Mr. Doe,

I am writing to express my interest in the open position of Financial Analyst at your company. With my background in finance and accounting, I am confident in my ability to contribute effectively to your team.

I have attached my resume for your review. Thank you for considering my application.

Sincerely,
Jane Smith]

2. Writing Informal Emails and Letters

Informal emails and letters are used for casual or friendly communication. They are common in personal correspondence and with people you know well.

a. Structure of an Informal Email

1. Subject Line

Keep it simple and relevant. For example: "Catch Up Soon?"

2. Greeting

Use a friendly greeting like "Hi Mike," or "Hello Sarah,".

3. Body

- **Introduction:** Start with a friendly or casual remark. For example, "I hope you're doing well!"

- **Main Content:** Share your news or ask questions. For example, "I just wanted to check in and see how your vacation was."

- **Conclusion:** Wrap up with a casual sign-off, like "Talk to you soon!"

4. Closing

Use an informal closing such as "Best," "Cheers," or "Take care," followed by your name.

Example of an Informal Email:

Subject: Weekend Plans

Hi Alex,

How's it going? I was thinking we could get together this weekend. Maybe grab lunch or go for a hike?

Let me know what you think!

Cheers,
Sam]

b. Structure of an Informal Letter

1. Sender's Address

Optional in informal letters, but you can include it at the top left.

2. Date

Write the date if you want to, but it's not always necessary.

3. Greeting

Use a casual greeting like "Hey Emma," or "Dear Tom,".

4. Body

- **Introduction:** Start with a friendly comment or question.
- **Main Content:** Share your news or thoughts.
- **Conclusion:** End with a casual remark.

5. Closing

Use an informal closing such as "Love," "Best wishes," or "See you soon," followed by your name.

Example of an Informal Letter:

123 Maple Street
City, State, ZIP Code

August 25, 2024

Dear Aunt Mary,

I hope you're having a great summer! I just wanted to write and tell you about my recent trip to the beach. It was so much fun, and I got a great tan!

Can't wait to see you soon. Let's plan a visit!

Love,
Lucy]

Tips for Effective Communication

1. **Know Your Audience:** Tailor your language and tone to the recipient. Use formal language for professional communications and informal language for friends and family.
2. **Be Clear and Concise:** Get to the point quickly. Avoid unnecessary details that might confuse the reader.
3. **Check Your Grammar and Spelling:** Always proofread your emails and letters before sending them to avoid mistakes.
4. **Be Polite and Respectful:** Use polite language and show respect in both formal and informal communications.

Chapter 4: Writing Essays

"Writing is a way to talk without being interrupted."

- Jules Renard

Writing essays is a necessary skill in both school and work. Essays help you share your thoughts and ideas clearly. In this chapter, we will learn the basics of writing essays, including how to plan and organize your ideas. We will also look at different types of essays and how to write each one effectively.

Introduction to Essay Writing

Essays are a common way to write about ideas and share information. They help us express our thoughts clearly and organize them in a way that is easy for others to understand. In this chapter, we will explore what essays are, how to plan them, and the basic structure of an essay. We will also discuss some simple tips for writing essays that are clear and effective.

What is an Essay?

An essay is a short piece of writing that explores a specific topic. It helps you explain your ideas and present your arguments. An essay usually includes an introduction, body paragraphs, and a conclusion. Let's look at each part in detail.

Parts of an Essay

1. **Introduction:**
   - **Hook:** This is the first sentence of your essay. It grabs the reader's attention. You can use a question, a quote, or an interesting fact to start.
   - **Background Information:** Provide some context for your topic. This helps the reader understand the subject better.
   - **Thesis Statement:** This is the most important part of your introduction. It tells the reader what your essay is about and what you will argue or explain.

2. **Body Paragraphs:**
   - **Topic Sentence:** Each paragraph should start with a topic sentence. This sentence tells the reader what the paragraph will discuss.
   - **Supporting Details:** After the topic sentence, include details, examples, and evidence that support your point.

- **Transition Sentences:** Use these to connect one paragraph to the next. Transitions help your essay flow smoothly.

3. **Conclusion:**

- **Restate Thesis:** Begin by restating your thesis in a new way. This reminds the reader of your main argument.

- **Summarize Main Points:** Briefly go over the key points you made in your essay.

- **Final Thought:** End with a final thought or a call to action. This can be a question, a prediction, or a recommendation.

Steps to Writing an Essay

1. **Choose a Topic:**

- Pick a topic that interests you and fits the assignment. If you have a choice, select something you are passionate about.

2. **Research:**

- Gather information about your topic. Use reliable sources like books, articles, and reputable websites. Take notes on important details and ideas.

3. **Create an Outline:**

- Plan the structure of your essay. An outline helps you organize your thoughts and ensures you cover all necessary points.

Sample Outline:

Part	Content
Introduction	Hook, Background Information, Thesis Statement
Body Paragraph 1	Topic Sentence, Supporting Details, Transition
Body Paragraph 2	Topic Sentence, Supporting Details, Transition
Body Paragraph 3	Topic Sentence, Supporting Details, Transition
Conclusion	Restate Thesis, Summarize Main Points, Final Thought

4. **Write the First Draft:**

Start writing your essay based on your outline. Don't worry about making it perfect. Focus on getting your ideas down on paper.

5. **Revise and Edit:**

After writing the first draft, read through your essay and make improvements. Check for spelling and grammar mistakes. Ensure your ideas are clear and logical.

6. **Get Feedback:**

Ask someone else to read your essay and provide feedback. They might notice errors you missed or offer useful suggestions.

7. **Finalize Your Essay:**

Make any final changes based on the feedback you received. Proofread your essay one last time to catch any remaining errors.

Types of Essays

1. **Descriptive Essay:**
   - **Purpose:** To describe a person, place, thing, or event in detail.
   - **Structure:** Focuses on vivid details and sensory descriptions.
   - **Example:** Describe your favorite place to visit.

2. **Narrative Essay:**
   - **Purpose:** To tell a story or recount an event.
   - **Structure:** Includes characters, a plot, and a setting.
   - **Example:** Write about a memorable experience you had on a vacation.

3. **Expository Essay:**
   - **Purpose:** To explain or inform about a topic.
   - **Structure:** Presents facts and information without personal opinions.
   - **Example:** Explain how a specific technology works.

4. **Persuasive Essay:**
   - **Purpose:** To convince the reader of a particular viewpoint.
   - **Structure:** Presents arguments and evidence to support a position.
   - **Example:** Argue for or against a school policy.

Tips for Effective Essay Writing

1. **Be Clear and Concise:**

Use simple language and clear sentences. Avoid unnecessary words or complex phrases.

2. **Stay on Topic:**

   Ensure each paragraph relates to your thesis and supports your main argument.

3. **Use Examples and Evidence:**

   Provide specific examples and evidence to back up your points. This makes your argument stronger.

4. **Proofread Your Work:**

   Check for spelling and grammar mistakes. Make sure your essay is well-organized and easy to read.

5. **Practice Regularly:**

   The more you write, the better you will become. Practice writing essays on different topics to improve your skills.

Structure of a Basic Essay

Writing a good essay involves understanding its structure. This chapter will help you learn how to build a basic essay step-by-step. We will cover each part of an essay: the introduction, body paragraphs, and conclusion. By the end, you will know how to organize your ideas clearly and effectively.

1. Introduction

The introduction is the first part of your essay. It sets up what you are going to talk about.

- **Hook:** Start with a sentence that grabs the reader's attention. This could be an interesting fact, a question, or a short story. For example:
  - "Did you know that people who read regularly have better problem-solving skills?"

- **Background Information:** Give some context about your topic. This helps the reader understand why it is important. For example:
  - "Reading is not just for pleasure; it also helps us think better and solve problems.

- **Thesis Statement:** This is the main point of your essay. It tells the reader what your essay will prove or explain. For example:
  - "This essay will show how reading regularly can improve your thinking and problem-solving abilities.

Example Introduction:

"Did you know that people who read regularly have better problem-solving skills? Reading is not just for pleasure; it also helps us think better and solve problems. This essay will show how reading regularly can improve your thinking and problem-solving abilities."

2. Body Paragraphs

The body of your essay is where you explain your main points. It usually has three parts: a topic sentence, supporting details, and a transition sentence.

- **Topic Sentence:** Start each paragraph with a sentence that tells the reader what the paragraph will be about. For example:
    - "First, reading can expand your vocabulary."
- **Supporting Details:** Include facts, examples, or explanations that support your topic sentence. For example:
    - "When you read, you come across new words. This helps you learn new vocabulary and use it in your own writing."
- **Transition Sentence:** End with a sentence that smoothly connects to the next paragraph. For example:
    - "In addition to improving vocabulary, reading also enhances critical thinking skills."

Example Body Paragraph:

"First, reading can expand your vocabulary. When you read, you come across new words. This helps you learn new vocabulary and use it in your own writing. In addition to improving vocabulary, reading also enhances critical thinking skills."

3. Conclusion

The conclusion wraps up your essay. It reminds the reader of your main points and leaves a final thought.

- Restate Thesis: Remind the reader of your main point by restating your thesis in a new way. For example:
    - "In summary, reading regularly helps improve your vocabulary and critical thinking skills."
- Summarize Main Points: Briefly go over the main points you made in your essay. For example:
    - "We have seen how reading can introduce new words and improve our ability to think critically."
- Final Thought: End with a final thought or call to action. This could be a question, a suggestion, or a reflection. For example
    - "So, next time you pick up a book, remember that you are not just enjoying a story but also making yourself smarter.

Example Conclusion:

"In summary, reading regularly helps improve your vocabulary and critical thinking skills. We have seen how reading can introduce new words and improve our ability to think critically. So, next time you pick up a book, remember that you are not just enjoying a story; you are also making yourself smarter."

Putting It All Together

Here is how the three parts come together in a complete essay:

1. **Introduction:** Hook, background information, thesis statement.
2. **Body Paragraphs:** Topic sentence, supporting details, transition sentence.
3. **Conclusion:** Restate thesis, summarize main points, and final thought.

Example Essay:

Introduction: "Did you know that people who read regularly have better problem-solving skills? Reading is not just for pleasure; it also helps us think better and solve problems. This essay will show how reading regularly can improve your thinking and problem-solving abilities."

Body Paragraph 1: "First, reading can expand your vocabulary. When you read, you come across new words. This helps you learn new vocabulary and use it in your own writing. In addition to improving vocabulary, reading also enhances critical thinking skills."

Body Paragraph 2: "Second, reading helps you think more critically. When you read, you analyze different characters, plots, and themes. This makes your brain work harder and improves your ability to think logically and solve problems."

Conclusion: "In summary, reading regularly helps improve your vocabulary and critical thinking skills. We have seen how reading can introduce new words and improve our ability to think critically. So, next time you pick up a book, remember that you are not just enjoying a story; you are also making yourself smarter."

Tips for Writing a Good Essay

1. **Plan Your Essay:** Before you start writing, make a plan. Outline your main points and organize them in a logical order.
2. **Use Clear and Simple Language:** Write in a way that is easy to understand. Avoid complicated words and long sentences.
3. **Revise and Edit:** After writing your essay, read it again. Check for mistakes and make sure your ideas are clear.
4. **Practice Regularly:** The more you practice writing essays, the better you will become.

Example Outline:

Part	Details
Introduction	Hook, Background, Thesis Statement
Body Paragraph 1	Topic Sentence, Supporting Details, Transition
Body Paragraph 2	Topic Sentence, Supporting Details, Transition
Conclusion	Restate Thesis, Summary, Final Thought

By following these steps and tips, you can write essays that are well-structured and easy to understand. Remember, practice makes perfect, so keep writing and improving your skills.

Visualizing Writing Essays:

Think of writing an essay as constructing a building. The introduction serves as the blueprint, outlining the main idea and purpose. The body paragraphs are the sturdy walls, each providing support and detail for your argument. Finally, the conclusion is the roof, summarizing the key points and providing closure. Together, they create a cohesive structure that effectively conveys your message and engages the reader.

HOW TO STRUCTURE AN ESSAY

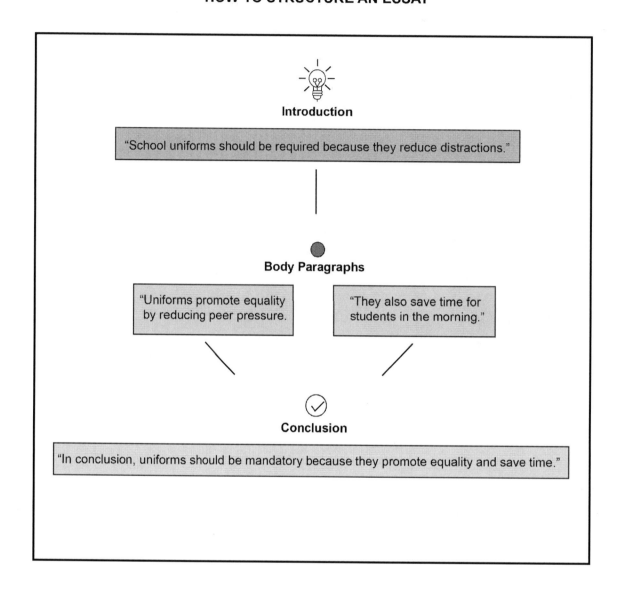

Introduction

"School uniforms should be required because they reduce distractions."

Body Paragraphs

"Uniforms promote equality by reducing peer pressure.

"They also save time for students in the morning."

Conclusion

"In conclusion, uniforms should be mandatory because they promote equality and save time."

Chapter 5: Writing for Social Media

"Social media is about the people, not about your business. Provide for the people and the people will provide for you."

— Matt Goulart

In today's digital world, social media is a crucial part of communication. Whether you are sharing personal thoughts, commenting on posts, or sending messages, how you write online can make a big difference. This chapter will guide you through the basics of writing effectively for social media. You will learn how to create engaging posts, write thoughtful comments, and send clear messages. By the end of this chapter, you will understand how to communicate well online, making sure your words are clear and appropriate for each social media platform.

Writing Posts, Comments, and Messages Online

Social media is a massive part of our lives in the digital age. It's where we share our thoughts, ideas, and connect with others. Understanding how to write effectively on social media is very important. This chapter will help you learn how to write clear and engaging posts, comments, and messages online. We will cover different types of social media writing and give you tips to make your communication effective and appropriate for different platforms.

1. Understanding Social Media Platforms

Before you start writing, it's important to understand the different social media platforms. Each platform has its own style and audience. Here's a quick guide to help you know where and how to write:

1.1. Facebook

- **Posts:** Facebook posts can be long or short. They often include personal updates, news, or questions.
- **Comments:** Comments are responses to other people's posts. They can be brief and should be relevant to the post.
- **Messages:** Private messages are for one-on-one conversations. They should be polite and clear.

1.2. Twitter

- **Tweets:** Tweets are short messages with a maximum of 280 characters. They should be concise and to the point.
- **Replies:** Replies are responses to other tweets. They should address the original tweet directly.

- **Direct** Messages: Private messages on Twitter are used for more personal conversations. Keep them brief and respectful.

1.3. Instagram

- **Captions:** Captions are short texts that go with your photos or videos. They can be descriptive, funny, or include hashtags.

- **Comments:** Comments on Instagram are short and should relate to the photo or video they are commenting on.

- **Direct Messages:** Instagram DMs are used for private conversations. Be friendly and clear in your messages.

1.4. LinkedIn

- **Posts:** LinkedIn posts are usually professional. They can include updates about your job, industry news, or professional achievements.

- **Comments:** Comments should be professional and add value to the discussion.

- **Messages:** LinkedIn messages are used for professional networking. Keep your messages formal and polite.

2. Writing Effective Posts

2.1. Start with a Strong Opening

Your opening sentence should grab attention. For example, if you're sharing a news article, start with an interesting fact or question to make people want to read more.

Example:

- Weak: "Here is a news article I found interesting."

- Strong: "Did you know that social media is changing the way we communicate? Check out this article!"

2.2. Be Clear and Concise

Use simple language and get straight to the point. Avoid long sentences and complicated words.

Example:

- **Complicated:** "In order to improve our communication efficiency, we must implement new strategies."

- **Simple:** "To communicate better, we need new strategies."

2.3. Add Value

Share useful information or exciting ideas. People follow you to learn or be entertained, so make sure your posts are valuable to them.

Example:

- **Less Useful:** "I had a great day."
- **More Useful:** "I had a great day at the workshop on social media marketing. Here are three tips I learned."

2.4. Use Visuals

Pictures and videos can make your posts more engaging. A good image or video can grab attention and help explain your message.

3. Writing Engaging Comments

3.1. Stay Relevant

Make sure your comment is related to the post. Avoid going off-topic.

Example:

- **Irrelevant Comment:** "I love pizza!" (on a post about travel destinations)
- **Relevant Comment:** "This travel destination looks amazing! I would love to visit someday."

3.2. Be Positive and Constructive

Keep your comments friendly and helpful. Even if you disagree, express your opinion politely.

Example:

- **Negative:** "This is a bad idea."
- **Constructive:** "I see your point, but I think there might be a better way to approach this."

3.3. Ask Questions

Engage with others by asking questions. This shows that you are interested in their opinions and keeps the conversation going.

Example:

- **Comment:** "Great post! What do you think are the most important skills for this job?"

4. Crafting Clear Messages

4.1. Be Direct and Clear

When writing messages, be clear about your purpose. State your main point early in the message.

Example:

- **Unclear:** "I wanted to talk to you about something important."
- **Clear:** "I would like to discuss the upcoming project deadline with you."

4.2. Use Proper Grammar and Spelling

Good grammar and spelling make your messages easier to understand. Always proofread your message before sending it.

Example:

- **Incorrect:** "I'm looking forward to the meetting."
- **Correct:** "I'm looking forward to the meeting."

4.3. Be Polite and Respectful

Use polite language and respect the other person's time. Start with a greeting and end with a closing.

Example:

- **Without Greeting:** "Can you send me the report?"
- **With Greeting:** "Hi [Name], Could you please send me the report? Thank you!"

5. Common Mistakes to Avoid

5.1. Overusing Jargon

Avoid using too many technical terms or slang that might confuse your audience.

Example:

- **With Jargon:** "We need to optimize the UX to increase CTR."
- **Without Jargon:** "We need to improve the user experience to get more clicks."

5.2. Ignoring Tone

Your tone can affect how your message is received. Be mindful of how your words might be interpreted.

Example:

- **Harsh Tone:** "You didn't follow the instructions."
- **Gentle Tone:** "It looks like there was a small mistake in following the instructions. Could you check it again?"

5.3. Neglecting Privacy

Be careful not to share private or sensitive information in public posts or comments.

Example:

- **Inappropriate:** "I had a tough day at work. My boss is really annoying."
- **Appropriate:** "I had a challenging day at work, but I'm working on finding solutions."

6. Practice Scenarios

6.1. Writing a Facebook Post

Scenario: You just completed a successful project at work.

Example Post: "I'm excited to share that our project was a big success! 🎉 Thanks to everyone who helped out. Here's a quick summary of what we achieved: [brief summary]."

6.2. Commenting on a LinkedIn Article

Scenario: You read an interesting article about career development.

Example Comment: "This article has great tips on career growth. I particularly liked the advice on networking. What do you think about the suggestion to attend industry events?"

6.3. Sending a Twitter Direct Message

Scenario: You want to ask a professional contact for advice.

Example Message: "Hi [Name], I hope you're well. I'm seeking advice on starting a career in [field]. Could we arrange a time to chat? Thank you!"

By understanding and practicing these tips, you can improve your social media writing and communicate more effectively online. Whether you are posting updates, commenting on others' posts, or sending messages, clear and engaging writing will help you connect better with your audience.

Writing for Different Social Media Platforms

Social media has become an essential part of communication. Different social media platforms have unique styles and rules for writing. To be effective on social media, you need to understand these differences. This chapter will guide you through writing for various social media platforms. We'll cover what works best on each platform and provide tips to help you communicate clearly and effectively.

1. Facebook

1.1. Writing Facebook Posts

Facebook allows for longer posts compared to other platforms. Here are some tips for writing posts:

- **Be Clear:** Start with a clear idea of what you want to say. Your first sentence should grab attention.
- **Be Engaging:** Ask questions or share interesting facts. This encourages people to comment or share.

- **Use Pictures or Videos:** Posts with images or videos are more engaging. They catch people's attention better than text alone.
- **Keep it Friendly:** Write in a friendly and conversational tone. This makes your post more relatable.

Example:

"Did you know that walking for just 30 minutes a day can improve your mood and health? ❊ What's your favorite way to stay active? Share your tips below!"

1.2. Writing Facebook Comments

Comments are responses to other posts. Here's how to write good comments:

- **Stay Relevant:** Make sure your comment relates to the original post.
- **Be Respectful:** Always be polite, even if you disagree.
- **Add Value:** Try to add something useful to the conversation.

Example:

"If you're looking for a fun workout, I highly recommend yoga! It's great for relaxation and fitness."

1.3. Writing Facebook Messages

Private messages are used for one-on-one conversations. Here's how to write effective messages:

- **Be Polite:** Always use polite language and greet the person at the start.
- **Be Clear:** State your purpose clearly. Avoid long-winded explanations.
- **Respond Promptly:** Try to reply quickly to keep the conversation going.

Example:

"Hi Sarah, I hope you're doing well! I wanted to ask if you're available for a meeting next week. Let me know what works for you. Thanks!"

2. Twitter

2.1. Writing Tweets

Twitter is known for its short messages. Here's how to write effective tweets:

- **Keep it Short:** You only have 280 characters, so be concise.
- **Use Hashtags:** Hashtags help others find your tweets. Use relevant ones, but don't overdo it.
- **Add a Call to Action:** Encourage your followers to do something, like clicking a link or retweeting.

Example:

"Excited for the new book release tomorrow! 📇🎉 Check it out here: [link] #BookRelease #Reading"

2.2. Writing Twitter Replies

Replies are responses to other tweets. Here's how to write good replies:

- **Be Direct:** Address the original tweet directly.
- **Keep it Short:** Since Twitter has a character limit, be brief.
- **Be Positive:** Even if you disagree, keep your tone positive and constructive.

Example:

"Great point! I agree that more research is needed on this topic. Thanks for sharing!"

2.3. Writing Twitter Direct Messages

Direct messages are private. Here's how to write them:

- **Be Formal:** Use a more formal tone compared to tweets.
- **Be Clear and Concise:** Clearly state your reason for messaging.
- **Respect Privacy:** Don't ask for personal information or make unsolicited requests.

Example:

"Hi John, I hope you're doing well. I wanted to discuss the upcoming project with you. Are you available for a quick call this week? Best, Emily."

3. Instagram

3.1. Writing Instagram Captions

Instagram captions accompany photos or videos. Here's how to write engaging captions:

- **Be Descriptive:** Describe what's in the photo or video.
- **Use Emojis:** Emojis can make your caption more lively and expressive.
- **Include Hashtags:** Use relevant hashtags to increase visibility.

Example:

"Enjoying a beautiful day at the beach! 🏖️☀️ #BeachDay #SummerVibes"

3.2. Writing Instagram Comments

Comments on Instagram should be brief and related to the post. Here's how to write good comments:

- **Be Positive:** Compliment or show appreciation for the post.
- **Keep it Short:** Instagram comments are often brief.

- **Engage:** Ask questions or add to the discussion.

Example:

"Wow, this photo is amazing! Where was it taken?"

3.3. Writing Instagram Direct Messages

Direct messages on Instagram are for private conversations. Here's how to write them:

- **Be Friendly:** Use a warm and friendly tone.
- **Be Clear:** State your purpose clearly.
- **Respect Privacy:** Avoid sending too many messages or being intrusive.

Example:

"Hey Alex, I loved your recent post! Can we discuss a potential collaboration? Let me know if you're interested. Thanks!"

4. LinkedIn

4.1. Writing LinkedIn Posts

LinkedIn is a professional network. Here's how to write effective LinkedIn posts:

- **Be Professional:** Use a formal tone and language.
- **Share Valuable Content:** Post industry news, career tips, or professional achievements.
- **Include a Call to Action:** Encourage others to comment, share, or follow a link.

Example:

"I'm excited to announce that I've joined ABC Company as a Marketing Manager. Looking forward to new challenges and opportunities ahead. #CareerMove #Marketing"

4.2. Writing LinkedIn Comments

Comments on LinkedIn should be professional and add to the discussion. Here's how to write good comments:

- **Be Constructive:** Add meaningful insights or ask thoughtful questions.
- **Be Respectful:** Always maintain a professional tone.

Example:

"Great article on digital marketing trends! I particularly found the section on social media strategies very useful. Thanks for sharing!"

4.3. Writing LinkedIn Messages

LinkedIn messages are for professional communication. Here's how to write effective messages:

- **Be Formal:** Use a polite and formal tone.

- **Be Clear:** Clearly explain the reason for your message.

- **Be Professional:** Keep your message focused on professional matters.

Example:

"Hello Ms. Johnson, I hope you're doing well. I'm reaching out to explore potential job opportunities at your company. I would appreciate any advice or referrals you might have. Thank you for your time. Best regards, Mark."

By understanding the different social media platforms and how to write effectively for each, you can communicate more clearly and professionally online. Each platform has its own style, and adapting your writing to fit these styles will help you connect better with your audience and achieve your communication goals.

Visualizing Writing for Social Media:

Think of writing for social media as crafting a catchy advertisement. The attention-grabbing headline is like the bold visuals that draw people in, while concise and engaging content is the message that keeps them interested.

HOW TO WRITE POSTS, COMMENTS, AND MESSAGES ON SOCIAL MEDIA

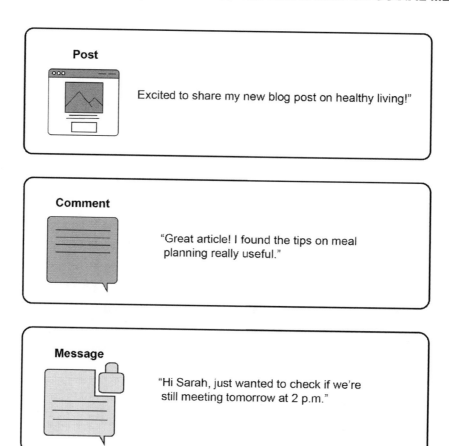

Post

Excited to share my new blog post on healthy living!"

Comment

"Great article! I found the tips on meal planning really useful."

Message

"Hi Sarah, just wanted to check if we're still meeting tomorrow at 2 p.m."

Chapter 6: Revising and Editing

"Writing is rewriting."

– Alan Ginsberg

Revising and editing are important steps in writing. They help make your writing clear and correct. This chapter will show you how to revise and edit your work. We will discuss simple techniques to help you improve your writing.

Techniques for Revising and Improving Writing

Writing is not just about putting words on paper. It's about making those words clear, correct, and engaging. Revising and editing are crucial steps in this process. They help ensure that your writing effectively communicates your ideas. In this chapter, we'll explore techniques for revising and improving your writing. We will cover how to check for mistakes, make your writing clearer, and enhance its overall quality.

Understanding Revising and Editing

Revising and editing are two important steps in the writing process. They are different but closely related:

- **Revising** is looking at your work to make big changes. This means changing ideas, adding or removing information, and making sure your writing is organized.
- **Editing** is checking your work for small mistakes. This includes fixing spelling errors, grammar issues, and punctuation problems.

Let's dive into these steps in more detail.

1. The Revision Process

Revising your writing means looking at it with fresh eyes and making improvements. Here are some simple steps to follow:

1.1. Take a Break

Before you start revising, take a short break from your writing. This helps you return to your work with a fresh perspective. You may see mistakes or areas for improvement that you missed before.

1.2. Read Your Work Aloud

Reading your writing out loud helps you catch mistakes and awkward sentences. When you hear your words, you might notice problems with the flow or clarity that are not obvious when reading silently.

1.3. Focus on the Big Picture

When revising, think about the overall structure of your writing:

- **Introduction:** Does it clearly state the main idea?
- **Body:** Are the ideas organized logically? Do the paragraphs support the main idea?
- **Conclusion:** Does it effectively summarize the main points?

Use a table to help organize your ideas:

Section	Checkpoints
Introduction	Clearly states the main idea
Body	Ideas are organized logically
Conclusion	Summarizes main points effectively

1.4. Improve Content and Structure

Ask yourself:

- Are there parts that need more detail or explanation?
- Are there sections that are unclear or confusing?
- Is there anything that does not fit with the main idea?

Add more details where needed and remove any unnecessary information.

1.5. Seek Feedback

Ask someone else to read your work. They can provide valuable insights and help you see problems you might have missed. Consider their feedback and make appropriate changes.

2. Editing Your Writing

Editing is about fixing the smaller details of your writing. Here's how to do it effectively:

2.1. Check for Spelling and Grammar Mistakes

Use spelling and grammar check tools in your word processor, but also review your work manually. These tools may miss errors.

2.2. Correct Punctuation

Ensure that your punctuation is correct:

- **Periods** (.) end sentences.
- **Commas** (,) separate items in a list or clauses.

- **Question Marks** (?) end questions.
- **Exclamation Marks** (!) show strong feelings.

2.3. Improve Sentence Structure

Look at your sentences:

- Are they too long or confusing?
- Can they be shortened or made clearer?
- Do they use simple and direct language?

Rewrite sentences that are too complex or unclear.

2.4. Check for Consistency

Ensure that your writing is consistent:

- **Tense:** Are you using past, present, or future tense consistently?
- **Style:** Is your tone and style uniform throughout the text?
- **Formatting:** Are headings, bullet points, and spacing used correctly?

2.5. Verify Facts and Information

Check any facts, dates, and names in your writing to ensure they are accurate. Incorrect information can undermine the credibility of your work.

3. Techniques for Effective Revising and Editing

Here are some simple techniques to make revising and editing easier:

3.1. Use a Checklist

Create a checklist of common mistakes to watch for:

- Spelling errors
- Grammar issues
- Punctuation problems
- Clarity and coherence

3.2. Work in Stages

Tackle different aspects of your writing in separate stages:

- **First Stage:** Focus on big-picture changes (organization, content).
- **Second Stage:** Focus on sentence structure and flow.
- **Third Stage:** Focus on spelling, grammar, and punctuation.

3.3. Take Your Time

Don't rush the revision and editing process. Give yourself plenty of time to review and improve your work. Rushing can lead to missed mistakes and less effective writing.

3.4. Use Editing Tools

There are many tools available to help with editing:

- **Grammarly:** Checks grammar, spelling, and style.
- **Hemingway Editor:** Highlights complex sentences and readability issues.
- **ProWritingAid:** Offers in-depth analysis of style and structure.

Proofreading and Editing

When you write, you should check your work carefully. This process is called proofreading and editing. It helps make your writing clear and free of mistakes. In this chapter, we will learn how to proofread and edit effectively. We will cover different techniques to find and fix errors, making your writing the best it can be.

1. What Is Proofreading and Editing?

Proofreading is the final step in the writing process. It means checking your work for errors and fixing them. This includes:

- **Spelling mistakes**
- **Grammar errors**
- **Punctuation problems**

Editing is about improving your writing by changing the content and structure. This includes:

- **Improving clarity**
- **Fixing awkward sentences**
- **Making sure the ideas are organized well**

2. Proofreading Techniques

2.1. Read Slowly

When proofreading, read your work slowly. This helps you catch mistakes you might miss when reading quickly.

2.2. Use a Checklist

A proofreading checklist can help you stay organized. Here's a simple checklist to follow:

Proofreading Checkpoints	What to Look For
Spelling	Misspelled words
Grammar	Subject-verb agreement, tense errors
Punctuation	Commas, periods, question marks
Formatting	Consistent font and spacing

2.3. Read Backwards

Read your text backwards, from the last word to the first. This technique helps you focus on each word and find spelling and grammar mistakes.

2.4. Use Tools

There are many tools online that can help with proofreading. Tools like spell checkers and grammar checkers can find errors, but they are not perfect. Always review their suggestions carefully.

3. Editing Techniques

3.1. Focus on Clarity

When editing, make sure your writing is clear. Ask yourself:

- **Is the main idea easy to understand?**
- **Are the sentences clear and concise?**

If a sentence is confusing, rewrite it to make it simpler.

3.2. Check for Consistency

Make sure your writing is consistent. This means:

- **Using the same tense throughout**
- **Keeping the same tone and style**
- **Consistent use of terms and names**

3.3. Improve Sentence Structure

Look at your sentences and check if they are varied and well-structured. Use a mix of short and long sentences to make your writing more interesting.

3.4. Ensure Proper Paragraph Structure

Check that each paragraph has a clear main idea and supporting details. Use this simple structure:

Paragraph Structure	What to Include
Topic Sentence	The main idea of the paragraph
Supporting Details	Information that explains or supports the main idea
Concluding Sentence	A sentence that wraps up the paragraph

3.5. Get Feedback

Ask someone else to read your writing. They might see mistakes you missed and offer suggestions for improvement.

4. Common Mistakes to Watch For

4.1. Homophones

Homophones are words that sound the same but are spelled differently and have different meanings. Examples include:

- **Their** vs. **There**
- **Your** vs. **You're**

Make sure you use the correct word in your writing.

4.2. Run-On Sentences

A run-on sentence happens when two or more sentences are joined together incorrectly. Use punctuation like periods or commas with conjunctions to fix run-on sentences.

4.3. Sentence Fragments

A sentence fragment is an incomplete sentence that lacks a main clause. Make sure each sentence has a subject and a predicate.

5. Tips for Effective Proofreading and Editing

5.1. Take Your Time

Don't rush through proofreading and editing. Take your time to carefully review each part of your writing.

5.2. Read Multiple Times

Read your work several times. Each time, focus on different aspects, like spelling, grammar, and clarity.

5.3. Use a Ruler or Pointer

Use a ruler or your finger to follow along as you read. This will help you stay focused and prevent you from skipping lines.

5.4. Keep a List of Common Mistakes

Make a list of common mistakes you often make. Look for these mistakes during proofreading to catch them more easily.

5.5. Practice Regularly

The more you practice proofreading and editing, the better you will become. Make it a habit to check your writing carefully before finalizing it.

Visualizing Revising and Editing:

Think of revising and editing as polishing a gemstone. Revising is like cutting and shaping the stone, refining the structure and content to enhance clarity and flow. Editing is the final polish, smoothing out any rough edges, correcting errors, and ensuring the piece shines. Together, these processes transform a rough draft into a sparkling final product, ready for presentation and appreciation.

HOW TO REVISE AND IMPROVE YOUR WRITING

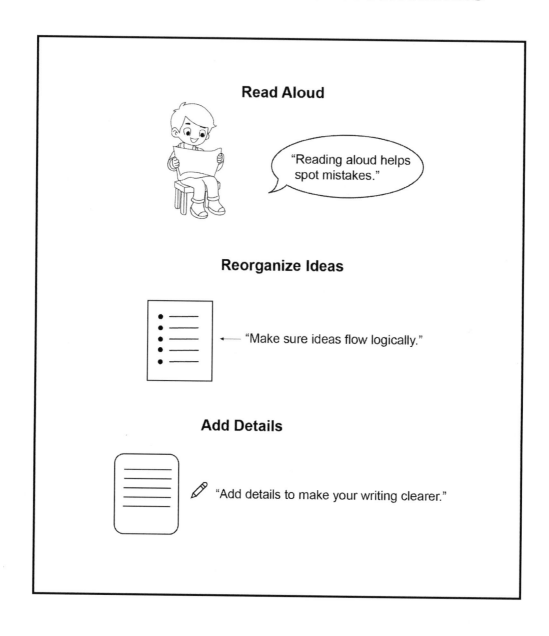

BOOK 7

Achieving Fluency

Reach English Fluency with Immersive Learning Techniques and Confidence-Building Practices

Explore to Win

Chapter 1: What Is Fluency?

"Language is the roadmap of a culture. It tells you where its people come from and where they are going."

– Rita Mae Brown

When we talk about fluency in a language, we are talking about more than just speaking or writing correctly. Fluency means being comfortable and confident in using a language in everyday situations. It is like being able to ride a bike smoothly after practicing a lot. In this chapter, we will explore what fluency really means, how it is different from just knowing a lot of words, and why it is crucial for effective communication. We will also look at how you can measure your own fluency and ways to become more fluent.

Defining Fluency in Language Learning

Fluency in a language is like being able to ride a bike smoothly. Just as riding a bike takes practice until it feels natural, using a language fluently means you can speak, read, and write easily without struggling. In this chapter, we will explore what fluency really means in language learning, how it differs from simply knowing a lot of words, and why it is important. We will also discuss how you can measure your fluency and tips to improve it.

Understanding Fluency

1. What is Fluency?

Fluency is the ability to use a language easily and confidently. When you are fluent, you can:

- **Speak Naturally:** You talk smoothly without pausing to find the right words.
- **Understand Quickly:** You can understand spoken and written language without needing to translate.
- **Use the Language in Real Situations:** You can handle everyday conversations and situations comfortably.

Think of fluency as a smooth conversation with a friend where you don't have to think too hard about what you're saying.

2. Fluency vs. Proficiency

It's important to know that fluency and proficiency are different:

- **Fluency:** This is about how easily and naturally you can use the language. It's more about the flow of your language use.
- **Proficiency:** This means how much you know about the language, including grammar, vocabulary, and rules. You might know a lot but still not be able to speak fluently if you find it hard to use what you know in real conversations.

3. Why Fluency Matters

Being fluent in a language helps in many ways:

- **Better Communication:** You can share your thoughts and ideas clearly and understand others better.
- **Increased Confidence:** You feel more comfortable and less anxious when using the language.
- **Social Interaction:** You can join in conversations, make friends, and enjoy social activities.

4. Measuring Fluency

Measuring fluency can be done in several ways:

- **Speaking Fluency:** How easily you can talk without many pauses or mistakes. It's about the flow of your speech.
- **Listening Fluency:** How well you understand spoken language in real-time. Can you follow conversations without having to stop and think too much?
- **Reading Fluency:** How quickly and easily you can read and understand written text.
- **Writing Fluency:** How smoothly you can write sentences and express your thoughts in writing.

Table 1: Comparing Fluency and Proficiency

Aspect	Fluency	Proficiency
Definition	Ease of use in real situations	Knowledge of grammar, vocabulary, and rules
Focus	Natural and smooth language use	Understanding and applying language rules
Measurement	Speaking without pauses, understanding spoken language quickly	Knowing grammar rules, vocabulary size
Importance	Communication, confidence, social interaction	Academic and professional use of language

5. How to Improve Fluency

Improving fluency involves practice and exposure:

- **Practice Regularly:** Speak, read, and write in the language as much as you can. The more you use it, the easier it becomes.

- **Engage with Native Speakers:** Talk with people who speak the language fluently. This helps you get used to how the language sounds and feels.

- **Read and Listen:** Read books, watch movies, and listen to music or podcasts in the language. This helps you get familiar with different ways the language is used.

- **Don't Be Afraid to Make Mistakes:** Making mistakes is a normal part of learning. The more you practice, the better you get.

Setting Realistic Goals for Achieving Fluency

Achieving fluency in a language is like climbing a mountain. It's a big goal, but with clear steps, you can reach the top. In this chapter, we will talk about how to set realistic goals for learning English or any language. Setting the right goals helps you stay motivated and makes learning easier. We will cover different types of goals, how to set them, and how to track your progress. Let's start this journey together!

What Are Realistic Goals?

Understanding Realistic Goals

A realistic goal is something you can actually achieve. It should be challenging but not impossible. For example, learning to speak basic phrases in a few weeks is a realistic goal, but speaking like a native speaker in that time might be too ambitious.

Why Set Realistic Goals?

Setting goals that are too big can be overwhelming. It might make you feel frustrated if you can't meet them. Realistic goals help you stay on track and feel successful. They also help you see your progress, which keeps you motivated.

Types of Goals

1. **Short-Term Goals:**

   - **What Are They?** Goals you want to achieve in a short time, like a few days or weeks.

   - **Examples:** Learn 10 new words this week, practice speaking for 15 minutes daily, or complete one chapter of a language course.

2. **Medium-Term Goals:**

   - **What Are They?** Goals you aim to achieve in a few months.

- **Examples:** Have a simple conversation with a friend in English, write a short essay, or pass a beginner's language test.

3. **Long-Term Goals:**
   - **What Are They?** Goals you want to achieve in a year or more.
   - **Examples:** Speak fluently, read a book in English without a dictionary, or get a job that requires English skills.

How to Set Realistic Goals

1. Start Small:
- Begin with small goals that are easy to achieve. This builds confidence and helps you stay motivated. For example, start by learning basic greetings and gradually move to more complex topics.

2. Be Specific:
- Make your goals clear and specific. Instead of saying "I want to get better at English," say "I will learn 5 new words every day."

3. Make Them Measurable:
- Decide how you will measure your progress. This could be through tests, quizzes, or just checking off completed tasks.

4. Set a Deadline:
- Give yourself a time frame for achieving each goal. This helps you stay focused and organized. For example, "I will complete my current language course by the end of this month."

5. Be Flexible:
- Sometimes things don't go as planned. Be ready to adjust your goals if needed. If you find a certain topic difficult, it's okay to spend more time on it.

6. Celebrate Success:
- Reward yourself when you achieve a goal. This could be as simple as taking a break or treating yourself to something special.

Visualizing Language Fluency:

Think of language fluency as riding a bike. At first, you may wobble and struggle to find your balance, but with practice, you gain confidence and control. Fluency allows you to navigate conversations smoothly, just as riding a bike lets you glide effortlessly along a path.

The more you practice speaking, listening, reading, and writing, the more natural and fluid your language skills become, enabling you to communicate freely and expressively.

WHAT DOES FLUENCY MEAN?

Chapter 2: Immersive Learning Techniques

"The best way to predict the future is to create it."

— Peter Drucker

In this chapter, we will explore how to use immersive learning techniques to become fluent in a new language. Immersive learning means surrounding yourself with the language you are learning as much as possible. We will look at how you can use media, culture, and conversations to help you become more fluent. You will learn how to make the most of these tools to practice and improve your language skills every day.

Using Media, Culture, and Conversation for Immersion

Learning a new language can be a fun adventure, and using immersive learning techniques can make it even more exciting! Immersion means surrounding yourself with the language in different ways. In this chapter, we will explore three main ways to use immersion: media, culture, and conversation. Each of these can help you learn and practice your new language in enjoyable and effective ways.

1. Using Media for Language Learning

Media includes things like TV shows, movies, music, and books. These can be great tools for learning a new language because they help you hear and see the language used naturally.

1.1 TV Shows and Movies

Watching TV shows and movies is one of the most fun ways to practice a new language. Here's how to make the most of it:

- **Start Simple:** Begin with children's shows or movies. They usually have simpler language and clear pronunciation.

- **Use Subtitles:** Start with subtitles in your own language to understand the story. Then, switch to subtitles in the language you are learning. As you get better, try watching without any subtitles.

- **Repeat Scenes:** Don't be afraid to watch the same scenes more than once. This helps you catch new words and phrases each time.

Example:

If you are learning Spanish, you might start with a cartoon like "Dora the Explorer" which has simple language and subtitles. As you progress, you can move on to movies like "Coco" which have more complex language.

1.2 Music

Listening to music in the language you are learning can help you practice listening skills and pronunciation.

- **Listen to Songs:** Find songs in the target language and listen to them regularly.
- **Read Lyrics:** Look up the lyrics and try to understand their meaning. Singing along can help you with pronunciation.
- **Create Playlists:** Make playlists of your favorite songs in the target language. Listen to them while doing other tasks.

Example:

If you are learning French, you might listen to songs by artists like Stromae. Look up the lyrics and sing along to improve your French skills.

1.3 Books

Reading books in the target language is another way to improve your skills.

- **Start Small:** Begin with children's books or simple stories. They are easier to understand and often include pictures.
- **Use a Dictionary:** Keep a dictionary handy to look up new words.
- **Read Aloud:** Try reading aloud to practice pronunciation and fluency.

Example:

If you are learning German, start with books like "Der Kleine Prinz" (The Little Prince). As you get more comfortable, you can move on to more complex books.

2. Exploring Culture to Enhance Learning

Understanding the culture of the language you are learning helps you use the language in real-life situations.

2.1 Festivals and Traditions

Learning about festivals and traditions can give you insights into how the language is used in different contexts.

- **Research:** Look up festivals and traditions in the countries where the language is spoken.
- **Participate:** If possible, attend local events or celebrations related to the culture.
- **Learn Vocabulary:** Learn new words and phrases related to the festivals and traditions.

Example:

If you are learning Japanese, you might research the festival "Hanami" which celebrates cherry blossoms. Learn the words related to this festival to enrich your vocabulary.

2.2 Cuisine

Trying foods from the culture can be a fun way to learn about the language.

- **Cook Recipes:** Find recipes in the target language and try cooking them. This helps you learn food-related vocabulary.
- **Visit Restaurants:** If there are restaurants that serve food from the culture, visit them and try speaking in the target language.
- **Learn Cooking Terms:** Understand cooking terms and ingredients in the target language.

Example:

If you are learning Italian, you might cook dishes like pasta or pizza using Italian recipes. Visit Italian restaurants and practice ordering in Italian.

2.3 History and Art

Exploring the history and art of the culture can give you more context for the language.

- **Visit Museums:** Look for museums or historical sites related to the culture. Many have information in the target language.
- **Read About History:** Find books or articles about the history of the countries where the language is spoken.
- **Explore Art:** Study the art from the culture and learn the vocabulary related to art and history.

Example:

If you are learning Russian, you might visit a museum with Russian art or read about Russian history to gain a deeper understanding of the language.

3. Engaging in Conversations

Conversation practice is essential for becoming fluent in a new language. Engaging in conversations helps you use the language in real-life situations.

3.1 Language Exchange

Language exchange involves practicing with someone who speaks the language you are learning.

- **Find a Partner:** Look for a language exchange partner who wants to learn your language.
- **Set Goals:** Decide on goals for each session, like practicing specific topics or skills.
- **Be Patient:** Be patient and supportive as you both practice and learn.

Example:

If you are learning Portuguese, find a Portuguese speaker who wants to learn English. Set up regular practice sessions to help each other improve.

3.2 Conversation Clubs

Join conversation clubs or groups where you can practice speaking with others.

- **Search for Groups:** Look for language clubs or groups in your area or online.
- **Participate Regularly:** Attend meetings regularly to practice speaking and listening.
- **Prepare Topics:** Prepare topics or questions in advance to help guide the conversation.

Example:

If you are learning Chinese, join a Chinese conversation club where you can practice speaking with others who are also learning or are native speakers.

3.3 Online Platforms

Use online platforms to practice speaking with native speakers or other learners.

- **Language Apps:** Use language learning apps that offer speaking practice and conversation.
- **Video Calls:** Set up video calls with language partners to practice speaking and listening.
- **Forums:** Participate in online forums or discussion groups related to the language.

Example:

If you are learning Arabic, use language learning apps like HelloTalk or Tandem to find native speakers and practice speaking with them.

By using media, exploring culture, and engaging in conversations, you can immerse yourself in the language and make learning more enjoyable and effective. Remember, the more you surround yourself with the language, the faster and easier it will be to achieve fluency. Keep practicing and stay motivated—your language skills will improve with time and effort!

Creating a Language-Rich Environment at Home

Learning a new language can be an exciting adventure, and you can make it even better by creating a language-rich environment right in your own home. This means surrounding yourself with the language you are learning so you can practice and get better every day. In this chapter, we will look at simple and fun ways to make your home a place where the new language is all around you.

1. Labeling Your Home

One easy way to start using the language daily is to label items around your home.

1.1 How to Label

- **Choose Items:** Pick common items like "door," "table," "chair," or "window."
- **Write Labels:** Write the names of these items in the new language on sticky notes.
- **Place Labels:** Stick the labels on the actual items in your home.

Example:

If you are learning Spanish, put labels on items like "puerta" (door), "silla" (chair), and "ventana" (window). Every time you see these labels, you'll practice the words.

2. Using Language Learning Apps

Apps can be great tools to practice the new language and make learning fun.

2.1 Popular Apps

- **Duolingo:** Offers lessons and exercises in many languages.
- **Babbel:** Provides interactive courses for various languages.
- **Rosetta Stone:** Focuses on immersion and speaking practice.

2.2 How to Use Apps Effectively

- **Set Goals:** Decide how much time you will spend on the app each day.
- **Practice Regularly:** Try to practice every day, even if it is just for a few minutes.
- **Use All Features:** Take advantage of speaking, listening, and writing exercises.

Example:

If you are learning French, set a goal to complete one lesson daily on Duolingo. Practice speaking by using the app's speaking exercises.

3. Listening to Language Radio and Podcasts

Listening to the language on the radio or through podcasts helps you get used to hearing it.

3.1 Finding Radio Stations and Podcasts

- **Search Online:** Look for radio stations or podcasts in the language you are learning.
- **Use Apps:** Apps like Spotify or Apple Podcasts have many options.

3.2 How to Listen

- **Choose Topics You Like:** Find shows or podcasts about interesting topics.
- **Listen Regularly:** Try to listen to a bit of the language every day.

Example:

If you are learning German, find a German radio station or a podcast about something you enjoy, like cooking or sports. Listen to it while doing other activities.

4. Watching TV Shows and Movies

Watching TV shows and movies in the new language can be fun and educational.

4.1 How to Choose Shows and Movies

- **Start Simple:** Begin with children's shows or animated movies that use simple language.
- **Use Subtitles:** Start with subtitles in your own language, then switch to subtitles in the new language.

4.2 Watching Tips

- **Repeat Scenes:** Watch the same scenes several times to catch more details.
- **Discuss What You Watch:** Try to talk about the show or movie with others who know the language.

Example:

If you are learning Japanese, start with an anime like "My Neighbor Totoro" and use Japanese subtitles. Watch it multiple times to learn new words and phrases.

5. Reading Books and Magazines

Reading helps you learn new vocabulary and see how sentences are formed.

5.1 Choosing Reading Material

- **Start with Simple Books:** Choose children's or beginner-level books in the new language.
- **Read Magazines:** Find magazines on topics you like.

5.2 Reading Tips

- **Read Aloud:** Practice speaking by reading aloud.
- **Use a Dictionary:** Look up words you don't know to build your vocabulary.

Example:

If you are learning Italian, start with a children's book like "Pinocchio" and use an Italian-English dictionary to help with new words.

6. Labeling Your Environment

Make your surroundings part of your learning process by labeling everyday items.

6.1 How to Label

- **Create Labels:** Write the names of objects in the target language on sticky notes.
- **Place Them Around:** Stick these labels where you can see them often, like on your desk or kitchen items.

6.2 Benefits of Labeling

- **Reinforces Learning:** Seeing the words regularly helps you remember them better.
- **Increases Exposure:** Surrounds you with the language in your daily life.

Example:

For someone learning Portuguese, label items like "geladeira" (refrigerator) and "televisão" (television) around your home.

7. Creating a Language Journal

A language journal is a great way to keep track of your progress and practice writing.

7.1 How to Start a Journal

- **Write Regularly:** Write a few sentences each day about your day or thoughts.
- **Include New Words:** Use the new vocabulary you've learned.

7.2 Benefits of Keeping a Journal

- **Tracks Progress:** Helps you see how much you've learned over time.
- **Improves Writing:** Gives you practice writing in the new language.

Example:

If you are learning Russian, write about your daily activities in a journal. Use new words and review your entries regularly.

Visualizing Immersive Learning Techniques:

Think of immersive learning techniques as diving into a deep pool. Just as you experience the water surrounding you, these techniques surround you with the language and culture, creating a rich learning environment. Activities like conversing with native speakers, watching films, or participating in cultural events engage your senses and encourage active participation. This deep dive helps you absorb the language naturally, leading to greater retention and understanding.

Media Immersion

"Watch movies or listen to music in the target language."

Cultural Immersion

"Engage with cultural experiences."

Conversational Immersion

"Practice speaking with native speakers or language partners."

Chapter 3: Practice Makes Perfect

"Practice does not make perfect. Only perfect practice makes perfect."

— Vince Lombardi

Learning a new language takes time and effort, but regular practice can make a big difference. In this chapter, we will explore why practicing the language every day is so important. We will look at how small, consistent efforts can lead to big improvements in your language skills. You will learn different ways to practice, find out what works best, and get tips on how to stay motivated.

The Importance of Regular Practice in Language Learning

Learning a new language can be exciting but also challenging. To become good at it, you need to practice regularly. This chapter will explain why practice is so important, how it helps you improve, and how you can fit practice into your daily life. We will look at different ways to practice, stay motivated and how regular practice leads to success.

1. Why Regular Practice Matters

1.1 Building Skills

Imagine learning to ride a bike. The more you practice, the better you get at balancing and steering. The same idea applies to learning a language. When you practice regularly, you help your brain get used to new words and rules. This helps you use the language more easily and naturally.

1.2 Keeping Knowledge Fresh

Learning new words and grammar rules is just the start. To keep them fresh in your mind, you need to use them often. If you stop practicing, you might forget what you learned. Regular practice helps you remember and use the language correctly.

2. Finding the Right Practice Methods

2.1 Speaking Practice

- **Conversation Partners:** Find a friend or someone who speaks the language to practice with. This helps you get used to speaking and listening.

- **Example:** If you are learning Spanish, find a Spanish-speaking friend or join a language exchange group to practice conversations.

- **Language Exchange:** Join online groups where people help each other learn languages. You can practice speaking and listening with native speakers.

- **Example:** Use apps like Tandem or HelloTalk to find language exchange partners.

- **Self-Talk:** Practice speaking by talking to yourself. Describe what you are doing or discuss your plans for the day.

- **Example:** While cooking, talk to yourself in the new language about the recipe and ingredients.

2.2 Listening Practice

- **Watch Movies and Shows:** Choose movies or TV shows in the language you are learning. This helps you hear how words are pronounced and used in different situations.

- **Example:** Watch a French movie with subtitles in English and then switch to French subtitles to test your understanding.

- **Listen to Podcasts:** Find podcasts that interest you in the new language. This helps with understanding different accents and speaking styles.

- **Example:** Listen to a podcast about a topic you like, such as sports or technology, in the language you are learning.

- **Listen to Music:** Enjoy songs in the new language and try to understand the lyrics. This can be a fun way to learn new words and phrases.

- **Example:** Listen to popular songs in Japanese and try to sing along, paying attention to the lyrics.

2.3 Reading Practice

- **Read Books:** Start with simple books and work your way up to more challenging ones. This helps with understanding sentence structure and vocabulary.

- **Example:** Read children's books or short stories in the language you are learning before moving on to more complex texts.

- **Read News:** Follow news websites or articles in the language. This helps you learn current vocabulary and expressions.

- **Example:** Read daily news headlines in German to improve your reading skills and stay updated on world events.

- **Read Signs and Labels:** Observe signs, labels, and advertisements in the language. This helps you learn practical vocabulary used in everyday life.

- **Example:** Read the ingredients and instructions on food packaging in Italian while grocery shopping.

2.4 Writing Practice

- **Write in a Journal:** Keep a diary where you write about your day or your thoughts in the new language. This helps with grammar and vocabulary.
- **Example:** Write a short entry every day about what you did, what you saw, and how you felt.
- **Write Emails:** Send emails or messages to friends or language partners in the new language. This helps with formal and informal writing skills.
- **Example:** Email a language partner asking about their weekend plans or discussing a recent event.
- **Write Stories:** Create short stories or essays in the language. This helps you practice using new words and grammar rules in context.
- **Example:** Write a short story about your favorite holiday or a recent adventure.

3. Staying Motivated

3.1 Setting Goals

Set clear, achievable goals for your practice. This helps you stay focused and see your progress. Goals can be short-term (like learning 10 new words each week) or long-term (like being able to have a 10-minute conversation in the language).

3.2 Tracking Progress

Keep track of your practice time and progress. This helps you see how much you have improved and where you need to focus more.

3.3 Finding Enjoyable Activities

Choose practice activities that you enjoy. This makes learning more fun and helps you stay motivated.

3.4 Joining Groups and Communities

Join language learning groups or communities where you can share your experiences and get support. This helps you stay motivated and learn from others.

1. **Chart of Skill Improvement with Regular Practice**
2. **Calendar with Practice Reminders**
3. **Language Exchange App Screenshot**
4. **Daily Practice Checklist**
5. **Goal-Setting Chart for Language Learning**
6. **Progress Tracking App Screenshot**

These visuals can help illustrate the concepts discussed and provide practical tools for learners.

Balancing Active and Passive Language Practice

Learning a new language takes effort and time. To become really good, you need to practice in different ways. This chapter will help you understand two main types of practice: active and passive. Both are important for improving your language skills. We will look at what each type of practice involves, how they help you learn, and how to balance them for the best results.

1. Understanding Active Practice

1.1 What Is Active Practice?

Active practice means doing things where you use the language directly. This includes speaking, writing, and having conversations. It's about using the language in real situations.

Examples of Active Practice:

- **Speaking:** Practice talking with someone who speaks the language. You might have conversations about daily life or ask questions.
- **Writing:** Write short stories, diary entries, or emails in the language you are learning. This helps you use new words and grammar rules.
- **Conversation Practice:** Join a language group or club where you can practice talking with others.

1.2 Benefits of Active Practice

- **Improves Communication Skills:** By speaking and writing, you get better at expressing your thoughts and understanding others.
- **Builds Confidence:** Regularly using the language helps you feel more comfortable and confident.
- **Fixes Mistakes:** When you practice actively, you notice and correct your mistakes, which helps you improve.

2. Understanding Passive Practice

2.1 What Is Passive Practice?

Passive practice involves activities where you are exposed to the language but not actively using it. This includes listening to music, watching TV shows or movies, and reading books. You hear or see the language but don't directly speak or write it.

Examples of Passive Practice:

- **Listening:** Listen to songs, podcasts, or radio shows in the language. This helps you get used to the sounds and rhythm of the language.

- **Watching TV Shows/Movies:** Watch shows or movies with subtitles. This helps you understand how the language is used in different situations.
- **Reading:** Read books, articles, or websites in the language. This helps you see how words and sentences are put together.

2.2 Benefits of Passive Practice

- **Improves Listening Skills:** You get better at understanding different accents and speeds of speech.
- **Increases Vocabulary:** You learn new words and phrases by seeing and hearing them used.
- **Enhances Language Sense:** You get a feel for how the language works and how sentences are structured.

3. Balancing Active and Passive Practice

3.1 Why Balance Is Important

Balancing active and passive practice helps you become a well-rounded language learner. Both types of practice support each other. For example, listening to a podcast (passive) helps you understand conversations better when you practice speaking (active).

Table: Comparison of Active and Passive Practice

Type of Practice	What It Involves	Benefits
Active Practice	Speaking, writing, conversation	Builds confidence, improves communication, fixes mistakes
Passive Practice	Listening, watching, reading	Improves listening skills, increases vocabulary, enhances language sense

3.2 How to Create a Balanced Routine

- **Set Goals:** Decide how much time you want to spend on each type of practice. For example, you might spend 30 minutes a day speaking and writing and 30 minutes listening and reading.
- **Mix It Up:** Combine active and passive activities. Listen to a podcast while commuting, then write a summary of it.
- **Use a Schedule:** Plan your practice sessions for the week. Make sure you include both active and passive activities.

3.3 Examples of Balanced Practice

- **Morning:** Listen to a podcast during breakfast (passive).

- **Afternoon:** Write a short paragraph about what you learned (active).
- **Evening:** Watch a TV show and try to repeat phrases you heard (passive).
- **Before Bed:** Have a conversation with a language partner (active).

4. Tips for Effective Practice

4.1 Be Consistent

Practice a little bit every day. Regular practice helps you get better and keeps what you've learned fresh in your mind.

4.2 Stay Motivated

Set small goals and reward yourself when you reach them. For example, treat yourself to something special after a week of good practice.

4.3 Mix Up Activities

Change your practice activities to keep things interesting. Try different types of media and practice methods to keep your learning fun.

4.4 Get Feedback

Ask for feedback from teachers, friends, or language partners. They can help you correct mistakes and improve faster.

Visualizing Why Regular Practice is Essential for Fluency:

Think of regular practice as watering a plant. Just as a plant needs consistent moisture to grow strong and healthy, language skills require frequent practice to develop and flourish. Each session of speaking, listening, reading, or writing nourishes your abilities, reinforcing connections in your brain.

WHY REGULAR PRACTICE IS ESSENTIAL FOR FLUENCY

Day 1

"I…like…go…store?"

Day 30

"I like to go to the store."

Day 90

"I went to the store yesterday to buy groceries."

"Consistent practice builds vocabulary, sentence structure, and confidence."

Chapter 4: Overcoming Language Plateaus

"The only way to do great work is to love what you do."

— Steve Jobs

Learning a new language is like climbing a hill. At first, you make fast progress, but sometimes you reach a point where it feels like you are stuck. This is called a "language plateau." In this chapter, we will explore what a language plateau is, how to recognize when you are on one, and ways to move past it.

Identifying Signs of a Language Plateau

When you learn a new language, you might feel like you're making significant progress. But sometimes, you might reach a point where it feels like you're not getting any better. This stage is called a "language plateau." In this chapter, we will discuss what a language plateau is, how to recognize if you are experiencing one, and why it happens. Understanding these signs can help you find ways to keep moving forward in your language-learning journey.

1. What Is a Language Plateau?

1.1 Definition of a Language Plateau

A language plateau is a time when it feels like you are not improving in your language skills, even though you continue practicing. Imagine climbing a hill; you might reach a flat area where it feels like you're not going up anymore. This flat area represents your plateau in language learning.

1.2 Why Do Plateaus Happen?

- **Routine Learning:** Doing the same type of exercises and activities repeatedly can make it hard to see new progress.

- **Lack of Challenge:** When you have mastered the basics, you may need more challenging material to keep improving.

- **Limited Practice:** If you are not using the language in different ways or situations, your progress may slow down.

2. Signs That You Are on a Language Plateau

2.1 Feeling Stuck

- **No New Vocabulary:** You might notice that you are not learning new words or phrases.

- **Difficulty with Advanced Topics:** When you try to learn more difficult grammar or vocabulary, you find it harder than before.

2.2 Reduced Motivation

- **Loss of Interest:** You might start to feel bored with your language lessons.
- **Skipping Practice:** You may find reasons to avoid studying or practicing the language.

2.3 Less Improvement in Communication

- **Struggling to Use What You Know:** You might know a lot of words but find it hard to use them correctly in conversations.
- **Misunderstanding Others:** Understanding native speakers or reading more complex texts becomes more difficult.

3. How to Identify a Language Plateau

3.1 Self-Assessment

Review Your Goals: Look at your language learning goals and see if you have achieved them. If you find that you have not made progress toward new goals, you might be experiencing a plateau.

Table: A simple table to track language learning goals and achievements.

Goal	Achieved	Not Achieved
Learn 100 new words	✔	
Hold a 10-minute conversation		✔

3.2 Track Your Progress

- **Monitor Your Skills:** Keep track of your speaking, listening, reading, and writing skills. If you see no improvement over time, you might be on a plateau.

3.3 Get Feedback

- **Ask for Help:** Talk to teachers or language partners and ask them if they notice any areas where you might be stuck.

4. Strategies to Overcome a Plateau

4.1 Change Your Routine

- **Try New Methods:** Experiment with different learning materials, such as books, apps, or videos, to make your practice more engaging.

4.2 Set New Goals

- **Create New Challenges:** Set specific, new goals that are more advanced. This can help push you out of your plateau and encourage progress.

Table: A table for setting new learning goals.

New Goal	Target Date	Progress
Learn 50 new phrases	2 months	
Read a book in the language	3 months	

4.3 Increase Practice

- **Use the Language More:** Find more opportunities to use the language in daily life, such as speaking with native speakers or writing essays.

Visualizing Overcoming Language Plateaus:

Think of overcoming language plateaus as climbing a mountain. When you reach a plateau, it may feel like progress has stalled, and the climb seems challenging. To push through, you might need to change your approach—try new techniques, engage in different activities, or seek support. Just as a climber adjusts their route to reach new heights, embracing varied learning methods helps you break through barriers and continue your journey toward fluency.

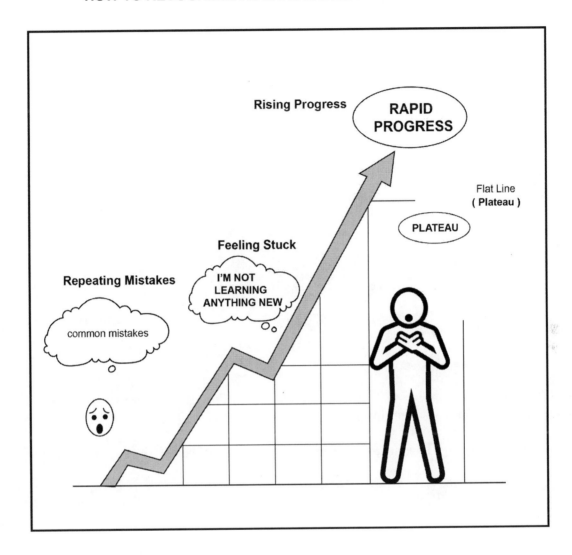

Techniques for Breaking Through Language Learning Plateaus

Reaching a language plateau can be frustrating. It feels like you are stuck and not improving, despite your best efforts. But don't worry! There are many effective techniques to help you break through this barrier and keep progressing in your language learning. In this chapter, we will explore various strategies to help you overcome plateaus, including changing your study habits, setting new goals, and using different resources.

1. Change Your Study Routine

1.1 Try New Study Methods

If you feel stuck, it might be time to change how you study. Here are some ideas:

- **Use Different Resources:** Switch from textbooks to language apps, podcasts, or videos. Different tools can offer new perspectives and learning experiences.
- **Incorporate Games:** Language learning games can make studying more fun and engaging. For example, you can play word games or complete language puzzles.

1.2 Add Variety to Your Practice

Variety keeps your learning fresh and exciting. You can:

- **Change Your Topics:** Study different subjects, such as travel, food, or culture, to expand your vocabulary and interests.
- **Practice with Different People:** Speak with new language partners or join a conversation group to experience various speaking styles and accents.

2. Set New Goals

2.1 Set Specific, Achievable Goals

When you reach a plateau, setting new goals can motivate you to push forward. Your goals should be:

- **Specific:** Instead of a general goal like "improve my speaking," try "learn 10 new phrases for ordering food in a restaurant."
- **Achievable:** Set goals that are challenging but possible. For example, aim to read a short article or watch a video in the target language each week.

Table: Examples of specific and achievable goals with deadlines.

Goal	Deadline	
Learn 10 new phrases	1 week	5 phrases learned
Watch a 10-minute video	3 days	Watched 1 video
Read a short article	2 weeks	Read 2 articles

2.2 Monitor Your Progress

Keep track of your improvements to stay motivated. You can:

- **Use a Language Journal:** Write about what you learn each day and note any new words or phrases.
- **Review Your Goals:** Regularly check your progress towards your goals and adjust them if needed.

3. Immerse Yourself in the Language

3.1 Use the Language in Real-Life Situations

The more you use the language, the better you will get. Try:

- **Speaking with Native Speakers:** Engage in conversations with native speakers or language exchange partners.
- **Participating in Language Events:** Attend events or meetups where you can practice speaking in a social setting.

3.2 Consume Media in the Target Language

Exposure to the language in different contexts helps with learning. You can:

- **Watch Movies and Shows:** Choose films or TV shows in the language you are learning. Turn on subtitles if needed.
- **Listen to Music and Podcasts:** Enjoy songs and podcasts in the target language to improve your listening skills and learn new expressions.

4. Seek Feedback and Adjust

4.1 Get Feedback on Your Skills

Feedback helps you understand what areas you need to improve. Consider:

- **Language Tutors:** Work with a tutor who can provide personalized feedback and guidance.
- **Language Exchange Partners:** Ask your language exchange partner for feedback on your speaking and writing.

4.2 Adjust Your Learning Strategies

Based on the feedback you receive, you may need to change how you study. For example:

- **Focus on Weak Areas:** If you struggle with grammar, spend extra time on grammar exercises and resources.
- **Improve Your Speaking Skills:** If speaking is difficult, practice more with conversation partners or join speaking clubs.

Table: Adjustments based on feedback.

Feedback Area	Adjustment Needed	
Struggles with grammar	More grammar exercises	Use grammar apps, worksheets
Difficulty in speaking	Practice speaking more	Join a conversation club

5. Stay Motivated

5.1 Find Your Language Learning "Why"

Understanding why you want to learn the language can keep you motivated. Your reasons might include:

- **Traveling:** Learning the language to travel and communicate with locals.
- **Cultural Interest:** Learning to understand and enjoy music, movies, and books in the target language.

5.2 Reward Yourself

Celebrate your achievements to stay motivated. You can:

- **Set Rewards:** Give yourself small rewards when you reach a goal, like a treat or a break.
- **Reflect on Your Progress:** Look back at how far you've come and be proud of your achievements.

Chapter 5: Speaking With Confidence

"Language is the roadmap of a culture. It tells you where its people come from and where they are going."

– Rita Mae Brown

When learning English, speaking can be scary. You might worry about making mistakes or not being understood. Building confidence is key to speaking English well. Confidence helps you feel comfortable and speak clearly. In this chapter, we will explore ways to boost your confidence when speaking English.

Building Confidence in Spoken English

In this chapter, we will learn how to build confidence when speaking English. You will discover simple ways to practice speaking, how to overcome nervousness, and how to use strategies to help you feel more comfortable in conversations. By the end of this chapter, you will have practical tools to help you speak English with greater ease and self-assurance.

Understanding Confidence in Speaking English

Confidence in speaking means feeling sure of yourself when you talk in English. It's about trusting your ability to communicate your ideas clearly. When you are confident, you can speak more naturally and enjoy your conversations more.

Why Confidence Matters:

- **Improves Communication:** When you are confident, you speak more clearly, and people understand you better.

- **Reduces Anxiety:** Confidence helps you feel less nervous and more relaxed during conversations.

- **Encourages Practice:** The more confident you feel, the more likely you are to practice speaking regularly.

1. Practice Regularly

To build confidence, you need to practice speaking English often. Regular practice helps you become more comfortable and familiar with the language.

- **Daily Speaking:** Try to speak English every day. Even short conversations can help. You can speak with friends and family or use language learning apps.

- **Language Exchange:** Find a language partner who speaks English and practice with them. You can help each other improve.

- **Self-Recording:** Record yourself speaking in English. Listen to the recordings to hear how you sound and notice areas where you can improve.

Table: Daily Practice Ideas

Activity	Description	Benefits
Talking with a Friend	Speak English with someone you know.	Builds familiarity and reduces nervousness.
Using Language Apps	Practice with apps designed for speaking.	Offers structured practice and feedback.
Reading Out Loud	Read English books or articles out loud.	Improves pronunciation and fluency.

2. Join Speaking Groups

Speaking groups are great for building confidence because they offer a supportive environment where you can practice with others.

- **Conversation Clubs:** Look for local conversation clubs where people gather to practice speaking English. These clubs often provide a friendly space to speak and improve.

- **Online Forums:** Join online forums or chat groups where you can participate in English conversations from home.

- **Language Meetups:** Attend meetups or social events focused on language practice. These gatherings can be fun and help you practice speaking in a relaxed setting.

3. Focus on Pronunciation

Good pronunciation helps you be understood clearly. When you work on pronunciation, you can speak more confidently.

- **Listen and Imitate:** Listen to native speakers and try to imitate their pronunciation. You can use movies, podcasts, or language learning videos.

- **Use Pronunciation Tools:** There are many tools and apps that help with pronunciation. These tools can give you feedback on how to improve.

- **Practice with Tongue Twisters:** Tongue twisters are fun ways to practice difficult sounds. They help you get used to making different sounds in English.

Table: Pronunciation Practice Tools

Tool	Description	Benefits
Pronunciation Apps	Apps that provide feedback on your pronunciation.	Helps you correct mistakes and improve.
Listening to Media	Using movies, podcasts, and songs to hear correct pronunciation.	Provides examples of natural speech.
Tongue Twisters	Phrases that help practice tricky sounds.	Improves clarity and fluency.

4. Overcome Nervousness

Feeling nervous when speaking English is common, but there are ways to manage this anxiety.

- **Deep Breathing:** Before speaking, take deep breaths to calm your nerves. This can help you feel more relaxed.
- **Positive Self-Talk:** Use positive affirmations to boost your confidence. Remind yourself of your strengths and improvements.
- **Prepare and Practice:** Prepare what you want to say in advance. Practice your speech or conversation to feel more ready.

Table: Tips for Overcoming Nervousness

Tip	Description	Benefits
Deep Breathing	Taking slow, deep breaths to relax.	Reduces anxiety and helps calm nerves.
Positive Self-Talk	Using affirmations to build confidence.	Boosts self-esteem and reduces fear.
Preparation	Preparing what to say ahead of time.	Increases readiness and reduces stress.

5. Set Realistic Goals

Setting goals helps you track your progress and stay motivated. Start with small, achievable goals and gradually increase their difficulty.

- **Small Steps:** Set simple goals, like introducing yourself or ordering food in English. These small successes build confidence.
- **Track Progress:** Keep a journal of your speaking practice. Note improvements and areas to work on.

- **Celebrate Achievements:** Celebrate your progress, no matter how small. Recognizing your achievements helps keep you motivated.

Table: Goal-Setting Example

Goal	Description	
Introduce Yourself	Practice saying your name and a few details.	1 week
Order Food in English	Practice ordering a meal at a restaurant.	2 weeks
Have a Short Conversation	Engage in a 5-minute conversation with a friend.	1 month

6. Use Technology for Practice

Technology offers many tools to help you practice speaking English and build confidence.

- **Language Learning Apps:** Use apps that focus on speaking and pronunciation. They often have exercises and feedback to help you improve.

- **Speech Recognition Software:** Some tools can analyze your speech and give you feedback on pronunciation and fluency.

- **Video Calls:** Practice speaking with friends or tutors through video calls. This allows you to practice real-life conversations.

Table: Technology Tools

Goal	Description	
Introduce Yourself	Practice saying your name and a few details.	1 week
Order Food in English	Practice ordering a meal at a restaurant.	2 weeks
Have a Short Conversation	Engage in a 5-minute conversation with a friend.	1 month

Visualizing Speaking With Confidence:

Think of speaking with confidence as standing on a stage. The spotlight represents your knowledge and preparation, illuminating your ideas for the audience. Your body language and tone are like the music that enhances your performance, drawing people in and keeping their attention. Just as a confident performer captivates their audience, speaking confidently allows you to communicate your thoughts clearly, engaging listeners and conveying your message effectively.

HOW TO BUILD CONFIDENCE IN SPEAKING ENGLISH

Feedback and Self-Assessment Strategies for Improvement

In this chapter, we will explore how to use feedback effectively and assess your own speaking skills to make real progress. You'll learn how to seek constructive feedback from others, use self-assessment techniques to track your improvement, and apply this knowledge to speak more confidently.

1. Seeking Constructive Feedback

Feedback is essential for improvement. It helps you understand your strengths and areas where you need to grow. Here's how to use feedback to become more confident:

A. Find a Feedback Partner

- **Language Exchange Partner:** Look for someone who speaks English fluently. They can listen to you and give you advice on how to improve.

- **Teacher or Tutor:** A professional can provide detailed feedback on your pronunciation, grammar, and fluency.

- **Friends and Family:** Ask people you trust to listen to your English and offer their honest opinions.

B. Ask Specific Questions

When asking for feedback, be specific about what you want to improve:

- **Pronunciation:** "Can you help me with my pronunciation of these words?"

- **Grammar:** "Do you notice any grammar mistakes in my sentences?"

- **Fluency:** "Am I speaking too slowly or too quickly?"

Table: Types of Feedback

Type	Description	Example
Pronunciation	How clearly you say words and sounds.	"Your pronunciation of 'th' is unclear."
Grammar	Correct use of language rules.	"You used past tense correctly here, but not in this sentence."
Fluency	Smoothness and speed of speaking.	"You speak too slowly; try to speed up a bit."

C. Use Feedback Constructively

- **Listen Carefully:** Pay attention to what others say and understand their comments.

- **Practice the Suggestions:** Work on the areas where you received feedback.

- **Ask for Examples:** If you don't understand the feedback, ask for examples to clarify.

2. Self-Assessment Techniques

Self-assessment helps you track your own progress. By evaluating your speaking skills regularly, you can see how you are improving and where you need more practice.

A. Record Yourself

- **How to Record:** Use a phone or computer to record your English speaking practice.

- **What to Record:** Try recording yourself reading a passage, describing a picture, or having a conversation.
- **Listening Back:** Play the recording and listen carefully to identify areas where you can improve.

B. Use Checklists

Create a checklist of key speaking skills to evaluate yourself. Here are some examples:

Table: Self-Assessment Checklist

Skill	Questions to Ask Yourself	Example
Pronunciation	Did I pronounce all the words clearly?	"Did I say 'hello' correctly?"
Grammar	Did I use correct grammar in my sentences?	"Did I use past tense properly?"
Fluency	Was I able to speak smoothly without long pauses?	"Did I speak at a good speed?"

C. Set Goals and Track Progress

- **Set Clear Goals:** Decide what you want to improve, like pronunciation or fluency.
- **Track Your Progress:** Use a journal or app to record your goals and check your progress regularly.
- **Celebrate Successes:** Acknowledge your improvements and keep motivated by celebrating small victories.

Chapter 6:
Continuing Your Language Journey

"The journey of a thousand miles begins with a single step."

– Lao Tzu

Learning a language is like taking a long journey. Even after you reach a certain level of fluency, it's essential to keep moving forward. In this chapter, we'll explore how to continue improving your English and maintain the skills you've worked hard to build. We will cover practical tips for keeping your language skills sharp, finding new ways to practice, and staying motivated. By following these steps, you can ensure that your language journey keeps growing and evolving.

Tips for Maintaining and Improving Fluency

Language learning is not just about reaching a goal; it's about keeping the skills you've gained and continuing to grow. In this chapter, we will explore practical ways to maintain and improve your English fluency even after you have achieved a good level. This includes regular practice, real-life conversations, setting goals, and finding new learning opportunities.

1. Practice Regularly

A. Establish a Routine

- **Daily Practice:** Set aside a little time each day for English practice. Consistency is key. Even short periods, like 10-15 minutes a day, help you stay fluent.
- **Diverse Methods:** To keep things interesting, use different methods for practice. These include reading, writing, listening, and speaking.

Table: Daily Practice Ideas

Activity	Description	Example
Reading	Read books, articles, or news in English.	Read a news article or a chapter from a book.
Speaking	Talk to others in English or practice speaking alone.	Have a brief conversation with a friend in English.
Listening	Listen to English media, like music or podcasts.	Listen to a podcast or an English song.

Writing	Write in English, such as keeping a journal.	Write a few sentences about your day or thoughts.

B. Make Practice Fun

- **Watch Movies and TV Shows:** Choose English-language movies or TV shows. This helps with listening skills and understanding different accents.
- **Play Language Games:** Use apps or games designed for learning English. They make practice enjoyable and interactive.

2. Engage in Real-Life Conversations

A. Join English-Speaking Groups

- **Language Exchange:** Find language exchange partners or groups where you can practice English with native speakers.
- **Social Clubs:** Join clubs or social groups that speak English. This could be a hobby group or a discussion club.

B. Practice Speaking in Everyday Situations

- **At Work:** Try to use English during work meetings or with colleagues.
- **In Public:** Speak English when shopping, at restaurants, or while traveling.

3. Set Personal Goals

A. Short-Term Goals

- **Weekly Goals:** Set small, achievable goals for each week. For example, learn ten new words or watch one English movie.
- **Track Progress:** Keep a journal of your achievements and what you want to improve.

B. Long-Term Goals

- **Monthly or Yearly Goals:** Plan larger goals, such as reading a whole book in English or improving your speaking skills.
- **Review and Adjust:** Regularly review your goals and adjust them based on your progress and needs.

Table: Goal Setting Example

Type of Goal	Goal	Action Plan
Short-Term	Learn ten new words	Write down and practice ten new words every week.
Medium-Term	Read a book in English	Choose a book and set a reading schedule.

| Long-Term | Improve speaking skills | Join a speaking club and practice regularly. |

4. Explore New Learning Opportunities

A. Take Advanced Classes

- **Online Courses:** Enroll in advanced English courses online that focus on specific skills, such as business English or advanced writing.
- **Local Classes:** Join local language classes or workshops to learn more and interact with other learners.

B. Use Technology

- **Language Apps:** Use apps for language learning that offer advanced practice options.
- **Online Communities:** Participate in online forums or social media groups where you can interact with native speakers.

5. Stay Motivated

A. Find Your Passion

- **Hobbies and Interests:** Engage with English content related to your hobbies, such as cooking shows if you like cooking or news if you enjoy current events.
- **Celebrate Achievements:** Reward yourself for reaching milestones and celebrate your progress.

B. Connect with Others

- **Language Buddies:** Find a language buddy who shares your learning goals. This can help keep you motivated.
- **Support Groups:** Join groups of learners who can provide encouragement and share experiences.

Resources and Strategies for Lifelong Language Learning

Learning a language is a journey that doesn't end after reaching fluency. To keep improving and to use your language skills effectively, it's important to use various resources and strategies. In this chapter, we will explore different tools and methods that can help you continue learning and growing in your language skills throughout your life.

1. Online Resources

A. Language Learning Apps

- **Duolingo:** A popular app that makes learning fun through games and quizzes. It offers lessons in many languages and helps you practice regularly.

- **Babbel:** This app focuses on practical language skills and conversation practice. It's good for learning phrases you can use in real life.

B. Websites for Practice

- **BBC Learning English:** Offers free resources, such as videos, quizzes, and articles to help with listening, reading, and grammar.
- **Quizlet:** Provides flashcards and games to help you learn vocabulary and grammar rules. You can create your own sets or use ones made by others.

2. Books and Audio Resources

A. Language Learning Books

- **Grammar Books:** Look for books that focus on grammar rules and exercises. They can help you understand and use correct grammar.
- **Vocabulary Books:** Books with lists of useful words and phrases can expand your vocabulary. Choose books with themes that interest you.

B. Audio Resources

- **Podcasts:** Find podcasts that are designed for language learners. They often have episodes on different topics and levels.
- **Audiobooks:** Listening to books in English helps improve listening skills and exposes you to different accents and speaking styles.

3. Language Exchange and Practice

A. Find Language Exchange Partners

- **Language Exchange Websites:** Websites like Tandem or HelloTalk connect you with native speakers who want to learn your language. You can help each other practice.
- **Local Language Meetups:** Look for local events or groups where people meet to practice speaking different languages.

B. Join Language Clubs

- **Conversation Clubs:** Many cities have clubs where people practice speaking English. Joining these can give you regular speaking practice.
- **Online Forums:** Participate in online forums or discussion groups where English is the main language. This helps with writing and reading skills.

4. Setting and Achieving New Goals

A. Set Specific Goals

- **Short-Term Goals:** These could be daily or weekly goals, like learning 10 new words or writing a short paragraph in English.
- **Long-Term Goals:** Aim for goals like being able to watch a movie without subtitles or giving a presentation in English.

B. Track Your Progress

- **Journals:** Keep a journal of your learning activities and progress. Write about what you have learned and areas where you need more practice.
- **Self-Assessment:** Regularly assess your skills to see how much you have improved and where you need to focus more.

5. Engaging with English-Speaking Culture

A. Explore English Media

- **Movies and TV Shows:** Watch a variety of genres and styles to understand different accents and cultural contexts.
- **Music and Lyrics:** Listen to English music and follow along with the lyrics. This helps with pronunciation and rhythm.

B. Participate in Cultural Events

- **Festivals and Holidays:** Join in local or online events related to English-speaking cultures. It's a fun way to practice and learn about cultural traditions.
- **Volunteering:** Volunteer for activities or organizations where English is the primary language. It's a practical way to use your skills.

6. Staying Motivated and Inspired

A. Find a Language Buddy

- **Practice Together:** Partner with someone who shares your language learning goals. You can motivate each other and practice together.
- **Share Achievements:** Celebrate milestones and successes with your language buddy. This helps keep you motivated.

B. Stay Curious and Open-Minded

- **Explore New Topics:** Read or listen to topics you are curious about in English. This keeps learning interesting and relevant.

- **Be Open to Feedback:** Accept and use feedback to improve your skills. It helps you grow and refine your language abilities.

Visualizing Continuing Your Language Journey:

Think of continuing your language journey as embarking on a long, adventurous road trip.

Each destination represents a new milestone—whether it's mastering a new skill, traveling to a new country, or engaging in conversations with native speakers. Along the way, you'll encounter detours and challenges, but these experiences enrich your journey.

Just as a road trip offers opportunities for exploration and discovery, staying committed to your language learning keeps the excitement alive and leads you to new horizons of understanding and communication.

HOW TO MAINTAIN AND IMPROVE YOUR FLUENCY OVER TIME

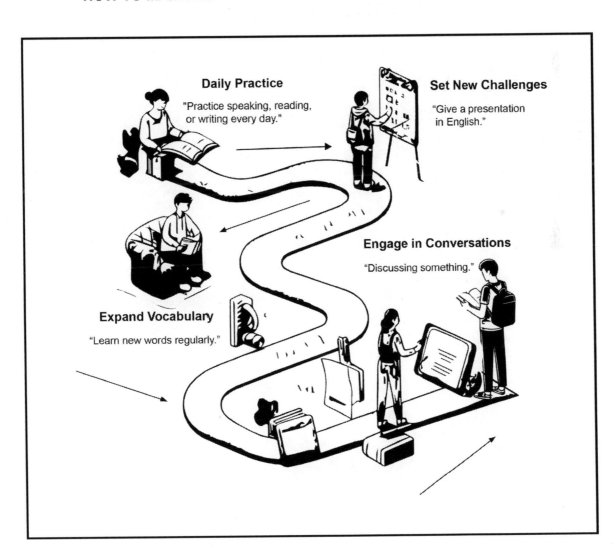

Made in the USA
Columbia, SC
22 November 2024

47369471R00178